VINTAGE TOYS

ROBOTS AND SPACE TOYS

VINTAGE TOYS

ROBOTS AND SPACE TOYS

JIM
BUNTE
◆
DAVE
HALLMAN
◆
HEINZ
MUELLER

ANTIQUE TRADER BOOKS
A DIVISION OF KRAUSE PUBLICATIONS

DEDICATIONS

To Alexander and Victoria — *J. B.*
To Sandy, Lauren, and Christopher — *D. H.*
To Fiona, Dwayne, Charlotte, Felicity, and Alexander — *H. M.*

ISBN: 1-58221-025-X
Library of Congress Catalog Card Number: 99-65831

Designed by American Eagle Entertainment Inc.   www.ameri-eagle.com

Select images courtesy of James D. Julia Auctions, Fairfield, Maine   www.juliaauctions.com
Select images courtesy of Kalmbach Publishing Co., Waukesha, Wisconsin   www.kalmbach.com
Select images courtesy of Robert Johnson / Comet Toys USA, Minneapolis   www.comettoys.com

ALL IMAGES FROM ABOVE SOURCES USED WITH PERMISSION.

Printed in the United States of America

To order additional copies of this book or to request a free catalog, please contact:

KRAUSE PUBLICATIONS
700 EAST STATE STREET
IOLA, WI 54990-0001
800-258-0929

Acknowledgments

There are many people who helped make this book a reality, and we would like to take this opportunity to thank each of them for their meaningful contributions to VINTAGE TOYS: ROBOTS AND SPACE TOYS. Without their efforts, this book would not be the same.

To CATHERINE SAUNDERS-WATSON, for her unparalleled knowledge of the toys; to LAURA DONNELLY, for her talented imaging work which appears throughout this book; to BOE KANAREK, for her always-accurate proofreading and keen insights; to DON HALLMAN, for his outstanding imaging work; to MARK FORSS, for his contributions at Classic Tin Toy; to BOB BURNS, for opening his legendary collection to us for photographic and research purposes; to STEVE BORRELLI, for invaluable legal assistance; to IRENE BOLDUC, of James D. Julia Auctions, who secured key images appearing in this book; to DICK CHRISTIANSON, of Kalmbach, who dug through old *Collecting Toys* files to unearth more key images; and to ROBERT JOHNSON, of Comet Toys USA, whose last-minute provision of a number of vital images helped provide a completeness to this book it otherwise would not have.

About this volume

VINTAGE TOYS: ROBOTS AND SPACE TOYS represents a comprehensive, but by no means complete, documentation of space-themed playthings created since the turn of the century. We've tried to include as many toys as possible from the huge range of product built mainly since the 1930s, but obviously 100% coverage is not possible. As such, we believe the materials included in this volume convey an excellent overview of this category of toymaking from builders the world over.

We have tried to provide accurate manufacturer and dating information with each and every listing. However, due to the nature of the historic toy industry, and vintage Japanese toys in particular, some information may be subjective and based on suppositional research rather than hard evidence (e.g. a manufacturer's mark on the toy or the toy's package). Wherever possible, we attempt to provide as much historical insight as possible into the provenance of each toy, but of course cannot certify the provenance of generally "unknown" toys. Regarding dating, most toys feature a "circa" listing, which denotes the most accurate, to-the-year estimation we can provide for the original release date of each toy. These dates are arrived at based on a number of factors, including decoration design, vintage catalog resource materials, close examination of similar toys and componentry, and analysis of package design trends. Toys with firm dating reflect their appearances in dated vintage publications.

We've included three valuations with each toy: good, excellent, and mint with original package. These prices are based on the authors' vast experience in buying and selling toys, as well as auction results and the prices realized from private sales. Please note that these valuations are provided as a guide to collectors, and should be considered entertainment and not actual appraisals of specific toys. Because of the fluid nature of aftermarket selling of vintage toys, particularly in the age of online auctioning, real-world values fluctuate daily, and are determined solely on a case-by-case basis. For up-to-the-minute valuations of toys, please consult a qualified antique toy appraisal service.

HOW TO USE THIS VOLUME

We've designed VINTAGE TOYS: ROBOTS AND SPACE TOYS to be the most easy-to-use reference guide ever. As you'll note in the illustration below, each page boasts a number of organizational elements designed to speed your searching. All toys are sorted first by DECADE OF MANUFACTURE. Within each DECADE, toys are sorted by their MANUFACTURER'S NAME, then by the TOY'S NAME, and finally, for identically named toys from different production runs, by YEAR OF MANUFACTURE.

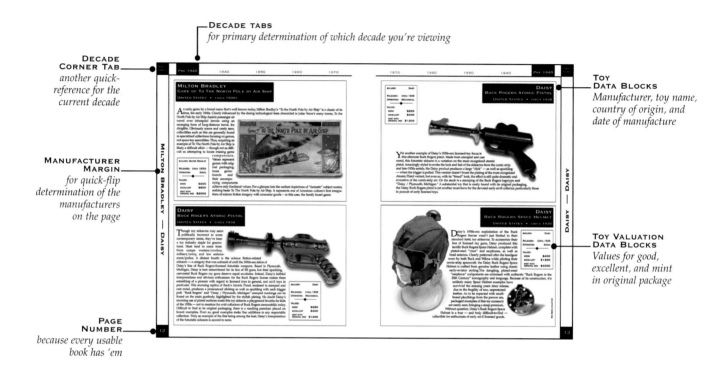

DECADE TABS
for primary determination of which decade you're viewing

DECADE CORNER TAB
another quick-reference for the current decade

MANUFACTURER MARGIN
for quick-flip determination of the manufacturers on the page

PAGE NUMBER
because every usable book has 'em

TOY DATA BLOCKS
Manufacturer, toy name, country of origin, and date of manufacture

TOY VALUATION DATA BLOCKS
Values for good, excellent, and mint in original package

CONDITION GRADING

Each toy documented in VINTAGE TOYS: ROBOTS AND SPACE TOYS is accompanied by a valuation data block. Within this block are three "condition" values: good, excellent, and mint with original box. Below are depictions of toys in each condition, to assist you in better understanding the subtle differences between each one, and to help assign a condition to your toy.

GOOD
Toy has been played with; small, minor scuffs and marks, but generally well cared for

EXCELLENT
Toy is free from scratches and scuffs; shows no real evidence of wear; hardly played with

MINT-ORIGINAL BOX
Toy is ABSOLUTELY pristine; NEVER played with; factory-new; accompanied by ALL original packaging

TABLE OF CONTENTS

BEFORE THE 1940s

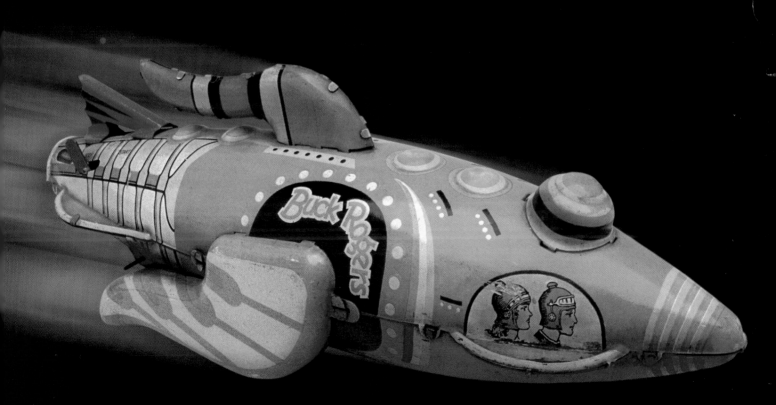

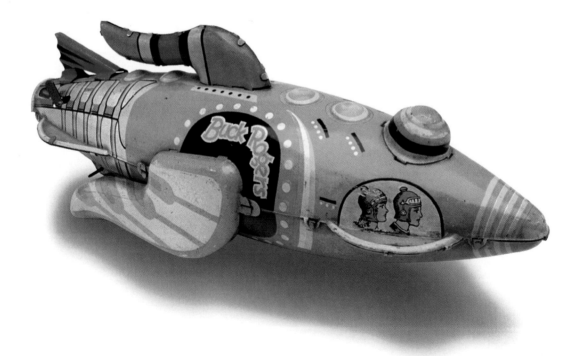

BUCK ROGERS 25TH CENTURY ROCKET SHIP

1934

BY LOUIS MARX & CO.

UNITED STATES OF AMERICA

BEFORE THE 1940s

In the beginning, science fiction as a cultural phenomenon didn't exist.
Certainly the literary work of Jules Verne and the silent films of Georges
Méliès (*A Trip to the Moon*, 1902) had established an awareness for science
fiction subject matter. But even so, Americans were simply more interested in
historical tableaux, comedies, and melodramas. Just as events like World
War II and Vietnam continue to mesmerize us today, historic events like the
American Revolution and Civil War (*Birth of a Nation*, 1915, D.W. Griffith)
held similar sway over the citizenry of the age.

Things began to change with the marketplace success of Fritz Lang's
Metropolis (1926), a stunningly dark cinematic vision of the future that
presented the popularity of movie melodrama against the emerging backdrop
of "science fiction." Pulp magazines like *Amazing Stories* were quick to adopt
the imagery and psychological dread of Lang's vision, commercializing it in
classic American fashion for popular consumption. The result was *Buck Rogers
in the 25th Century* — first a series of articles in *Amazing Stories*, then a
syndicated comic strip. American-style science fiction had been born.

U.S. toymakers were quick to react to the trend, and by the end of the 1930s,
playthings based on *Buck Rogers* (and later, *Flash Gordon*) had become staples
in toy stores and playgrounds everywhere. Across the Pacific, Japanese
toymakers watched in earnest. For despite the conflict which loomed on the
horizon, the destiny of Japanese toymakers was now clear. Only a decade after
the close of World War II, imported Japanese robots and space toys would
dominate this segment of the toy industry — a segment that had been born
only a few short years earlier.

MILTON BRADLEY
GAME OF TO THE NORTH POLE BY AIR-SHIP
UNITED STATES • CIRCA 1900S

An early game by a brand name that's well known today, Milton Bradley's To the North Pole by Air-Ship is a classic of its time, the early 1900s. Clearly influenced by the daring technological feats chronicled in Jules Verne's many tomes, To the North Pole by Air Ship depicts passenger air travel over inhospitable terrain using an emerging form of long-distance travel, the dirigible. Obviously scarce and rarely seen, collectibles such as this are generally found in specialized collections focusing on games, not space-toy assemblies. Thus, acquiring an example of To The North Pole by Air-Ship is likely a difficult affair — though not as difficult as attempting to locate missing game components. Values represent games with original packaging; loose gameboards and accompanying components achieve only fractional values. For a glimpse into the earliest depictions of "fantastic" subject matter, nothing beats To The North Pole by Air-Ship. It represents one of American culture's first integrations of science fiction imagery with consumer goods — in this case, the family board game.

BUILDER: MILTON BRADLEY	
RELEASED: CIRCA 1900S	
OPERATION:	STATIC
VALUES:	
GOOD	$200
EXCELLENT	$800
MINT WITH ORIGINAL BOX	$2000

DAISY
BUCK ROGERS ATOMIC PISTOL
UNITED STATES • CIRCA 1938

Though toy sidearms may seem politically incorrect to some contemporary tastes, they've been a toy industry staple for generations. Most tend to come from three camps: western/cowboy, military/army, and law enforcement/police. A distant fourth is the science fiction-related sidearm — a category that was unheard of until the 1930s-era debut of Daisy's line of *Buck Rogers*-licensed futuristic weapons. Based in Plymouth, Michigan, Daisy is best remembered for its line of BB guns, but their sparkling, cast-metal Buck Rogers ray guns deserve equal accolades. Indeed, Daisy's faithful interpretations and obvious enthusiasm for the *Buck Rogers* license makes them something of a pioneer with regard to licensed toys in general, and sci-fi toys in particular. This stunning replica of Buck's Atomic Pistol, rendered in stamped and cast metal, produces a pronounced clicking as well as sparkling with each trigger pull. "*Buck Rogers*" and "Daisy / Plymouth, Michigan" stamped markings can be found on the main gunbody, highlighted by the stylish plating. No doubt Daisy's stunning use of plated surfaces made this toy sidearm a playground favorite for kids of the 1930s — not to mention for avid collectors of *Buck Rogers* memorabilia today. Difficult to find in its original packaging, there is a resulting premium placed on boxed examples. Even so, good examples make fine additions to any respectable collection. Truly an example of the first being among the best, Daisy's interpretation of the futuristic sidearm is second to none.

BUILDER:	DAISY
RELEASED:	CIRCA 1938
OPERATION:	MECHANICAL
VALUES:	
GOOD	$250
EXCELLENT	$400
MINT WITH ORIGINAL BOX	$1200

DAISY
BUCK ROGERS ATOMIC PISTOL
UNITED STATES • CIRCA 1938

BUILDER:	DAISY
RELEASED:	CIRCA 1938
OPERATION:	MECHANICAL

VALUES:

GOOD	$250
EXCELLENT	$400
MINT WITH ORIGINAL BOX	$1200

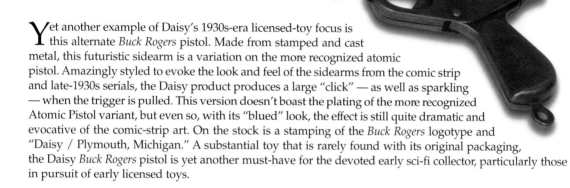

Yet another example of Daisy's 1930s-era licensed-toy focus is this alternate *Buck Rogers* pistol. Made from stamped and cast metal, this futuristic sidearm is a variation on the more recognized atomic pistol. Amazingly styled to evoke the look and feel of the sidearms from the comic strip and late-1930s serials, the Daisy product produces a large "click" — as well as sparkling — when the trigger is pulled. This version doesn't boast the plating of the more recognized Atomic Pistol variant, but even so, with its "blued" look, the effect is still quite dramatic and evocative of the comic-strip art. On the stock is a stamping of the *Buck Rogers* logotype and "Daisy / Plymouth, Michigan." A substantial toy that is rarely found with its original packaging, the Daisy *Buck Rogers* pistol is yet another must-have for the devoted early sci-fi collector, particularly those in pursuit of early licensed toys.

DAISY
BUCK ROGERS SPACE HELMET
UNITED STATES • CIRCA 1936

Daisy's 1930s-era exploitation of the *Buck Rogers* license wasn't just limited to their standard forte, toy sidearms. To accessorize their line of licensed ray guns, Daisy produced this terrific *Buck Rogers* Space Helmet, complete with plated-steel "visor" and earphones, as well as head antenna. Clearly patterned after the headgear worn by both Buck and Wilma while piloting their comic-strip spacecraft, the Daisy *Buck Rogers* Space Helmet is crafted from genuine leather using classic early-aviator styling. The dangling, plated-steel "earphone" components are embossed with authen-tic *Buck Rogers in the 25th Century* iconography and language. Because of its construction, it's unlikely many Space Helmet examples have survived the ensuing years since release, due to the fragility of raw, unprotected leather. As to be expected with small-brand playthings from the prewar era, packaged examples of this toy accessory are rarely seen, bringing a steep premium. Without question, Daisy's *Buck Rogers* Space Helmet is a true — and truly diffi-cult-to-find — collectible for enthusiasts of early sci-fi licensed goods.

BUILDER:	DAISY
RELEASED:	CIRCA 1936
OPERATION:	STATIC

VALUES:

GOOD	$400
EXCELLENT	$1200
MINT WITH ORIGINAL BOX	$4000

BOB BURNS COLLECTION

DAISY

5

MARX

LOUIS MARX & CO.
BUCK ROGERS 25TH CENTURY ROCKET SHIP
UNITED STATES • 1934

As the 1930s progressed, the success of *Buck Rogers* in pop culture — first as a featured character in *Amazing Stories*, later as a syndicated comic strip, radio program, and movie serial — became too obvious to ignore. Louis Marx learned, early in his career as a product marketer at Ferdinand Strauss, that shrewd licensing deals could provide big profits. So in 1934, when he became one of the first toy manufacturers to gamble on a *Buck Rogers* license, he was handsomely rewarded. Highly desirable today, Marx's *Buck Rogers* 25th Century Rocket Ships are classic icons of the mid-1930s era of toy manufacture. Twelve inches in length, the wind-up Rocket Ship floor toy cruises along during operation, its rear exhaust port sparkling all the way. The stylized litho features Buck and Wilma at the helm, with stylized tin "fins"

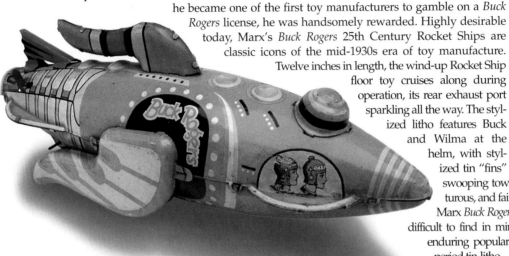

BUILDER:	MARX
RELEASED:	1934
OPERATION:	WIND-UP
VALUES:	
GOOD	$550
EXCELLENT	$900
MINT WITH ORIGINAL BOX	$3800

swooping toward the rear. Colorful, adventurous, and faithful to comic strip design, the Marx *Buck Rogers* 25th Century Rocket Ship is difficult to find in mint-boxed condition, owing to enduring popularity as well as the fragility of period tin-litho.

LOUIS MARX & CO.
BUCK ROGERS 25TH CENTURY ROCKET SHIP
UNITED STATES • 1934

Lithography is such an imprecise art, at times — particularly when it comes to color. Registration problems are inherent to the lithographic process; slight movement in a sheet of tin's location as it is struck by plates in the press, and whamo! Wasted steel. Of course, collectors don't count registration issues as major variations — but they do document color shifting wherever possible. Take this 1934 Marx *Buck Rogers* 25th Century Rocket Ship. The orange is decidedly more muddy and brown in color — likely due to alternate level

BUILDER:	MARX
RELEASED:	1934
OPERATION:	WIND-UP
VALUES:	
GOOD	$550
EXCELLENT	$900
MINT WITH ORIGINAL BOX	$3800

of ink application during the lithographic printing process. In addition, this version boasts a revised treatment for the rear dorsal fin. Note the

alternate litho in comparison to the other Rocket Ship. Minor variations such as this often occur during large production runs, with the net result being more convoluted documentation across the many differing versions of a single toy.

BUILDER:	MARX
RELEASED:	1935
OPERATION:	WIND-UP

VALUES:	
GOOD	**$400**
EXCELLENT	**$800**
MINT WITH ORIGINAL BOX	**$2800**

LOUIS MARX & CO.
BUCK ROGERS ROCKET POLICE PATROL
UNITED STATES • 1935

Following on the success of the original *Buck Rogers* 25th Century Rocket Ship of 1934, Louis Marx & Co. released the Rocket Police Patrol variant in 1935. This 12-inch wind-up includes the rear-exhaust sparkling and swept-back fins and wings of the original Rocket Ship platform, but also includes a "three-dimensional" Buck peering over his windscreen, with his atomic pistol at the ready. Though it has noticeably different visuals from the Rocket Ship, Rocket Police Patrol actually shares a number of major components in classic Marx tool-recycling fashion. Many collectors believe Rocket Police Patrol's litho suggests a "space fish" (or similar creature), citing the ship's "eyes" and apparent smile, two decades before Japan's Yoshiya would conquer space with whales, dogs, and elephants (1950s). Also noteworthy is Marx's camouflaging of the Rocket Ship's swept-back wings through the application of linear "exhaust pipe" lithography. Slightly less desirable than the first Marx *Buck Rogers* ship, Rocket Police Patrol still commands strong response from seasoned collectors of most genres, primarily due to its famous license and the colorful litho inherent in period Marx pieces.

LOUIS MARX & CO.
FLASH GORDON RADIO REPEATER GUN
UNITED STATES • CIRCA 1936

Covering all the bases, Louis Marx, around 1936, obtained the *Flash Gordon* license concurrent to his *Buck Rogers* endeavors. One of the first products issued under the new license was this iconic play sidearm — a tooling design that would see endless reuse during the next 25 years. Sporting a bold comic-based illustration of Flash on the stock, the Radio Repeater Gun — a combination space-age and wild-west name — is loaded with 1930s-style science-fiction graphic design. Space-themed icons, Saturn, stars, and Flash himself factor largely in the sidearm's lithography. To be expected, the toy clicks with a loud report when the trigger is pulled. As this was an inexpensive, hollow-bodied ten-inch click toy, the Radio Repeater Gun didn't survive in large quantities, particularly in mint-original package condition. Valued by both *Flash Gordon* fans as well as toy gun enthusiasts, Marx's *Flash Gordon* Radio Repeater is a colorful reminder of a simpler sci-fi era.

BUILDER:	MARX
RELEASED:	CIRCA 1936
OPERATION:	MECHANICAL

VALUES:	
GOOD	**$600**
EXCELLENT	**$900**
MINT WITH ORIGINAL BOX	**$2200**

BOB BURNS COLLECTION

MARX

7

LOUIS MARX & CO.
FLASH GORDON ROCKET FIGHTER
UNITED STATES • 1939

Use and use again! Marx's famous penchant for repeatedly using the same tools couldn't be bothered by the presence of competing licenses. How else to explain 1935's *Buck Rogers* Rocket Police Patrol transforming into 1939's *Flash Gordon* Rocket Fighter? Sporting the comic strip's logotype, this 12-inch wind-up features all-new lithography over stampings and operation that are identical to the 1935 Buck Rogers original. As with the 1935 version, Rocket Fighter includes forward motion, clicking sounds, and rear-exhaust sparkling during operation. Not as desirable as Buck, either, yet *Flash Gordon* Rocket Fighter commands ongoing, solid interest from contemporary collectors,

BUILDER:	MARX
RELEASED:	1939
OPERATION:	WIND-UP
VALUES:	
GOOD	$400
EXCELLENT	$800
MINT WITH ORIGINAL BOX	$1800

particularly in mint-original box condition. The *Flash Gordon* Rocket Fighter would re-emerge in 1951 in a nearly identical format — except for the marked absence of the *Flash Gordon* licensing.

TOOTSIETOY
BUCK ROGERS ATTACK SHIP
UNITED STATES • 1937

The licensors of *Buck Rogers* no doubt put a full-court press on American toy manufacturers in the mid-1930s period. How else to explain the rash of products from companies which had never previously issued anything even remotely sci-fi related? Tootsietoy, that American icon of prewar die-cast ingenuity, fidelity, and creativity, left their mark on the pantheon of *Buck Rogers* product with their line of space ships. In 1937 they released a licensed die-cast line packaged in stylized second-color boxes, with fully decorated die-cast

BUILDER:	TOOTSIETOY
RELEASED:	1937
OPERATION:	STATIC
VALUES:	
GOOD	$150
EXCELLENT	$250
MINT WITH ORIGINAL BOX	$650

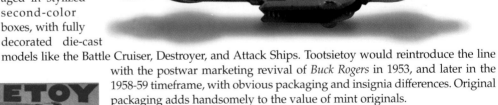

models like the Battle Cruiser, Destroyer, and Attack Ships. Tootsietoy would reintroduce the line with the postwar marketing revival of *Buck Rogers* in 1953, and later in the 1958-59 timeframe, with obvious packaging and insignia differences. Original packaging adds handsomely to the value of mint originals.

TOOTSIETOY
No. 1033 Attack Ship
BUCK ROGERS 25th CENTURY

TOOTSIETOY
BUCK ROGERS DESTROYER
UNITED STATES • 1937

With the 1937 launch of *Buck Rogers* die-cast toys, to the delight of children everywhere, Dowst's Tootsietoy brand enjoyed an enhanced level of success. The long-term merit of science-fiction licensing was once again proven with yet another successful execution of the *Buck Rogers* license, this time in 1937. Always looking to add to success, Tootsietoy immediately brought out color variations to help assist children in more complex play patterns — as well as helping them to separate themselves from their money. Without question, this Destroyer's cream and blue are particularly appealing. Classic pocket-money toys even Depression-era kids could afford, Tootsietoy *Buck Rogers* die-cast today has strong value, particularly when found boxed. Considering the stylized art and bold typography, it's easy to see why. Reissued in 1953, and again in the 1958-59 time period, with altered copyright lines in relief lettering on each piece.

BUILDER:	TOOTSIETOY
RELEASED:	1937
OPERATION:	STATIC
VALUES:	
GOOD	$150
EXCELLENT	$250
MINT WITH ORIGINAL BOX	$650

TOOTSIETOY
BUCK ROGERS FLASH BLAST ATTACK SHIP
UNITED STATES • 1937

This variation on the standard Tootsietoy *Buck Rogers* Attack Ship features alternative coloring and the enhanced branding of "Flash Blast Attack Ship." Amazingly faithful to the designs seen in *Amazing Stories* and the *Buck Rogers* comic strip, pieces such as the Attack Ship demonstrate the leadership role Tootsietoy had established in die-cast by the late 1930s. Re-released in 1953, and again in the 1958-59 period. Original packaging dramatically enhances the value of virtually any Tootsietoy *Buck Rogers* die-cast piece.

BUILDER:	TOOTSIETOY
RELEASED:	1937
OPERATION:	STATIC
VALUES:	
GOOD	$150
EXCELLENT	$250
MINT WITH ORIGINAL BOX	$650

TOOTSIETOY

TOOTSIETOY
BUCK ROGERS VENUS DESTROYER
UNITED STATES • 1937

Toy success generally results in one thing: more of the same. And that's just what Dowst's Tootsietoy, of Chicago, did when it first experienced success with its new *Buck Rogers* die-cast toy line in the mid-1930s. The easiest way to reissue toys is to alter coloration, so revised versions of the first-issue toys soon appeared on the market — in fact, in many cases, the revised toys occupied shelf space concurrent with the first issues. That's likely the case with this red-and-cream Venus Destroyer. Faithfully re-created from the *Buck Rogers* comic strip artwork, this Destroyer has an alternate color scheme that allowed children to engage in multi-toy play patterns without the confusion of identically decorated spacecraft. And it helped part them from their cash — always a good thing, in the mind of a toymaker. This somewhat more valuable color variation is particularly desirable when found with its original packaging. Reissued in 1953, again in the 1958-59 time period.

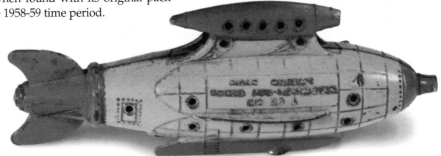

BUILDER:	TOOTSIETOY
RELEASED:	1937
OPERATION:	STATIC
VALUES:	
GOOD	$150
EXCELLENT	$350
MINT WITH ORIGINAL BOX	$800

UNKNOWN
ROBOT LILLIPUT
JAPAN • CIRCA 1939

For every collectible genre, there is a first — and for robots, this is believed to be IT. No matter whose opinion is solicited, most contemporary robot collectors consider Robot Lilliput, by an unknown Japanese manufacturer, to be the earliest-known toy automaton. Originally believed to be an early postwar product, the contemporary thinking about Lilliput now holds that it predates World War II. (Close examination of original packaging and other factors now point toward a circa-1939 release.) Standing six inches in height, Robot Lilliput is a mechanical wind-up who straight-leg walks while swinging his arms. Lithographically crude by postwar standards, Lilliput features oversized rivets and large, hand-drawn chest gauges complemented by a snaking hose from the robot's head to its "heart." The robot's block-style head and expressionless gaze undoubtedly helped establish these now-iconic robot features. Lilliput also boasts the inexplicable "N.P. 5357" designation on its lower torso. Relatively affordable in good condition — suggesting solid sales during its original period of availability — examples with original packaging bring a steep premium. However humble when judged by postwar operational standards, Robot Lilliput nonetheless commands serious respect due to its seminal role in the establishment of the robot and space-toy genre.

BUILDER:	UNKNOWN
RELEASED:	CIRCA 1939
OPERATION:	WIND-UP
VALUES:	
GOOD	$450
EXCELLENT	$1200
MINT WITH ORIGINAL BOX	$2000

JAMES D. JULIA AUCTIONS IMAGE

WYANDOTTE
BUCK ROGERS ROCKET FIGHTER
UNITED STATES • CIRCA 1936

The era of pressed-steel playthings reached its zenith in the prewar period, with brands like Buddy "L", Nylint, Structo, and Wyandotte all competing for the "sandbox" dollar — toy purchases that parents would expect to survive multiple years of hard play. Rugged and generally less sophisticated in design, most pressed-steel toys were traditionally automotive in inspiration. However, in the 1936 timeframe, Wyandotte bucked the trend (as it were) with the fascinating *Buck Rogers* Rocket Fighter. Created from pressed steel, the six-inch teardrop/zeppelin-shaped toy is far more "Wyandotte" than *Buck Rogers* in terms of design and construction technique. Enameled steel is tabbed together in a three-color deco format. As a mechanical wind-up, the Fighter scoots along the floor, its wheels housed in 1930s-style teardrop-shaped "boots." An affordable toy in good and excellent condition, Wyandotte's *Buck Rogers* Rocket Fighter is uncommon in mint-original box condition. Given its "rough and tumble" nature, this toy doesn't command higher prices the way some fragile Buck Rogers litho toys do — but to an entry-level collector, that's just fine. For an uncommon toy at an undervalued price, Wyandotte's *Buck Rogers* Rocket Fighter is a best bet.

BUILDER:	WYANDOTTE
RELEASED:	CIRCA 1936
OPERATION:	WIND-UP
VALUES:	
GOOD	**$200**
EXCELLENT	**$400**
MINT WITH ORIGINAL BOX	**$1200**

WYANDOTTE
ROCKET SPACE SHIP
UNITED STATES • CIRCA 1938

Because so many of Wyandotte's early toys were crafted from pressed-steel, their early tin-litho toys are easily overlooked. That's a shame, because examples like Rocket Space Ship, from the 1938 time period, are wondrous examples of the art of printed tin. This eight-inch friction toy is believed to be Wyandotte's attempt to cash in on the popularity of Marx's space-oriented tin-litho toys of the same era. Though Wyandotte had a *Buck Rogers* license (PRE-1940s), it was for a pressed-steel toy only. Thus, it's likely Rocket Space Ship — with its swept-back lines, Streamline Moderne litho design, and sturdy friction motor — was Wyandotte's marketplace answer. Something of a cross between an airplane, streamlined diesel locomotive, and airship from Fritz Lang's silent sci-fi opus *Metropolis*, Rocket Space Ship is tin-litho creativity in a compact package. Affordable except when original packaging is present, and stylish in its own right — licensed or not.

BUILDER:	WYANDOTTE
RELEASED:	CIRCA 1938
OPERATION:	FRICTION
VALUES:	
GOOD	**$150**
EXCELLENT	**$450**
MINT WITH ORIGINAL BOX	**$1200**

WYANDOTTE

WYANDOTTE
ROCKET SPACE SHIP
UNITED STATES • CIRCA 1939

Wyandotte's second iteration of Rocket Space Ship debuted only a year or so after the debut of the original in 1938. This version features a more color-coordinated chassis, as well as an improved, more modernized friction drive and wheelsets.

A handful of slight lithographic alterations are also key to the main differences. Not surprisingly, collectors don't see much fiscal difference between the two eight-inch toys, resulting in identical values across both variations. For those with a penchant for completeness, the Rocket Space Ship pair by Wyandotte make a fine complementary display alongside other tin-litho space toys of the prewar era.

BUILDER:	WYANDOTTE
RELEASED:	CIRCA 1939
OPERATION:	FRICTION

VALUES:

GOOD	$150
EXCELLENT	$450
MINT WITH ORIGINAL BOX	$1200

THE 1940s

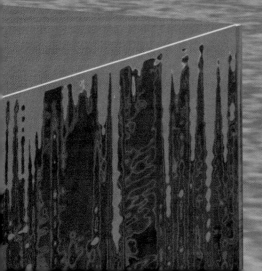

ATOMIC ROBOT MAN

CIRCA 1949

BY AN UNKNOWN MANUFACTURER

OCCUPIED JAPAN

THE 1940s

The war years weren't good for anything except ridding the world of fascist imperialism — for a time, anyway. The 1940s were particularly hard on the toy industries of the period. As the giant of early mass-production toymaking, Germany found itself on the losing end of World War II. Most of its historic toy builders had either been forcibly converted to war materiel manufacture, or had been so badly destroyed during Allied bombing raids that rebuilding proved impossible. And some, like E. P. Lehmann Patentwerk, found themselves in Red Army territory at the close of the war, forcing wholesale relocation overnight simply to retain their freedom. Overall, toys would not be a significant part of Germany's postwar rebuilding effort.

On the other side of the world, Japan also lay in ruins, its infrastructure badly damaged by both atomic and conventional attacks. What had been before the war a promising new power in toy design and manufacture was mostly rubble, thanks to Doolittle's bombing runs over Tokyo's industrial sectors.

Yet amazingly, within a decade both nations would be rebuilt, brick by brick, industry by industry. And key to both nations' recoveries would be the methodical export of key consumer goods — in the case of Japan, toys. Though the process of rebuilding was slow, almost painful, the end result was not only economic rejuvenation and fledgling democracy, but the creation of an entirely new generation of playthings — powered, in part, by the new consumer dry-cell battery and miniature can motors.

The battery age was beginning.
But it wouldn't truly unfold until the early 1950s.

AMERICAN PENCIL COMPANY
BUCK ROGERS CRAYON SHIP
UNITED STATES • CIRCA 1940

BOB BURNS COLLECTION

Packaging ingenuity has long been a hallmark of toymaking. From early wooden boxes to today's complex marriages of paper, glassine, and plastic, toy packaging is often as meaningful as the toy inside. There's no better example of this concept than American Pencil's *Buck Rogers* Crayon Ship, circa 1940. This stunning, yet simply elegant, five-inch box containing eight crayons is a marvel: not only does it serve as a receptacle for coloring instruments, it ingeniously leverages the best properties of the license as well. Outside, there are two pieces of art; one is the "*Buck Rogers* Crayon Ship," while the opposite side shows Buck and Wilma intently watching a view port. The "port" is actually a die-cut opening which displays an animated sequence of passing spaceships and meteors as the inner tray is removed from the outer package. As a container for crayons, American Pencil's *Buck Rogers* Crayon Ship is both functional and protective, but as a metaphor for both the *Buck Rogers* license and its symbolism of space travel, the Crayon Ship is unparalleled. Note all values reflect the presence of original packaging.

BUILDER:	AMERICAN PENCIL COMPANY
RELEASED:	CIRCA 1940
OPERATION:	STATIC
VALUES:	
GOOD	$65
EXCELLENT	$200
MINT WITH ORIGINAL BOX	$450

DAISY
BUCK ROGERS ATOMIC PISTOL
UNITED STATES • CIRCA 1940

There's nothing like a solid run of success, particularly in the notoriously fickle toy industry. For a company like medium-sized Daisy, their profitable *Buck Rogers* streak would be profound enough to ultimately characterize the company's 1930s efforts. By the 1940s, Daisy was marketing a complete set of *Buck*-inspired sparkling ray guns, though the line was clearly getting a little long in the tooth. So designers integrated this stylish and clearly Western-influenced holster featuring *Buck* artwork and typography in custom-tooled leather As most period leather has by now disintegrated — without the power of ray guns — finding fine examples such as this is highly uncommon. Note all values reflect the presence of the original leather holster. Mint-original condition assumes the presence of virtually unheard-of original packaging. For collectors of *Buck Rogers* ephemera, this may be one of the last remaining pinnacles.

BUILDER:	DAISY
RELEASED:	CIRCA 1940
OPERATION:	MECHANICAL
VALUES:	
GOOD	$500
EXCELLENT	$1000
MINT WITH ORIGINAL BOX	$3000

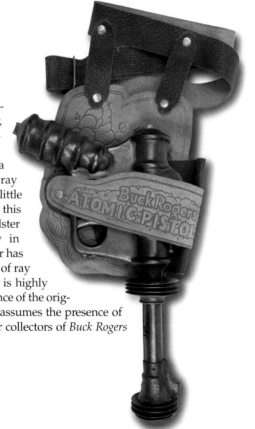

BOB BURNS COLLECTION

DAISY
ZOOKA POP PISTOL
UNITED STATES • CIRCA 1940

Not every toy sidearm by Daisy was a cast-metal affair. Like many of its contemporaries, Daisy also marketed a selection of cost-reduced tin-litho guns, such as the Zooka Pop Pistol from the 1940 timeframe. Merging sci-fi, gangster movies, and military lingo, the seven-inch Zooka Pop Pistol is just that — a classic sparkling pop gun loaded with colorful artwork. In fact, it's often mistaken for a Marx toy at first glance — the artistic resemblance is that close. Fun and inexpensive, relatively easy to find, and loaded with classic '40s styling — it's pure Daisy.

BUILDER:	DAISY
RELEASED:	CIRCA 1940
OPERATION:	MECHANICAL
◆	
VALUES:	
GOOD	$55
EXCELLENT	$95
MINT WITH ORIGINAL BOX	$165

BOB BURNS COLLECTION

HILLER
ATOM RAY GUN WATER PISTOL
UNITED STATES • CIRCA 1949

A lasting benefit of the wartime industrial build-up was the establishment of a huge metallurgical casting base. With military contracts drying up in the early postwar period, these casting companies couldn't *all* crank out hose spigots and auto parts. Some relied on innovation; indeed, the little-known casting firm of Hiller kept ahead of its competition by creating this stunning Atom Ray Gun water pistol during the late-1949 period. Military-level tolerances and an ingenious watertight design were matched with *Buck Rogers* styling in a 6½-inch package. Just fill the top tank with water, screw it back into place, and start the blasting; the water jet travels upwards of twenty feet with liquid accuracy. A rarely seen water sidearm borne of wartime engineering know-how and obscure branding — in short, the perfect space toy. And quintessentially American, as well.

BUILDER:	HILLER
RELEASED:	CIRCA 1949
OPERATION:	MECHANICAL
◆	
VALUES:	
GOOD	$200
EXCELLENT	$350
MINT WITH ORIGINAL BOX	$900

BOB BURNS COLLECTION

DAISY — HILLER

MILTON BRADLEY
CAPTAIN VIDEO SPACE GAME
UNITED STATES • 1949

Nearly forgotten today, Captain Video starred in the 1949-1955 television series of the same name on the short-lived DuMont television network. Perhaps owing to the series' rather cerebral bent, or the inept capabilities of DuMont licensors, few *Captain Video* toys were produced, and fewer exist today. A super-brilliant scientist of the future, Captain Video and his youthful sidekick, the Video Ranger, battled all sorts of villians, usually resorting to reasoning and knowledge, rather than fights, to resolve each episode's conflicts. This Milton Bradley game hails from the earliest *Captain Video* days, when the show was appearing in daily strip form on DuMont. Colorful graphics and the terrific stand-up control panel set the game apart from its pedestrian MB gameplay peers. Values represent complete games in varying conditions.

BUILDER: MILTON BRADLEY	
RELEASED:	1949
OPERATION:	STATIC
◆	
VALUES:	
GOOD	$100
EXCELLENT	$300
MINT WITH ORIGINAL BOX	$650

UNKNOWN
ATOMIC ROBOT MAN
OCCUPIED JAPAN • CIRCA 1949

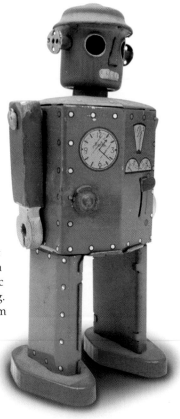

Considered by many space-toy enthusiasts to be the "second" robot toy ever produced (after Robot Lilliput, PRE-1940s), Atomic Robot Man, by an unknown Japanese manufacturer, boasts all of the genre's best features: a blank facial expression; barrel chest; crude, oversized gauges; and straight-legged eccentric-wheel/pin walking. A diminutive toy, Atomic Robot Man stands a mere five inches in height. Yet, what it lacks in stature, Atomic Robot Man more than covers in style. Its lightbulb ears and mechanical "hat" are outdone only by the red feet and chest-mounted on/off slide switch. Along with Robot Lilliput, Atomic Robot Man makes a terrific display of early Japanese space-themed toymaking. Though recently reproduced and imported from China in lookalike packaging, original Atomic Robot Men have not experienced value deflation as a result. Being second, it would seem, isn't so bad after all.

BUILDER:	UNKNOWN
RELEASED:	CIRCA 1949
OPERATION:	WIND-UP
◆	
VALUES:	
GOOD	$300
EXCELLENT	$500
MINT WITH ORIGINAL BOX	$1600

UNKNOWN
SPACE PATROL SPACE GAME
OCCUPIED JAPAN • CIRCA 1948

One of the earliest toys to bear the venerable means-nothing brand "Space Patrol," this carnival giveaway was imported from Occupied Japan in relatively high quantities during the late-1940s timeframe. Bulk-packed in 24-counts for easy distribution as prizes in the carnival and sideshow channel, Space Patrol Space Games feature a gear-driven push-and-spin mechanism which turns the toy's inner dial. Wherever the rocket lands becomes the participant's "destination." Numeric scores can be integrated for enhanced play. As this toy never had retail packaging, the mint value represents "mint, loose only." Marked "Occupied Japan," Space Patrol Space Game is a colorful collectible that boasts excellent lithographic artistry, a basic yet durable mechanism, and enough mystery to make it worthy of additional inquiry.

BUILDER:	UNKNOWN
RELEASED:	CIRCA 1948
OPERATION:	MECHANICAL
VALUES:	
GOOD	$100
EXCELLENT	$175
MINT	$250

UNKNOWN

THE 1950s

SPACE WHALE

CIRCA 1957

BY YOSHIYA (KO)

JAPAN

THE 1950S

The golden age. As with every phenomenon, it only happens once, and for robots and space toys, that time was the decade of the 1950s. There are countless reasons for this explosion in popularity, but perhaps the greatest influences come down to motion pictures and the 1956 launch of Sputnik. These two factors contributed greatly to the public's awareness of "outer space" as a concept, and robots and flying saucers in particular.

Though science fiction had been around for decades — and had gained momentum in the 1930s with the rise of pop-culture icons like *Buck Rogers* and *Flash Gordon* — it underwent a profound maturation in the 1950s. To be sure, most sci-fi content was still aimed at children; from the *Captain Video* television series to the hapless relaunches of the anachronistic *Rogers* and *Gordon*, kids were awash in goofy, silly, and often trite portrayals of science fiction.

But films like *Destination Moon* (1950) and *The Day the Earth Stood Still* (1952) demonstrated the increasing seriousness and maturity that sci-fi subject matter was enjoying. Just as the kids of the 1930s had grown up, so too had their sci-fi entertainment. This enhanced respectability had widespread social impact, including an embracing of space toys by toymakers and consumers alike.

Combine this increased pop-culture awareness with the reality of the 1956 launch of Sputnik, and American consumers in particular had plenty of reason — good *and* bad — to focus on the skies when they shopped for toys.

And no one was better positioned to respond than the toymakers of Japan. D cells, can motors, and lithographed tin — three basic components of a product strategy that would rule toy design and marketing for a generation.

ALPS
(DOOR) ROBOT
JAPAN • CIRCA 1958

BUILDER:	ALPS
RELEASED:	CIRCA 1958
OPERATION:	BATTERY
VALUES:	
GOOD	$2000
EXCELLENT	$3500
MINT WITH ORIGINAL BOX	$6000

The tale of Alps is that of a survivor. This company rose from the ashes of World War II to become one of Japan's most revered postwar toybuilders, then transitioned itself into a manufacturer of consumer and manufacturing electronics. Back in the late 1950s, Alps was yet another Tokyo-based toymaker, searching for that magic formula to hit it big with American consumers. With the 1956 release of *Forbidden Planet*, Alps — and virtually every other Tokyo toymaker — had a wellspring of inspiration from which to draw. Their battery-operated Robot — Door Robot to collectors — exhibits clear indebtedness to Robby, yet it transcends imitation. During operation, the 9¼-inch remote-control robot "walks" forward using eccentric wheels housed in the leg-feet assembly; twin antennae inside its clear dome spin; an illuminated color light-show ensues through the robot's mouth grille; and its arms swing to and fro. Plus, when this isn't enough, there's its namesake chest door to open. (Could this toy be the inspiration for Matt Groening's Bender the Robot, as seen on Fox's *Futurama*? Only Matt knows for sure.) As a very desirable robot from the classic period, Door Robot has become one of Alps' most popular products.

ROBERT JOHNSON / COMET TOYS USA IMAGES

ALPS
MR. ROBOT THE MECHANICAL BRAIN
JAPAN • CIRCA 1954

Likely the first Alps space toy, Mr. Robot the Mechanical Brain boasts many of the classic design elements which would come to characterize the leading school of robot design. Among its more notable features, Mr. Robot includes a boxy body with a central row of rivets; outward, immovable, forward-facing hands; straight-legged locomotion; ear-muff headsets; coiled head-brain and telescoping backpack antennae; and an unchanging, emotionless gaze. All are design icons today, but they came from somewhere — and that somewhere was toys like Mr. Robot. Interestingly, Alps chose to integrate battery power with this wind-up toy, but not to automate its movement — battery power provides illumination for Mr. Robot's impenetrable gaze. It's unclear which came first — Alps' Mr. Robot, or Nomura's Zoomer the Robot (1950s) — but it's obvious they emerged around the same time, likely in the 1954 era. Alps would, in a few short years, be issuing some of the more innovative and collectible space-toy playthings, so it's interesting to see where it all began. A mid-priced robot in terms of collectible value, the diminutive Mr. Robot by Alps symbolizes the beginning of something big.

BUILDER:	ALPS
RELEASED:	CIRCA 1954
OPERATION:	WIND-UP
VALUES:	
GOOD	$900
EXCELLENT	$1500
MINT WITH ORIGINAL BOX	$2800

JAMES D. JULIA AUCTIONS IMAGES

ALPS
TELEVISION SPACEMAN
JAPAN • CIRCA 1959

It's unclear which Japanese manufacturer was first to integrate the decade's biggest phenomenon — television — with the robot toy, but Alps definitely had an early lock on coolness with Television Spaceman. The boxy battery-op from around 1959 defines the TV space toy genre: during operation, it slowly walks and swings its arms, the gears in its "eyes" turning, while the illuminated TV screen rolls a space-themed "program." Standing nearly 15 inches to its antenna top, this impressive toy isn't uncommon in today's collector market, making it a popular choice among new enthusiasts looking to upgrade the sophistication of their collections. Often found without its antenna, Alps' Television Spaceman should be inspected for functioning illumination within the TV set — without it, repairs will soon follow. Many color variations are known, as well as plastic feet on later versions. Television Spaceman by Alps has it all: terrific packaging, great action, and iconic classic-period industrial design.

BUILDER:	ALPS
RELEASED:	CIRCA 1959
OPERATION:	BATTERY
VALUES:	
GOOD	$550
EXCELLENT	$800
MINT WITH ORIGINAL BOX	$1200

AMERICAN PLASTICS COMPANY
SMOKE RING GUN
UNITED STATES • CIRCA 1954

With western toy guns, there was more than just flash and panache — there was also the BAM! of tiny gunpowder caps. Toy ray guns didn't usually employ caps for effect, requiring kids to fill in the blanks with imagination. American Plastics realized this when marketing their Smoke Ring Gun, an ingenious nine-inch device that literally blows western cap guns away. Drop the magic pellet into the nose of the gun, then pull the trigger. Pronounced smoke rings emanate from the gun's barrel, floating toward your adversary in slow-motion dread. Ultra-cool, it's likely these guns were a kid's favorite toy — that is, until the pellets ran out. Rarely found with original smoke pellets today, Smoke Ring Gun is now more interesting and collectible for its industrial design. In addition, it's a great example of nonlicensed creative product design.

BUILDER:	AMERICAN PLASTICS COMPANY
RELEASED:	CIRCA 1954
OPERATION:	MECHANICAL
VALUES:	
GOOD	$150
EXCELLENT	$350
MINT WITH ORIGINAL BOX	$650

BOB BURNS COLLECTION

AMERICAN TOY PRODUCTS
ROCKET PATROL MAGNETIC TARGET GAME
UNITED STATES • CIRCA 1955

Toy industry bottomfeeders like magnetic dart games were quick to ride the tidal wave of science fiction that swept over American popular culture in the early 1950s. In fact, they were among the first to adopt the trend, if for no other reasons than commercial expedience and an easy lithographic plate change. American Toy Products' circa-1955 Rocket Patrol Magnetic Target Game bears the definite look of a bandwagon toy. A standard play pattern — shooting at a tin-litho board with magnet-tipped "darts" — is merged with colorful (if not unique) sci-fi artwork to create a toy that likely was given as an unrequested gift far more than it was directly solicited by children. Still, the game board itself (14 x 16 inches) provides a wonderful and colorful look at third-tier toy product design and marketing. Interestingly, American Toy no doubt wanted to cover all of its bases, as the reverse side of the Rocket Patrol game is the "Name-A-State" dart game. Choose your weapon, choose your side — it's dart time.

BUILDER:	AMERICAN TOY PRODUCTS
RELEASED:	CIRCA 1955
OPERATION:	STATIC
VALUES:	
GOOD	$100
EXCELLENT	$150
MINT WITH ORIGINAL BOX	$250

ARCHER
ROCKETSHIP KIT
UNITED STATES • CIRCA 1955

BUILDER:	ARCHER
RELEASED:	CIRCA 1955
OPERATION:	STATIC
VALUES:	
GOOD	$35
EXCELLENT	$125
MINT WITH ORIGINAL BOX	$350

As a toymaker specializing in thermoplastic construction, Archer is best known for their "Space People" (1950s) line of plastic figures. But their less-recognized Rocket Ship Kit is just as deserving of attention, as it represents an interesting early hybrid (or cross-category) toy: a plastic model kit with an outer-space theme. Issued before the Willy Ley-designed Revell kits of the late 1950s and early '60s, Archer's take-apart/put-together kit borrows heavily on 1930s-era design concepts, such as the dorsal fin and vertical-launch motif, to create an interesting (and mildly entertaining) play pattern from mere mold-in-color plastic. The Rocketship Kit includes three primary "stages" (rocket components) as well as the "launcher pad." Good and excellent valuations do not necessitate the presence of original packaging. Not common, yet not highly desirable, the Archer Rocket Ship Kit more than lives up to its billing, promising "you be the space engineer." That is to say, put it together yourself, if you want to have any fun at all!

L ong before Hanna-Barbera's Jetsons, there were Archer's Space People. Dating back to roughly 1947, these four-inch plastic figures perfectly capture the hilariously strange perceptions postwar America had of The Future. Outfits, hairstyles, even footwear and helmets, all suggested a tomorrow that was straight out of an Ed Wood movie. As the package stated boldly, the set includes "space men, space women [and] space children" — the entire gravity-challenged brood! Depicted here is a later release from the same tools, hailing from around 1955. This set includes Archer's distinctive removable helmets. Note how the innovative window packaging leverages the space theme with a glassine rocket-shaped window. Reproductions from original tooling in recent years means boxed originals help ensure authenticity and collectibility. The figures' best quality: hilarious poses and stylized interpretations of tomorrow's fashions. Individual loose figures vary wildly in value, depending on seller, condition, and completeness. For static displays among tin toys, nothing beats the character and intrinsic comedy of Archer's Space People.

BUILDER:	ARCHER
RELEASED:	CIRCA 1955
OPERATION:	STATIC
VALUES:	
GOOD	$250
EXCELLENT	$450
MINT WITH ORIGINAL BOX	$800

A rnold, of Germany, is one of the world's most storied toymakers, with a history dating to the 19th century. Now known for its model trains, Arnold was a full-line toy company during the 1950s when they produced the Flying Saucer Airplane. This curiously named product is exactly what it says: a friction toy that, when pushed along the floor, launches one of two included "flying saucers." The airplane itself has extremely colorful lithography, and the box is nothing short of a period sci-fi visual opus: multiple UFOs seem to be attacking the aircraft as it speeds across a cloud-dotted blue sky. Interestingly, the toy's play pattern is opposite that which the package lid depicts (now *there's* a toymaking rarity). When found today, Flying Saucer Airplane is generally lacking one or both of the UFOs. A basic toy with vivid visuals, Arnold's Flying Saucer Airplane is a budget-priced item that adds European charm to any collection's overall product mix.

BUILDER:	ARNOLD
RELEASED:	CIRCA 1954
OPERATION:	FRICTION
VALUES:	
GOOD	$350
EXCELLENT	$475
MINT WITH ORIGINAL BOX	$850

ARCHER — ARNOLD

ASAHI
SPACE PATROL
JAPAN • CIRCA 1957

Take one off-the-shelf Mercedes-Benz racer toy, add a hood-mounted laser cannon, and pilot the entire affair with a stern-faced robot. Put it all together, and you've got Space Patrol, built in the 1957 timeframe by Asahi (ATC). Clearly a shotgun-marriage hybrid toy, Space Patrol is typical in leveraging existing tooling (in this case, the Mercedes-Benz racer) and merging it with a contemporary fad (in this case, space toys in general, and robots in particular). Speaking of robots, the Asahi automaton design features a classic blockheaded format, circular, expressionless eyes, and wireform ears and head antennae. The friction-drive, 11-inch Mercedes produces a distinctive whine during operation, but does precious little additionally. Owing largely to the weirdness of the toy, it's a highly pursued piece in today's collecting environment — and even more so when the toy is found mint with its original package. Look for this robot head subassembly on other period Asahi toys, as well. Cars, guns, and robots — if this amalgam doesn't define postwar Japanese toymaking, nothing does.

BUILDER:	ASAHI
RELEASED:	CIRCA 1957
OPERATION:	FRICTION

◆

VALUES:	
GOOD	$1200
EXCELLENT	$1800
MINT WITH ORIGINAL BOX	$3500

ASAHI
SPACE PATROL
JAPAN • CIRCA 1958

Many Japanese toy builders quickly filled their space-toy lines by combining off-the-shelf products with "outer space" elements to create instant hybrids. Asahi was in the forefront of the trend with products like the 1958-ish Space Patrol. Based on the then-new MGA created for their vehicle-toy line, Asahi's 10-inch toy features friction drive and a timing mechanism which causes the astronaut to periodically raise and fire his ray gun as the car speeds along. Taking a page from the science fiction pulps of the day, Asahi's helmeted astronaut design accurately foretells the later real-life gear of NASA explorers. Colorful lithographic decoration and the incongruity of it all make this a terrific must-have for collectors. Boxed examples are particularly desirable, reflecting the quality of the package illustration and the scarcity of the box itself. And, when placed next to the standard Asahi MGA friction toy, there's no better illustration of postwar Japanese hybrid toymaking than Space Patrol.

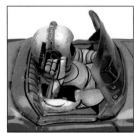

BUILDER:	ASAHI
RELEASED:	CIRCA 1958
OPERATION:	FRICTION

◆

VALUES:	
GOOD	$800
EXCELLENT	$1600
MINT WITH ORIGINAL BOX	$3000

ASAKUSA
THUNDER ROBOT
JAPAN • CIRCA 1957

Little is known about Japanese toymaker Asakusa, other than its name being a manufacturing district on the outskirts of Tokyo. Yet Asakusa's amazing legacy, Thunder Robot, speaks for itself. With its confident stride, head-mounted spinning antenna, and scary palm-mounted guns, this stylized bullet-shaped automaton has but a single life purpose: to destroy everything in its path. During operation, eyes and headlight flash as the 11-inch toy walks along, its head antenna spinning. Then it stops, raises its arms, and begins firing with guns located in its palms. Thunder Robot is a huge collector favorite due to its unique Mayan-like industrial design, as well as rarity; it has been estimated that this toy had an extremely short production run, compounded by ineffective distribution in the United States, resulting in the extreme present scarcity. Not surprisingly, Thunder Robot commands top dollar whenever exchanges take place. The toy is generally found without its original antenna, and reproductions exist; values provided reflect complete and original toys only. An amazing battery-op from a forgotten manufacturer, Asakusa's Thunder Robot is one of the contemporary collecting environment's most pursued toys, and rightly so.

BUILDER:	ASAKUSA
RELEASED:	CIRCA 1957
OPERATION:	BATTERY
VALUES:	
GOOD	$6000
EXCELLENT	$9000
MINT WITH ORIGINAL BOX	$18000

KALMBACH IMAGES

BALLEIS
SPACE TOP
WEST GERMANY • 1957

Spinning tops have been around in one form or another for thousands of years, so it figures that the space-toy explosion of the 1950s — fueled by Hollywood motion pictures as much as by real-life events — would result in a themed spinning-top product. Balleis, of Germany, stepped up with their 1957 release, Space Top. Clearly influenced by the launch of Sputnik, Space Top features the standard "pump and spin" action used by most 20th-century mechanical tops. The space-toy connection is revealed on the inside, where Balleis product designers included tin-litho globe-toy artwork and two tiny Sputniks, which circumnavigate the "earth" whenever the top is in action. Outfitted with this terrific play pattern, Space Top is one of those oddball items that add character and depth to any space-toy accumulation. The toy is marked "© 1957 Balleis." Scarce in mint-original box condition, most examples are found loose and in good condition, where pricing is far more affordable. Little is known about Balleis, but their Sputnik-influenced Space Top speaks volumes about event-based product design.

BUILDER:	BALLEIS
RELEASED:	1957
OPERATION:	MECHANICAL
VALUES:	
GOOD	$400
EXCELLENT	$800
MINT WITH ORIGINAL BOX	$2100

ASAKUSA — BALLEIS

BANDAI
SPACE PATROL SUPER CYCLE
JAPAN • CIRCA 1957

The merging of Today with Imagined Tomorrow tends to produce readily recognizable results. Consider Bandai's Space Patrol Super Cycle. The future; super heroes; motorcycles — it all adds up, doesn't it? Heavily indebted to period comic book designs, Bandai's Super Cycle is an extremely desirable piece, owing both to its iconic styling, as well as its rarity, particularly in complete condition. As this image attests, most Super Cycles lack their original, molded green-rubber super hero rider; some riders are believed to have come outfitted with fabric capes in traditional superhero fashion. Bold styling, colorful litho, a prodigious sparkling mechanism that displays through a red gel located over the rear wheel, and friction drive — in sum, a truly memorable tin-toy presentation. A red Super Cycle variation, created from slightly altered stamping tools, is also known. (Note all prices reflect the presence of an original rider in complete condition. Toys lacking drivers plummet in value.) Red or blue, Bandai's Space Patrol Super Cycle reigns supreme among two-wheeled space toys. Let's ride!

KALMBACH IMAGE

BUILDER:	BANDAI
RELEASED:	CIRCA 1957
OPERATION:	FRICTION

VALUES:

GOOD	$6000
EXCELLENT	$8000
MINT WITH ORIGINAL BOX	$12000

BANDAI-ALPS
MOON EXPLORER
JAPAN • CIRCA 1958

MARKETER:	BANDAI
BUILDER:	ALPS
RELEASED:	CIRCA 1958
OPERATION:	BATTERY

VALUES:

GOOD	$1200
EXCELLENT	$2000
MINT WITH ORIGINAL BOX	$4500

The developmental chain interconnecting the many tiers of postwar Tokyo toymaking led to unexpected alliances. Consider Moon Explorer, by Bandai and Alps. Though the two companies competed vigorously in the vehicle- and character-toy categories, Bandai simply wasn't much of a player in space toys. By 1958, when Moon Explorer was likely released, Alps had already staked out a solid piece of real estate in robot and space-toy exporting. It's clear Bandai simply chose the path of least resistance for capitalizing on the robot craze — work with an existing player (and their tools) to create a new product.

Fourteen-inch (to the antenna tip) Moon Explorer is the metallic offspring of Alps products like Television Spaceman (1950s), though it boasts its own intriguing set of exclusive features, like the stylized death masque face (with backlit illumination) and the truly weird chest-mounted clock which counts down to who-knows-what. Obvious Alps influences include the Marconi-style antenna; leg and arm assemblies; main torso frame; and additional small visible components, as well as the drive train. Found in a small variety of colors and variations, with packaged examples at a strong premium, Moon Explorer is a desirable automaton that illustrates the more-than-friendly interconnections found between players in the Japanese toy industry of the 1950s.

ROBERT JOHNSON / COMET TOYS USA IMAGES

BEEMAK PLASTICS
SPACE PATROL OUTER SPACE PLASTIC HELMET
UNITED STATES • CIRCA 1954

BOB BURNS COLLECTION

It was around 1954, and Beemak Plastics ("Los Angeles 23, California") saw the opportunity to cash in on the sci-fi craze among kids. Their Space Patrol outer space plastic helmet probably wasn't a licensee of the 1950-55 *Buzz Corry Space Patrol* TV program, but that mattered little to the lucky kids who owned one. Featuring an inflatable "tank" and "air tubes" on which the molded-clear, two-piece nine-inch plastic dome is affixed, the Beemak Space Patrol helmet was a robust-enough toy — until that fateful (and inevitable) first puncture put the inflatable section out of business. While domes are not uncommon, complete Beemak Space Patrol helmets are exceedingly difficult to find, particularly ones which can still inflate. "Good" values reflect both helmet and inflatable portions present, while mint-original box values reflect the presence of all original packaging, including inserts and the instruction sheet, as well as a mint, unused helmet itself.

BUILDER:	BEEMAK PLASTICS
RELEASED:	CIRCA 1954
OPERATION:	STATIC

◆

VALUES:	
GOOD	$500
EXCELLENT	$900
MINT WITH ORIGINAL BOX	$1800

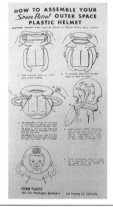

CRAGSTAN-ASAHI
SPACE ROBOT PATROL
JAPAN • CIRCA 1959

ROBERT JOHNSON / COMET TOYS USA IMAGE

No one hates a languishing investment more than a toy manufacturer, so any opportunity to reuse old, dated tooling is always a welcome opportunity. When Cragstan was looking for its first imported products, they left Asahi with a contract to import one of that firm's older space-toy products, 11-inch Space Patrol (1950s). New lithography was designed, this time more colorful and child-focused; friction drive was retained; and new packaging was approved. Speaking of packaging, Space Robot Patrol's box is a classic example of early-period Cragstan packaging: custom toy-specific graphics grace the lid and side panels; the "It's Cragstan for toys" logotype anchors the bottom-left corner; and stylized, yet crude, illustrations convey a simple charm. To no one's surprise, Asahi would flog this platform one final time in the early 1960s with Prop Flying Robot Car (1960s). All three examples, positioned with one another, constitute a great little troika in space-toy variation collecting.

MARKETER:	CRAGSTAN
BUILDER:	ASAHI
RELEASED:	CIRCA 1959
OPERATION:	FRICTION

◆

VALUES:	
GOOD	$700
EXCELLENT	$1200
MINT WITH ORIGINAL BOX	$3500

CRAGSTAN-YOSHIYA
FLYING SAUCER WITH SPACE PILOT
JAPAN • CIRCA 1959

Yoshiya (KO) created a number of flying saucer toys, and this example, Flying Saucer with Space Pilot, is their contribution to the early Cragstan family of badge-engineered product. Now shrouded in legend, Cragstan was comprised of New York City-based toy sales veterans who, over a 15-year period, imported thousands of different Japanese toys for sale in the American market-place. Though the term "selfless" doesn't come to mind when reflecting on the shamelessly self-promoting Cragstan, they were big enough to allow their manufacturing partners some visibility, as this "KO"-marked box demonstrates. Flying Saucer with Space Pilot is a basic saucer-format toy, with a centrally located dome housing a humanoid astronaut. Actions include a "swivel lited engine" (sic); mystery action; turning antenna; and even "real space noise." Obviously part of the post-Sputnik era, Yoshiya's Flying Saucer with Space Pilot is a basic toy that sells at reasonable values in the contemporary environment. Alternate versions of this toy platform were marketed directly by Yoshiya, and include Space Patrol 3; Sky Patrol Flying Saucer; and close variant New Flying Saucer. As a saucer toy, Yoshiya's creation isn't that groundbreaking. But as an example of early Cragstan importation, it's practically historic.

MARKETER:	CRAGSTAN
BUILDER:	YOSHIYA
RELEASED:	CIRCA 1959
OPERATION:	BATTERY

VALUES:	
GOOD	$250
EXCELLENT	$450
MINT WITH ORIGINAL BOX	$700

FLORIAN
TOM CORBETT SPACE CADET PUSHOUTS
UNITED STATES • CIRCA 1952

Compared to its sci-fi competition, *Tom Corbett Space Cadet* was something of a renegade TV program. Set in the distant future (around 2350), the show followed the exploits of a group of teenage Space Cadets studying to become officers of the Solar Guard. Rather than focus on monsters or other fantastic subject matter, the writers of *Tom Corbett Space Cadet* featured more human-based exploits and adventures, helping to endear the show to its preteen audience. A strong licensing program boosted *Tom Corbett*'s visibility, with numerous toys and play-things marketed during its initial 1950-55 run. This pushout book by specialty publisher Florian, from the 1952 period, is filled with terrific artwork based on the characters and situations from the TV series. In general, most pushout books are found with one or more of the objects removed from the pages; note that the value for mint-original denotes a complete book. Not as popular as *Buck Rogers* or *Flash Gordon*, *Tom Corbett Space Cadet* toys none-theless have their own loyal following, making items such as this pushout book less common than one might expect.

BUILDER:	FLORIAN
RELEASED:	CIRCA 1952
OPERATION:	STATIC

VALUES:	
GOOD	$100
EXCELLENT	$200
MINT WITH COMPLETE BOOK	$350

GAMA
ZOOMING SATELLITE
WEST GERMANY • CIRCA 1959

German toy manufacturer Gama jumped on the Sputnik launchpad around 1959 with Zooming Satellite, a twist on the by-then standard "satellite" toy. Mounted on a suction cup-footed tripod is a tin-litho globe with a clockwork mechanism inside. Wind the globe, then release it — the earth begins to spin, causing the attached satellite to spin around as well, replicating a truly "zooming" form of planetary orbit. Simple yet ingenious, Gama's toy features a nice package which depicts the satellite as a direct thematic descendant of Sputnik, polar antennae and all. Gama wasn't a solid importer to the United States, so it can be difficult to find this toy domestically. However, space-toy demand means many have found their way here through the collectibles channel. Sure, it may only be a globe toy with a grafted-on space angle, but Gama's Zooming Satellite more than lives up to its name, action-wise.

BUILDER:	GAMA
RELEASED:	CIRCA 1959
OPERATION:	WIND-UP
VALUES:	
GOOD	**$300**
EXCELLENT	**$450**
MINT WITH ORIGINAL BOX	**$900**

GESCHA
SATELLIT ROTARIJO MAGNETA
WEST GERMANY • CIRCA 1959

BUILDER:	GESCHA
RELEASED:	CIRCA 1959
OPERATION:	MECHANICAL
VALUES:	
GOOD	**$200**
EXCELLENT	**$350**
MINT WITH ORIGINAL BOX	**$650**

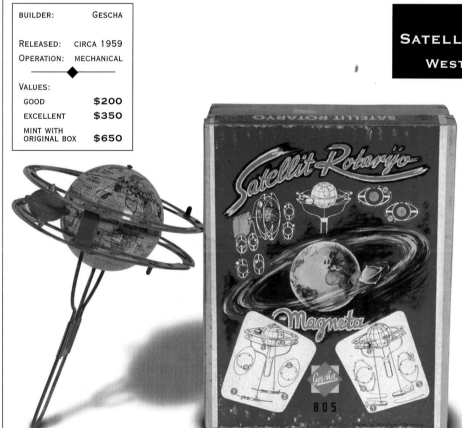

Think of it as a sci-fi sceptre. Gescha's Satellit Rotarijo Magneta is an odd toy that was designed to profit from Sputnik-era fascination with orbiting man-made objects. Hold the toy's handle in hand, then rotate the orb portion (actually, a tin-litho globe) in a circular manner. A small gyroscope-equipped "satellite" begins to generate momentum within its raceway. With enough momentum generated, the satellite then navigates the globe under its own power, until its gyroscope winds down. Designed for the European market, Satellit Rotarijo Magneta is yet another Sputnik-era plaything that survives more as a curiousity than a true icon of ingenious toymaking. Still, the gyroscope factor makes this toy more than a little special, even if collectible values don't necessarily agree.

HAJI
SPACE TROOPER
JAPAN • CIRCA 1955

This exquisite example of early-period toymaking is from Haji, that lower-echelon toymaker who created a wide variety of products throughout the postwar era, but precious few in the space-toy category. Best known for its later flying saucers, Haji spent much of the 1950s creating vehicle toys pulling Lucy-and-Desi-style travel trailers. Their circa-1955 Space Trooper manifests none of this domestic bliss. The tin-litho wind-up has the sober look of a youth being sent to war, with all the self-doubt and suppressed fear one might expect from an actual person, only here it's lithographed onto an Asian-style face. Interesting colors combine to create an unusual presentation. The toy's "space" elements are quite muted: a crudely shaped and formed helmet with headphones, and what appears to be breathing apparatus on the chest and back. Finally, of course, there's the characteristic rifle, intricately lithographed and stamped, carried cross-shoulder style as the toy lumbers along with its straight-legged walk. While not exceedingly rare, this toy is highly uncommon, and original packaging is virtually unheard of. Only a small lithoed "Haji" (as well as "Japan" on the rifle stock) provides the needed provenance. There's a seriousness and sense of pathos in Haji's Space Trooper that just doesn't manifest too often in toys from any period or nation, making this desirable wind-up unique in design as well as execution.

BUILDER:	HAJI
RELEASED:	CIRCA 1955
OPERATION:	WIND-UP

VALUES:

GOOD	**$700**
EXCELLENT	**$1200**
MINT WITH ORIGINAL BOX	**$2500**

HORIKAWA
ROBOT
JAPAN • CIRCA 1958

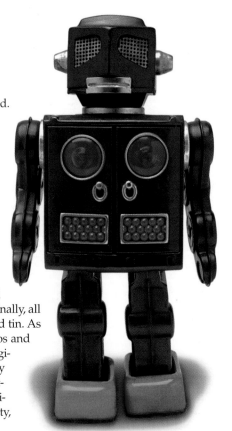

This is quite possibly the most successful robot toy platform ever introduced. First released around 1958, Horikawa's Robot/Astronaut is the ultimate outer-space conqueror, having survived in various incarnations through the 1980s, and selling millions of units worldwide. What accounts for its success? The Horikawa formula was ingeniously simple: market a walking automaton which could be sold in two adversarial formats with a simple change of heads (robots have fly-like eyes; astronauts have human faces peering behind plastic shields); include illumination; and most important, feature a camouflaged chest-firing cannon — a feature that not only defines Horikawa today, but has become toymaking legend, as well. Horikawa Robot/Astronauts can be charted through time by their level of plastic content; originally, all major components were fashioned from enameled tin. As time passed, arms, feet, legs, and ultimately torsos and even heads would be manufactured from plastic, displacing the metallic originals. Values for Horikawa Robot/Astronauts vary wildly, but generally speaking, the older and more metallic, the more valuable they are. For whatever reason — huge production numbers, stout mechanical design, or a combination thereof — Horikawa Robot/Astronauts have survived in great quantity, so prices are quite reasonable. As a rule, aim for earlier models.

BUILDER:	HORIKAWA
RELEASED:	CIRCA 1958
OPERATION:	BATTERY

VALUES:

GOOD	**$300**
EXCELLENT	**$450**
MINT WITH ORIGINAL BOX	**$750**

Horikawa
Shoot Down Floating Satellite Target Game
Japan • circa 1958

Here's a toy that capitalizes on human nature — that is, to attack that which is new or foreign. (*Just kidding!*) Actually, Horikawa's Shoot Down Floating Satellite target game is more than just a thinly veiled Western philosophical reponse to the orbital threat presented by Sputnik. It's also a classic hybrid, merging space toys and toy weapons into a predictable product. Using a battery-powered blower fan, the toy floats a small styrofoam ball above the killer-litho backdrop. The child then lowers an enameled-tin dart pistol and fires, hopefully striking the floating satellite and saving the world for capitalism. Normally missing darts, gun, and satellites, complete-condition Shoot Down games are difficult to find, but not expensive to own. Indeed, Shoot Down is worthy for no other reason than its terrific package art and the stunning rocket/moonbase artwork on the blower fan backdrop. Horikawa's Shoot Down Floating Satellite target game is great on display and even more fun in action.

BUILDER:	HORIKAWA
RELEASED:	CIRCA 1958
OPERATION:	BATTERY
VALUES:	
GOOD	**$200**
EXCELLENT	**$450**
MINT WITH ORIGINAL BOX	**$800**

Horikawa
Space Station
Japan • circa 1959

To many collectors, this is the greatest space-station toy ever released by a postwar Japanese toymaker. Created by Horikawa in the 1959 timeframe, Space Station is based on the forward-thinking designs of futurist Willy Ley and German-turned-American rocket scientist Werner von Braun, both of whom worked with toy and model-kit companies to create reality-based space toy products. Of course, Horikawa didn't have such networked luxury, so they built their battery-op the old-fashioned way — by purchasing one of Willy Ley's books and copying his designs. The result: a torus-shaped station with five animated "bays" (Engine Room, Communication Room, Rest & Recreation Room, Dining Room, Controller Room) in which vibration-animated space explorers conduct their scientific duties. A centrally located communications dish also spins during operation, and the entire station "floats" about using mystery action, while each bay features illumination. Horikawa would cost-reduce this toy in the early 1960s as "New Space Station" (1960s). Desirable, but difficult to repair, seek only operating examples. When it comes to vintage space station toys, Space Station by Horikawa is the best, period. Intellectual piracy does have its benefits, it would appear.

BUILDER:	HORIKAWA
RELEASED:	CIRCA 1959
OPERATION:	BATTERY
VALUES:	
GOOD	**$1200**
EXCELLENT	**$1800**
MINT WITH ORIGINAL BOX	**$2600**

KALMBACH IMAGE

HORIKAWA

37

IDEAL
ROBERT THE ROBOT
UNITED STATES • 1954

In the world of space-toy collecting, plastic is generally indicative of cheapness and decline. Not so with Ideal's Robert the Robot. Carried by Sears in its 1954 Christmas catalog (original retail: $5.79), this 14-inch plastic automaton represents early-form American interpretation on a traditionally "Japanese" design concept — the "skirted" robot. So called because of a lack of legs, skirted robots not only appear industrial and imposing, they also allow manufacturers to easily conceal mystery-action drivetrains inside the spacious skirted cavity. Because Robert is such an early toy, however, he lacks mystery action, instead relying on a cabled trigger device which connects to the robot's drivetrain, enabling forward, left, right, or backward movement. Turn the crank located on his back and he announces, "I am Robert the Robot." For on-the-road repairs, Robert also carries his own tools (hammer and screwdriver) behind a round panel on his torso. Though essentially a mechanical-movement toy, Robert does feature battery-powered eye illumination. Note that early Roberts (including this example) have clear eye lenses; later versions lack them. For classic American robot design, Ideal's Robert the Robot sets the standard.

BUILDER:	IDEAL
RELEASED:	1954
OPERATION:	MECHANICAL
VALUES:	
GOOD	**$200**
EXCELLENT	**$600**
MINT WITH ORIGINAL BOX	**$1200**

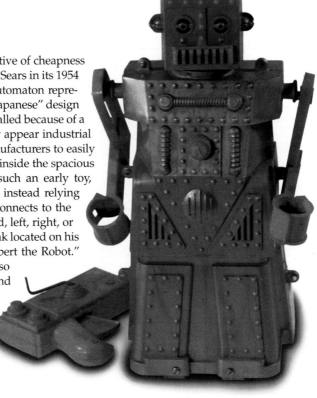

JOUSTRA
TERRE-MARS SPACE SHIP
FRANCE • CIRCA 1955

Not every interpretation of futuristic design necessitates the trappings of technology. Consider this simple yet evocative design from French toymaker, Joustra. Called the Terre-Mars Space Ship, the circa-1955 tin-litho friction toy incorporates many of the century's more esoteric and emotional design concepts, rather than the cold and calculating icons of our technological present. (It also bears uncanny resemblance to Masudaya spacecraft from the early 1950s. Coincidence?)

BUILDER:	JOUSTRA
RELEASED:	CIRCA 1955
OPERATION:	FRICTION
VALUES:	
GOOD	**$200**
EXCELLENT	**$350**
MINT WITH ORIGINAL BOX	**$900**

Two large, swept-back wings protrude from the ship's fuselage. Its nose features clamshell sculpting, from nose to cockpit, as if to channel the winds of space up and over the ship's body during flight. The rear-third location of the cockpit recalls the receding cockpits of prewar racers like Bugattis and Bentleys. And the colorful litho — rendered in soft reds, yellows, and blues — evoke something decidedly different than space travel. Nonetheless, Joustra's design is definitely intended for extraterrestrial adventure, as the "Terre-Mars" ("Earth-Mars") fuselage name suggests. An available collectible that, from a design standpoint, is just slightly behind its time.

ROBERT JOHNSON / COMET TOYS USA IMAGE

LINEMAR-MARUSAN (ROBOTRAC) BULLDOZER
JAPAN • CIRCA 1958

Linemar, the Japanese import subsidiary of Louis Marx & Co., played the field when it came to choosing products. During their era, which extended from the late 1950s through the late 1960s, Linemar would work with every major Tokyo toy builder. Most of the time, Linemar insisted on exclusive branding, making it difficult to accurately determine a toy's real builder. Robotrac Bulldozer, as it's called by collectors today, is believed to be a Marusan product, owing to the presence of a nearly identical blue Marusan toy called "Bulldozer Space Tractor." This, and all robot-on-bulldozer toys, are indebted to Marvelous Mike by Saunders (1950s). During operation, Robotrac employs a form of mystery action which allows the toy to reverse direction whenever it strikes an impedance, producing a back-and-forth action. The robot adds to the toy's appeal, "shifting" the controllers in response to mystery-action directional changes. Combine this animation with backlit eyes, a head-mounted light, and an electric horn which sounds whenever the mystery-action kicks into gear, and it's clear Robotrac is more than just a Marvelous Mike ripoff.

MARKETER:	LINEMAR
BUILDER:	MARUSAN
RELEASED:	CIRCA 1958
OPERATION:	BATTERY
◆	
VALUES:	
GOOD	$600
EXCELLENT	$1100
MINT WITH ORIGINAL BOX	$1500

LINEMAR-MASUDAYA? (GOLDEN) ROBOT
JAPAN • CIRCA 1958

This grinning Linemar automaton is best known as "Golden Robot" for its coloration. As with many Linemar products, this toy's manufacturer is not identified, but it is believed to be a Masudaya product, based on shared components with other robots sold under Masudaya's branding. During operation, the six-and-half-inch corded-remote battery-op "walks" forward and reverse using eccentric-wheel motion, swinging its claw arms and flashing its illuminated eyes. The stylized block head sports a mischievous grin, suggesting all is well in this robot's universe. Interestingly, Golden Robot's package art depicts a toy more like Masudaya's R-35 Robot (1960s) than it does Golden Robot. Key to this connectivity is the illustrated toy's "ROBOT" lettering, which, like R-35's, is based on A.C. Gilbert's logotype. Without question, it's an odd non sequitur that furthers the hypothesis of Golden Robot being a Masudaya robot. Definitely a desirable automaton, Golden Robot's value doubles in mint-boxed condition. Smiling all the way — that's Linemar's Golden Robot.

MARKETER:	LINEMAR
BUILDER:	MASUDAYA?
RELEASED:	CIRCA 1958
OPERATION:	BATTERY
◆	
VALUES:	
GOOD	$800
EXCELLENT	$2000
MINT WITH ORIGINAL BOX	$4000

JAMES D. JULIA AUCTIONS IMAGES

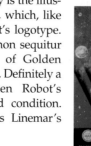

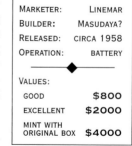

LINEMAR-MARUSAN — LINEMAR-MASUDAYA?

LINEMAR-MASUDAYA?
(LANTERN) ROBOT
JAPAN • CIRCA 1955

MARKETER:	LINEMAR
BUILDER:	MASUDAYA?
RELEASED:	CIRCA 1955
OPERATION:	BATTERY
VALUES:	
GOOD	$800
EXCELLENT	$1600
MINT WITH ORIGINAL BOX	$3800

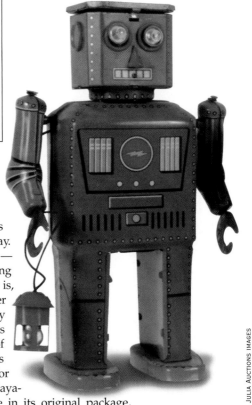

Louis Marx's importing subsidiary Linemar is responsible for literally hundreds of fascinating toy products sold in the United States between the early 1950s and the late 1960s. But they didn't build anything; they simply contracted with Japanese (and later, Hong Kong) vendors to either re-brand an existing product or create an entirely new one, then provided importation expertise for their American corporate parent. Lantern Robot, built in the 1955 period and sold at a $2.77 original retail, is a highly desirable example of this corporate relationship. During operation, the eight-inch corded-remote battery-op walks forward on eccentric pin-wheels, swinging his illuminated lantern all the way. As an added effect, Lantern Robot also blows "smoke" from his mouth — believed by some to actually be baby powder as opposed to a chemical smoking process. Though a few Linemar toys were marked by their builder, this toy is, like most, devoid of such lineage, making the establishment of its true builder

more difficult. However, many collectors point to Lantern Robot's legs and feet as clear indication of Masudaya's involvement in this product; they are dead-ringers for the components used on Masudaya-branded robots. Highly valuable in its original package, Lantern Robot is among the more desirable 1950s-era automatons.

JAMES D. JULIA AUCTIONS IMAGES

LINEMAR-NOMURA?
SPACEMAN
JAPAN • CIRCA 1958

Linemar's Spaceman is one of the more popular astronaut-themed space toys. Rarity certainly has something to do with it, as the toy is uncommon and particularly valuable in mint-original package condition. Like so many of its 1950s contemporaries (and fellow Linemar toys in particular), eight-inch Spaceman's lineage is unclear. Careful examination of components (legs, feet, and in particular, the ray gun/rifle) suggest the toy is by Nomura. Its small-face helmet/head design also suggests a general design connection to Naito Shoten (1950s), which itself is believed to have been allied with Nomura. (Confused yet?) Its operation is familiar, though not characteristic of any particular brand; the battery-op walks with a

MARKETER:	LINEMAR
BUILDER:	NOMURA?
RELEASED:	CIRCA 1958
OPERATION:	BATTERY
VALUES:	
GOOD	$600
EXCELLENT	$3000
MINT WITH ORIGINAL BOX	$6500

terrific special effect: a lighted facial area within the space helmet. The original box for this toy is very scarce, hence the large jump in value when found in mint-boxed condition. Though historic provenance for this toy may never fully be established, Linemar's Spaceman is one of the nicest small-format astronaut toys Nomura may — or may not — have built.

JAMES D. JULIA AUCTIONS IMAGES

LINEMAR-YONEZAWA
(EASEL-BACK) ROBOT
JAPAN • CIRCA 1959

Imagine the embarrassment. You design toys for Yonezawa, and your project for American client Linemar is now due. You bring the prototype to the handoff meeting, and during the demonstration, the toy robot keeps falling backwards due to an inherently unstable vertical design. As you smile nervously, it hits you: using that monster butterfly paper clip from the client's presentation packet, you might just have a solution. Hurriedly, you fashion your stabilizer; you pick up the six-and-one-half-inch toy's remote; and you re-initiate the demo. It works perfectly. No Window A for *you* — this week, anyway. Reality was likely less dramatic, but it's possible that Linemar-Yonezawa's Robot (popularly known as Easel-back Robot) had something of a development by fire. After all, what could account for Yonezawa's bizarre use of a butterfly-paperclip stabilizer on the robot's back? Note this version includes the desirable clear-plastic dome; alternate versions, marketed directly by Yonezawa, lack this feature. A remote-control toy, Easel-Back Robot also features stylized lithography and simple walking action during operation. The basic, yet colorful package adds to the value of loose mint examples. Easel-back Robot is yet another example of Linemar bringing the artistry of Japanese toymaking — no matter how unstable — to American shores.

JAMES D. JULIA AUCTIONS IMAGES

MARKETER:	LINEMAR
BUILDER:	YONEZAWA
RELEASED:	CIRCA 1959
OPERATION:	BATTERY
VALUES:	
GOOD	$800
EXCELLENT	$1600
MINT WITH ORIGINAL BOX	$2600

LION
LION ANNUAL 1954
UNITED KINGDOM • 1954

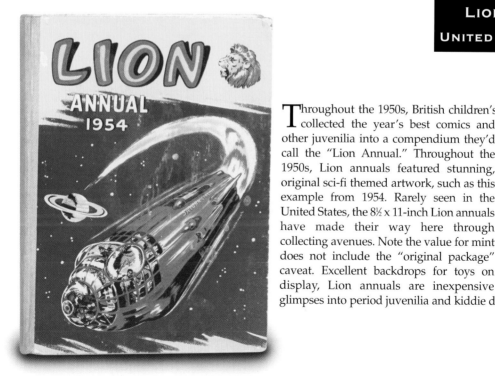

Throughout the 1950s, British children's publisher, Lion, regularly collected the year's best comics and other juvenilia into a compendium they'd call the "Lion Annual." Throughout the 1950s, Lion annuals featured stunning, original sci-fi themed artwork, such as this example from 1954. Rarely seen in the United States, the 8½ x 11-inch Lion annuals have made their way here through collecting avenues. Note the value for mint does not include the "original package" caveat. Excellent backdrops for toys on display, Lion annuals are inexpensive glimpses into period juvenilia and kiddie depictions of space themes.

BUILDER:	LION
RELEASED:	1954
OPERATION:	STATIC
VALUES:	
GOOD	$80
EXCELLENT	$120
MINT	$250

LION
LION ANNUAL 1955
UNITED KINGDOM • 1955

This Lion Annual, from 1955, features a futuristic city populated by all sorts of interesting people. As the Lion cover art progressed through the 1950s, unfolding trends in futurism were presented in a juvenile (yet detailed) manner. Lion's 8½ x 11-inch annuals were compendiums of children's comics and related juvenilia, compiled by the U.K.-based publisher and sold during a limited window of availability. Not widely available in the United States, Lion annuals make excellent toy-display backdrops at an affordable price. Note mint value does not include the standard packaging caveat.

BUILDER:	LION
RELEASED:	1955
OPERATION:	STATIC
VALUES:	
GOOD	$80
EXCELLENT	$120
MINT	$250

LION
LION ANNUAL 1956
UNITED KINGDOM • 1956

BUILDER:	LION
RELEASED:	1956
OPERATION:	STATIC
VALUES:	
GOOD	$90
EXCELLENT	$160
MINT	$280

For 1956, the Lion Annual publishers chose a space-walk theme that depicts two jetpack-equipped astronauts floating over a lunar surface, just a short distance from their vehicle. Published in the United Kingdom, the 8½ x 11-inch annuals compiled "year's best" comics and related juvenilia for child buyers. To be expected with a U.K.-focused product, Lion annuals are not often seen in the United States. The mint valuation does not include the standard "original package" caveat.

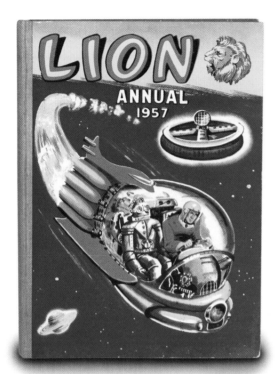

The 1957 Lion Annual features a torus-shaped space station which has just dispatched a streaking spacecraft filled with interesting futuristic lifeforms. Created by a U.K.-based publisher for the child market, the 8½ x 11-inch annuals were compendiums of comic strips and related juvenilia. Terrific backdrop material for space-toy collections, Lion annuals are generally not found in great quantities in the United States.

BUILDER:	LION
RELEASED:	1957
OPERATION:	STATIC
VALUES:	
GOOD	$80
EXCELLENT	$120
MINT	$250

Lion's 1958 cover depicts one of its more interesting images from their entire decade of annuals — that of a mechanical walking beast being piloted by astronaut explorers. As a compendium of children's comics and other juvenilia, the 8½ x 11-inch annuals were top-sellers in the United Kingdom, but are rarely seen in the United States. Perfect as backdrops to other sci-fi objects from the period, Lion annuals are affordable examples of period art targeted at school-age children during the golden years of robot and space toy production.

BUILDER:	LION
RELEASED:	1958
OPERATION:	STATIC
VALUES:	
GOOD	$100
EXCELLENT	$160
MINT WITH ORIGINAL BOX	$300

LION

LONE STAR — MARX

LONE STAR
SPACE ACE SPACE PHONE WALKI-TALKI SET
UNITED KINGDOM • CIRCA 1955

The mid- to late-1950s period in toy design saw an explosion of wire-based communication devices. Though companies like Marx had experimented with such toys as early as the 1940s, the novelty was still manifest by the middle of the '50s. Most toy manufacturers chose the "walkie talkie" name, owing to that wireless device's popularity during World War II. A good example is Lone Star's Space Ace Space Phone Walki-Talki set, a British product from the 1955 time period. As with most of these toys, the packaging promises far more than the toy delivers, and Space Ace is no exception. As perhaps the toy's best feature, the cover art is quite striking yet quaintly pre-Sputnik in its innocence. The components are nothing more than vibratory speaker-phone combinations, hardwired together, which allow the child users to speak to one another from the distance the wires permit. A classic case of overpromise-underdeliver, Lone Star's Space Ace Space Phones still make terrific complements to all kinds of related period collectibles.

BUILDER:	LONE STAR
RELEASED:	CIRCA 1955
OPERATION:	MECHANICAL
VALUES:	
GOOD	$65
EXCELLENT	$125
MINT WITH ORIGINAL BOX	$250

LOUIS MARX & CO.
FLASH GORDON ARRESTING RAY GUN
UNITED STATES • CIRCA 1952

When Hearst Corporation reintroduced the *Flash Gordon* property to the American public in 1951, they wanted more than enhanced awareness for the venerable space hero — they also wanted enhanced bank accounts from a revived licensing program. Louis Marx & Co. was quick to sign, having enjoyed success back in the 1930s. Marx limited exposure by reintroducing many of the exact same 1930s *Flash* toys in the 1950s. Not every toy was a reissue; though built from the same stamping and forming tools as 1936's Radio Repeater Gun (PRE-1940s), the 10-inch *Flash Gordon* Arresting Ray Gun enjoys more contemporary lithographic art. Of course, by the 1950s, this 10-inch approach to click guns was rather anachronistic; smaller, more cost-effective click-weapons had become the norm. As a result, it's unlikely Marx did big numbers, resulting in relative scarcity today, particularly in mint-original package condition.

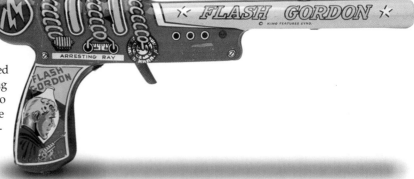

BUILDER:	MARX
RELEASED:	CIRCA 1952
OPERATION:	MECHANICAL
VALUES:	
GOOD	$200
EXCELLENT	$600
MINT WITH ORIGINAL BOX	$2000

BOB BURNS COLLECTION

LOUIS MARX & CO.
JUPITER ROCKET TRUCK
UNITED STATES • CIRCA 1957

Whereas its Japanese counterparts tended to focus on, and celebrate, the more fanciful of playthings, Louis Marx & Co. was firmly grounded in reality — largely due to licensing constraints. But even some nonlicensed product was reality-based, such as Jupiter Rocket Truck. This circa-1957 litho-tin truck (13½ inches in length) merges the Marx Lumar service-truck with a newsworthy load concept: a Jupiter-C rocket. First launched in September 1956, the Army's Jupiter-C was the first U.S. rocket that could reach sufficient orbit to launch a secondary vehicle, like a satellite. Marx's molded-plastic model of the Jupiter is astonishingly close to the real thing. Sears marketed an alternative version of this vehicle in the 1958 Wish Book as "USAF Rocket Carrier / Rocket Squadron." An interesting addition to any reality-based space-toy assembly, Jupiter Rocket Truck skyrockets in value when found in mint-original package condition. Which, come to think of it, is pretty darn appropriate.

BUILDER:	MARX
RELEASED:	CIRCA 1957
OPERATION:	FRICTION
VALUES:	
GOOD	$300
EXCELLENT	$450
MINT WITH ORIGINAL BOX	$1200

LOUIS MARX & CO.
REX MARS PLANET PATROL SPARKLING TANK
UNITED STATES • CIRCA 1952

Louie Marx, founder of the company that bore his name, was never accused of humility. Marx loved selling toys that employed variations of his own name — a kind of low-rent, in-house branding strategy. Consider just a few: Lumar, Big Loo, Garloo, Linemar, Marlines, Marxville, Magic Marxie — the list is prodigious indeed. It's been suggested that Rex Mars brand (found on a number of Marx toys) was a house brand. Then again, it might be from a forgotten television serial or radio program; the fact is, it's unclear. Nonetheless, this standard 10-inch Doughboy-style tank features terrific lithography and a long pedigree dating to the 1930s. Wound up, the tank cruises, then an astronaut-themed gunner emerges, fires, and clambers back into the tank. Turret sparkling accompanies the action. Preferred for its colorful litho, the toy also features a terrific package. Interestingly, this is the only space-themed version of the Doughboy tank ever produced by Marx, licensed or otherwise.

BUILDER:	MARX
RELEASED:	CIRCA 1952
OPERATION:	WIND-UP
VALUES:	
GOOD	$600
EXCELLENT	$900
MINT WITH ORIGINAL BOX	$1600

TOY: BOB BURNS COLLECTION

MARX

LOUIS MARX & CO.
ROBOT AND SON

UNITED STATES • CIRCA 1956

BUILDER:	MARX
RELEASED:	CIRCA 1956
OPERATION:	BATTERY
VALUES:	
GOOD	**$350**
EXCELLENT	**$550**
MINT WITH ORIGINAL BOX	**$1100**

The robot craze engendered by seminal products like Nomura's Zoomer (1950s) wasn't lost on savvy toy titans like Louis Marx. His manufacturing company had pioneered innovative, affordable, mass-produced playthings for the American market, and the Japanese weren't about to upstage him. Marx's first foray into robot toys was the Robot and Son. Created circa 1956 from plastic as an endearing paternal pairing, 15-inch Robot and Son was a solid hit for Marx, selling through the late 1950s, by which point Marx had founded Linemar to compete (and cooperate) with Japanese toymakers. Borrowing the "skirted" design pioneered by Ideal's Robert the Robot (1950s), Marx's battery-powered toy rolls forward and backward on concealed wheels, turning his head left and right as he goes. For added play value, there's a Morse code buzzer located in his chest plate. To cap it all, the robot totes his blockheaded son on a gym-style bar wherever he goes. Today, Robot and Son is a popular entry-level piece that must include the oft-missing son figure in order to command the accompanying values. Original packaging substantially affects overall value. Good, simple fun, Marx's Robot and Son is a must-have for any complete robot presentation.

LOUIS MARX & CO.
ROCKET FIGHTER

UNITED STATES • 1951

Rocket Fighter by Marx is an interesting toy for a number of reasons. It's a sharp reissue of the 1930s original which formerly carried *Flash Gordon* (and even *Buck Rogers*) licensing. It's also an amazing example of good lithographic-plate storage; Marx hadn't run this toy's plates in nearly 15 years, yet the finish and print quality is equal to that of the 1930s original. And finally, it's unclear why Marx didn't market a *Flash* version of this toy; they were creating *Flash*-licensed goods in the early 1950s — why not this toy? Virtually identical to the 1939 *Flash Gordon* version, this 12-inch wind-up has the forward motion,

BUILDER:	MARX
RELEASED:	1951
OPERATION:	WIND-UP
VALUES:	
GOOD	**$300**
EXCELLENT	**$450**
MINT WITH ORIGINAL BOX	**$1200**

exhaust sparkling, and "firing" action of the original, but lacks the "*Flash Gordon*" logotypes on the swept-back wings and fuselage. With the early-1950s television explosion of sci-fi programming like *Captain Video* and *Space Patrol*, reissuing old space-themed playthings just made sense, it would appear (with or without licensing). Two versions of this reissue are known; one with the numeral "5" on the wings (part of the the *Flash Gordon* original), the other without. As might be expected, collectors today don't regard either version with the same financial attention as the 1930s originals. Still, Marx Rocket Fighter is an affordable variant, particularly at lower condition grades.

Louis Marx & Co.
Space Satellites with Launching Site
United States • circa 1953

One of Louis Marx & Co.'s key strengths was the mighty "playset" — a collection of tin-litho structures accompanied by loads of molded-plastic figures and accessories. A playset could be about practically anything, and thanks to Marx product planners, they were; hundreds of sets were marketed over three decades. In the early 1950s, with films like *Destination Moon* and *The Day the Earth Stood Still* in the public consciousness, Marx offered their peek into the future with the Space Satellites with Launching Site playset. Issued years before the Sputnik revolution in "satellite" toys, the playset features the now-common wind-up propeller concept, launched from a stylish tin-litho base (measures 9¼ x 12 inches). Marx parts-sharing means most plastic rockets and accessories hail from *Tom Corbett Space Academy* playset. Space Satellites with Launching Site is pursued by both space-toy enthusiasts and dedicated Marx playset collectors. Values reflect playsets which are factory-complete; mint means never-assembled tin-litho structures.

BUILDER:	MARX
RELEASED:	CIRCA 1953
OPERATION:	WIND-UP
◆	
VALUES:	
GOOD	$600
EXCELLENT	$900
MINT WITH ORIGINAL BOX	$2000

Louis Marx & Co.
Space Satellites with Launching Station
Japan • circa 1954

Believed to be the second version issued by Marx, the slightly renamed Space Satellites with Launching Station playset has altered lithography on the 9¼ x 12-inch base, as well as the more obvious large-format wind-up propeller "satellite." It's believed Marx converted to this larger satellite to enhance its flying capabilities. The revised packaging includes stylized hand-drawn typography that suggests a science-fiction premise. Other differences include the large, molded-gray plastic antenna positioned just off the tin-litho launching station, as well as the lack of the vertical rocket-launcher originally "borrowed" from the *Tom Corbett Space Academy* playset. An alternate version of this toy would be marketed in the 1955 Sears Wish Book for the value-priced sum of $2.69. Collectors generally don't assign a premium to either version of this set. Pursued by both space-toy fans and Marx enthusiasts, Space Satellites with Launching Station is a desirable early space toy from the king of all playsets, Louis Marx & Co.

BUILDER:	MARX
RELEASED:	CIRCA 1954
OPERATION:	WIND-UP
◆	
VALUES:	
GOOD	$600
EXCELLENT	$900
MINT WITH ORIGINAL BOX	$2000

MARX

MARX

LOUIS MARX & CO.
TOM CORBETT SPACE CADET SPACE GUN
UNITED STATES • CIRCA 1951

One of Louis Marx's earliest *Tom Corbett Space Cadet*-licensed toys is the venerable 10-inch click gun. Interestingly, this toy dates to about 1936, when Marx used it for its then-hot *Flash Gordon* license (Radio Repeater Gun, PRE-1940s). It would appear that even in the 1951 timeframe, when this piece was first marketed, Marx was still making money off these 15-year-old stamping and forming tools — nothing short of an inspiration to toymakers and their accountants everywhere. Best of all, the *Tom Corbett Space Cadet* Space Gun features fine lithography, including a striking likeness of Tom himself (Frankie Thomas, star of the original television series). Pulling the trigger produces a loud clicking sound. A must-have for early-TV sci-fi collectors and Marx enthusiasts alike, the *Tom Corbett Space Cadet* Space Gun is a colorful reminder of Marx's undying ability to make money from fully amortized tooling.

BUILDER:	MARX
RELEASED:	CIRCA 1951
OPERATION:	MECHANICAL

VALUES:

GOOD	$300
EXCELLENT	$900
MINT WITH ORIGINAL BOX	$2000

BOB BURNS COLLECTION

LOUIS MARX & CO.
TOM CORBETT SPACE CADET SPACE GUN
UNITED STATES • CIRCA 1952

BUILDER:	MARX
RELEASED:	CIRCA 1952
OPERATION:	

VALUES:

GOOD	$150
EXCELLENT	$350
MINT WITH ORIGINAL BOX	$800

BOB BURNS COLLECTION

Nobody did licensed goods better than Marx in the early 1950s, and based on this *Tom Corbett Space Cadet* Space Gun from circa 1952, it's easy to see why. Starting with an existing toy platform — the double-trigger tommy gun — Marx designers created colorful lithographic art to accompany the plastic stocks and handle assemblies. The result is an obviously cobbled-together toy that still undoubtedly entertained its intended audience. Pulling the trigger produces a loud, rhythmic clicking sound, similar to the *rat-tat-tat* found in many gangster-style weapons. The coiled wireform on the gun's top suggests a science fiction raison d'etre. A typical low-end Marx toy, the *Tom Corbett Space Cadet* Space Gun is a must-have for early-TV sci-fi collectors, as well as dedicated Marx gun and space-toy enthusiasts.

BUILDER:	MASUDAYA
RELEASED:	CIRCA 1959
OPERATION:	BATTERY

VALUES:	
GOOD	**$3500**
EXCELLENT	**$7000**
MINT WITH ORIGINAL BOX	**$15000**

ROBERT JOHNSON / COMET TOYS USA IMAGE

MASUDAYA
GIANT SONIC (TRAIN) ROBOT
JAPAN • CIRCA 1959

Giant Sonic Robot, better known as Train Robot, is one of Masudaya's famed "Gang of Five" large skirted robots. They're a "gang" because they share body and arm stampings, as well as drive mechanisms, but each is unique in its own, ultra-collectible way. This example is called "Train Robot" by space-toy enthusiasts because the 15-inch automaton emits a loud "wooooo" (as the package describes) during mystery-action operation. Knowledgeable toy collectors recognize it as a basic sound generator from Masudaya's commonplace tin train toys of the same period. Train Robot is also the only member of the Gang to sport this rather unremarkable head design. Exceedingly scarce, Giant Sonic Robot is probably the least desirable of all the Gang members, simply because it is also the most mundane visually — and perhaps because no one can really stand that train sound for very long. Even so, for any veteran collector, this and all Gang of Five Masudaya robots occupy the pinnacle of collecting, with values to match.

MASUDAYA
LIGHTED SPACE VEHICLE
JAPAN • CIRCA 1959

As one of the majors of the postwar Japanese toy industry, Masudaya produced enough iconic toys to leave a unique sense of style across their entire legacy. Lighted Space Vehicle (also known as Space Tank), circa 1959, reveals many such style trends. Examples: the continuous-toned metallic finish; accents like lights, portholes, lightning bolts, and grilles; taillights protected by coil-wireform spring assemblies; and much more. But perhaps most distinguishing is the "floating ball" concept, which found enduring popularity in the post-Sputnik Age of Satellites. During operation, the battery-op mystery-action toy "floats" a styrofoam ball using an airstream generated by an internal fan. Today, Lighted Space Tank is common, suggesting strong original sales. That makes Lighted Space Tank a good "early purchase" by new space-toy collectors, owing both to its value pricing as well as good availability.

BUILDER:	MASUDAYA
RELEASED:	CIRCA 1959
OPERATION:	BATTERY

VALUES:	
GOOD	**$200**
EXCELLENT	**$400**
MINT WITH ORIGINAL BOX	**$900**

MASUDAYA

49

MASUDAYA

MASUDAYA
NON-STOP (LAVENDER) ROBOT
JAPAN • CIRCA 1956

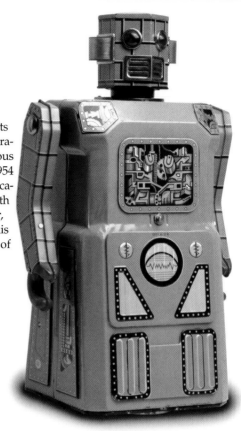

Easily the most visually arresting robot ever created, Non-Stop ("Lavender") Robot by Masudaya is a Cubist tour de force that puts everything great about robot design into one outrageous package. As part of Masudaya's famous Gang of Five skirted robot family, this circa-1954 robot employs mystery action to glide about, occasionally swinging its arms while eyes and mouth flash. What it lacks in animation, however, Lavender *more* than makes up for in visuals. This toy is clearly the design accomplishment of numerous people, as its various regions seem to be borne of independent creative founts.

BUILDER:	MASUDAYA
RELEASED:	CIRCA 1956
OPERATION:	BATTERY
VALUES:	
GOOD	**$2000**
EXCELLENT	**$6000**
MINT WITH ORIGINAL BOX	**$10000**

Perhaps the most accomplished of all these regions is the chest plate, with its determined swirl of mechanical elements. Extremely valuable, Non-Stop Robot also boasts an iconic package, one which depicts the robot serving Man on a desolate lunar surface, as father and son watch from the safety of a nearby transport tube. Outrageous by any standard, then or now, the singular design triumph of Non-Stop Robot earns Masudaya an important place in the pantheon of over-the-top toy design.

ROBERT JOHNSON / COMET TOYS USA AND JAMES D. JULIA AUCTIONS IMAGES

MASUDAYA
NON-STOP SPACE PATROL WITH FLOATING SATELLITE
JAPAN • CIRCA 1958

BUILDER:	MASUDAYA
RELEASED:	CIRCA 1958
OPERATION:	BATTERY
VALUES:	
GOOD	**$200**
EXCELLENT	**$350**
MINT WITH ORIGINAL BOX	**$900**

One of hundreds of toys to carry the "Space Patrol" name, Masudaya's Non-Stop Space Patrol with Floating Satellite is a classic post-Sputnik toy that no doubt inspired a heavy dose of buyer's remorse. Why? The "artist's conception" saucer box art features far better proportioning than does the actual toy, which looks like a mystery action-equipped Brown Derby Restaurant. As usual, "non-stop" refers to the eight-inch diameter saucer's mystery action feature, wherein it "hovers" around the floor while lights blink through various plastic lenses. As a bonus, Masudaya included their trademark floating-styrofoam ball trick, in

which a "satellite" floats above the saucer, no matter where it goes. This feature alone makes the toy a winner, but goofy lithography and terrific package art also add to the toy's appeal. Indeed, thanks to that artwork, mint-original package values are solid, and not out of reach for even the more modest of collecting budgets.

BUILDER:	MASUDAYA
RELEASED:	CIRCA 1958
OPERATION:	BATTERY

VALUES:	
GOOD	**$1600**
EXCELLENT	**$2500**
MINT WITH ORIGINAL BOX	**$5000**

JAMES D. JULIA AUCTIONS IMAGE

MASUDAYA
SPACE COMMANDO
JAPAN • CIRCA 1958

Masudaya isn't known for astronaut toys; they focused on robots and space vehicles. Among the rarest of their few astronauts is the circa-1958 Space Commando. Clocking in at 7½ inches, the toy is a corded remote-control battery-op that moves using Masudaya's eccentric-wheel mechanism for walking without actual articulation. Interesting touches include the battery box's cool litho art; a flashing helmet light; and a poseable head, a rare feature among astronaut toys of the period. Values reflect an original battery box. Note that an alternate version of Space Commando exists, sporting red lithography and a silver belly-box. The battery box's red astronaut art has led many to speculate the highly scarce red version was part of an initial run by Masudaya. Highly valued, Space Commando by Masudaya is a very desirable first-tier battery toy from the classic period.

MASUDAYA
SPACE EXPLORER
JAPAN • CIRCA 1957?

Though yet to be definitively identified, it's believed Space Explorer is the product of Masudaya. A number of compelling reasons support this hypothesis: the lithographic design of the tank-tread section; the "saucer" art on the rear dorsal fin; and the general litho and forming-tool design of the astronaut driver — the kind Masudaya often put inside cockpits or domes. A friction toy, Space Explorer

BUILDER:	MASUDAYA
RELEASED:	CIRCA 1957?
OPERATION:	FRICTION

VALUES:	
GOOD	**$1000**
EXCELLENT	**$2500**
MINT WITH ORIGINAL BOX	**$5500**

KALMBACH IMAGE

boasts a novel feature for its obviously budget-minded market placement: the pilot shifts gears as the toy moves along the floor. During operation, the toy also sparkles. Its long, rounded nose section and rear dorsal fin foretell the look and feel of North American Rockwell's Space Shuttle design, nearly 20 years in advance. A valuable toy, Space Explorer serves to remind collectors that the search isn't over for identity and provenance, even among the more desirable pieces of the postwar era.

MASUDAYA
(TARGET) ROBOT
JAPAN • CIRCA 1958

Target Robot, as he is known to collectors today, is yet another member of Masudaya's famed Gang of Five family of 15-inch skirted robots. Unlike his battery-op brothers, however, Target Robot boasts an interactive play pattern that encourages hours of repeat play-time with child owners. It's a great concept: switched on, the toy moves slowly toward the child, who fires Masudaya's dart gun at the robot's chest target disc. When the child hits it, the robot stops dead in its tracks and flashes its eyes and mouth, then backs away from the child in retreat. Thereafter, the robot again heads forward, in the direction of the child. Target Robot includes very nice lithographic art — not as over-the-top as its Non-Stop (Lavender, 1950s) brother, but nice nonetheless. As a Gang member, this is an extremely desirable toy, particularly when found in mint-original box condition, complete with the original dart gun and original darts. (Note that since original gun and darts were off-the-shelf items, it's difficult to determine originality.) Take aim and fire — Masudaya's Target Robot comes ready to play.

BUILDER:	MASUDAYA
RELEASED:	CIRCA 1958
OPERATION:	BATTERY
◆	
VALUES:	
GOOD	$4000
EXCELLENT	$7000
MINT WITH ORIGINAL BOX	$15000

ROBERT JOHNSON / COMET TOYS USA IMAGE

MASUO
U.S. AIR FORCE X-15
JAPAN • CIRCA 1959

Though its exploits are now lost in time, North American's X-15 endures as aviation legend. First flown in 1959, this amazing rocket-powered aircraft still holds two records for fixed-wing planes: 4,534 miles per hour max speed, and 354,200 feet top altitude. Masuo of Japan (MS) couldn't have chosen a more fitting subject for their eight-inch space-aircraft toy, which dates to 1952, and US Army Jupiter Space Ship (1950s). The tin-litho friction piece features Masuo's "patent pending" nose-lift actuator; when the craft strikes an object with its nose, a hidden chassis lift arm immediately deploys, standing the toy up on end. The large rocket port is clearly replicated, as are the authentic North American markings of the real-life planes (four were built). North American used the research gained from flying the X-15 to help create the Space Shuttle in the 1970s, when the successor company was known as North American Rockwell. An inexpensive toy, Masuo's X-15 provides a real-life connection between the worlds of science fiction and Tomorrow.

BUILDER:	MASUO
RELEASED:	CIRCA 1959
OPERATION:	FRICTION
◆	
VALUES:	
GOOD	$65
EXCELLENT	$150
MINT WITH ORIGINAL BOX	$350

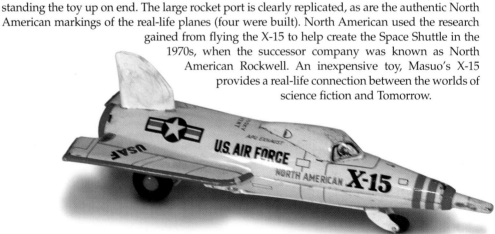

MASUO
U.S. ARMY JUPITER SPACE SHIP
JAPAN • CIRCA 1952

Little is known today about Japan's Masuo. Its mark, a stylized M logotype with an S inside, can be found on some, but not all, of their toys. Likely, Masuo was a skilled subcontractor for top-tier companies, but on occasion had the opportunity to release toys under their own branding. Most Masuo toys are friction-powered, like this U.S. Army Jupiter Space Ship from around 1952. Essentially a horizontal version of the classic vertical, finned rocketship design, Jupiter Space Ship features colorful litho that seems better placed on a candy wrapper than a tin toy. No matter — give the toy a push, and it careens across the floor. When it strikes an impedance with its "patent pending" nose-lift actuator, the toy deploys a hidden chassis lift-arm which raises the toy to a launch-ready vertical orientation. Masuo rocket toys are generally very affordable, even in mint-original box condition, encouraging variation collecting. Other toys in this family include the US Air Force X-15 (1950s) and later versions of Jupiter Space Ship (1960s) that feature similar, yet distinctive, litho treatments.

BUILDER:	MASUO
RELEASED:	CIRCA 1952
OPERATION:	FRICTION
VALUES:	
GOOD	$90
EXCELLENT	$160
MINT WITH ORIGINAL BOX	$350

MATTEL
FUTURE CAR
UNITED STATES • 1953

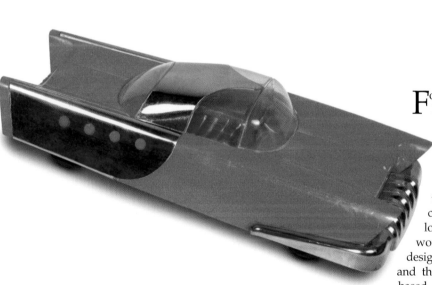

Founded in the early 1950s, Mattel, of Hawthorne, California, will be forever remembered as the company that gave the world Hot Wheels and Barbie. But long before either of these landmark product lines, Mattel was just another toy company struggling to find its identity among the postwar crush of builders and product. It wasn't long after their founding that a toy would emerge which hinted at future design greatness. That toy was Future Car, and though clearly based on Detroit's outré concept cars of the period, it also demonstrates a unique sense of style that would later emerge in the 1960s with the landmark Hot Wheels line. Offered in the 1953 Sears Christmas catalog for $1.79, Mattel's 10½-inch friction-drive plastic vehicle has it all: an eat-anything front grille, Buick-like perforated exhaust ports running down the rear quarterpanels, and prescient fins on the rear — in short, Mattel designers really were ahead of their time. Plus, the removable clear hardtop gave kids additional play value — though at a price to contemporary collectors: Future Cars are generally found lacking these components today. Accompanying values reflect complete-condition examples; original packaging is somewhat lackluster and as such doesn't greatly enhance mint-original boxed condition. Roll into tomorrow today with the Mattel Future Car.

BUILDER:	MATTEL
RELEASED:	1953
OPERATION:	FRICTION
VALUES:	
GOOD	$150
EXCELLENT	$250
MINT WITH ORIGINAL BOX	$450

MASUO — MATTEL

MERIT-RANDALL
JET MORGAN SPACE SUIT
UNITED KINGDOM • CIRCA 1952

Wearing costumes provides a child with the feeling of being someone else, which is key to understanding one's own sense of self. This British costume from the early 1950s let kids dress up as Jet Morgan, star of the BBC Radio's *Journey Into Space*. Created by J. & L. Randall Limited and marketed under the Merit brand, the incredible costume is Hollywood quality, complete with hood, tunic, and pants. Created from satin and sporting brass buttons and custom embroidery, the costume proudly features the Jet Morgan logotype, as well as stars, moons, and planets.

MARKETER:	MERIT
BUILDER:	RANDALL
RELEASED:	CIRCA 1952
OPERATION:	STATIC

VALUES:	
GOOD	$400
EXCELLENT	$1200
MINT WITH ORIGINAL BOX	$1400

Even the box sports spectacular visuals. Nearly impossible to find, Merit-Randall's Jet Morgan Space Suit is an example of the workmanship that was once found in every aspect of toymaking.

NAITO SHOTEN
DEEP-SEA ROBOT
JAPAN • CIRCA 1956

One of robot collecting's great enigmas is Naito Shoten. This presumably Tokyo-based toy manufacturer produced a small selection of toys in the mid-1950s designed around a key set of humanoid tooling. The most famous of these toys is Deep-Sea Robot, which by any standard is actually an eight-inch astronaut on underwater duty. After considerable research, toy legend Teruhisa Kitahara ascribed the Naito Shoten name to the equally enigmatic AN/AHI Toys, whose logotypes grace Deep-Sea Robot's original packaging. There is contemporary speculation that Naito Shoten and its AN/AHI Toys brands were resellers of rare-variation Nomura toys. This theory is supported by design similarities and identical-component sharing between toys like Deep-Sea Robot and Nomura's Earth Man (1950s) and Space Commando (1950s). Deep-Sea Robot is a valuable toy in the extreme, considered first-tier by most knowledgeable collectors and dealers, with hyperbolic pricing to match. Original packaging is colorful, and adds to an already expensive purchase.

BUILDER:	NAITO SHOTEN
RELEASED:	CIRCA 1956
OPERATION:	WIND-UP

VALUES:	
GOOD	$8000
EXCELLENT	$16000
MINT WITH ORIGINAL BOX	$24000

Ensure originality of the Robot's gun and spring "air hoses" between helmet and tanks, as these are often missing, yet are easily reproducible, components. Alternate versions, including a South Pole "skiing" variation, have emerged in recent years and are considered equally rare. For the ultimate in obscurity and true collectibility, there's no beating Naito Shoten toys like Deep-Sea Robot.

NOMURA
ATOMIC FIRE CAR
JAPAN • CIRCA 1959

Hybrid toys — playthings that merge two distinct categories to create a third — were common among the output of postwar Japanese toymakers. Atomic Fire Car by Nomura is hybrid toymaking at its finest, wherein toy marketers hope that no matter what the buyer's preferred interest, some element will motivate the purchase. In the case of the 10½-inch Atomic Fire Car, three key elements are at work: a helmeted doll figure; a 1959 Ford Fairlane; and a large, menacing "atomic fire" cannon mounted directly in the middle of the toy. Where most toys with the fire theme are traditionally involved in fire suppression, Atomic Fire Car seems designed to actually *initiate* blazes. During mystery-action operation, Atomic Fire Car goes through an "atomic fire" sequence, during which lights illuminate in the clear-plastic gun base and sparkling emits from the gun barrel — and all of it from the platform of Ford's new-for-1959 Fairlane. Who knew passenger cars had such a heinous undercurrent? A basic toy with values to match, Nomura's hybrid Atomic Fire Car has something for every toy buyer.

BUILDER:	NOMURA
RELEASED:	CIRCA 1959
OPERATION:	BATTERY
VALUES:	
GOOD	**$200**
EXCELLENT	**$600**
MINT WITH ORIGINAL BOX	**$1100**

NOMURA
EARTH MAN
JAPAN • CIRCA 1957

Here's yet another interesting entry in the "who made it?" derby between Nomura and Naito Shoten. Earth Man, a nine-inch, battery-operated toy with corded remote control, walks along, and, when commanded, raises his gun and fires. The toy shares components with Nomura's wind-up Space Commando toy (1950s), and appears to share feet and possibly leg assemblies with the Naito Shoten Deep-Sea Robot family (1950s). Colorful and distinctive lithography graces this astronaut toy, where a combination of flashy and subdued colors work together to create a more mature presentation than is typically found on such battery-ops. The toy's box is a more humble member of the Japanese family of package design, and markedly adds to a mint toy's value when present. Rare is the Japanese space toy that actually refers to astronauts as "earth" men, so Nomura's creation is somewhat unique in that regard. Not an inexpensive toy by any standard, Earth Man is held in high esteem among knowledgeable collectors for only the best of reasons: operational and lithographic quality.

BUILDER:	NOMURA
RELEASED:	CIRCA 1957
OPERATION:	BATTERY
VALUES:	
GOOD	**$1200**
EXCELLENT	**$2100**
MINT WITH ORIGINAL BOX	**$4500**

NOMURA

NOMURA

NOMURA
MECHANIZED ROBOT
JAPAN • CIRCA 1957

BUILDER:	NOMURA
RELEASED:	CIRCA 1957
OPERATION:	BATTERY

VALUES:

GOOD	**$1800**
EXCELLENT	**$2500**
MINT WITH ORIGINAL BOX	**$3500**

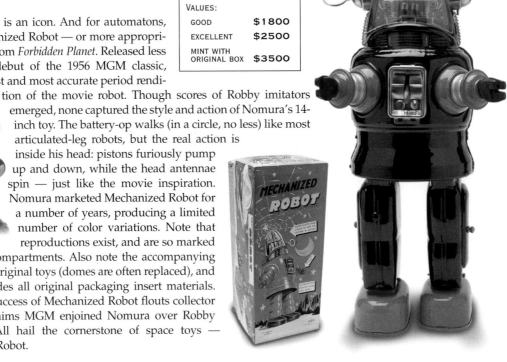

For every genre, there is an icon. And for automatons, it's Nomura's Mechanized Robot — or more appropriately, Robby the Robot from *Forbidden Planet*. Released less than a year after the debut of the 1956 MGM classic, Nomura's is both the first and most accurate period rendition of the movie robot. Though scores of Robby imitators emerged, none captured the style and action of Nomura's 14-inch toy. The battery-op walks (in a circle, no less) like most articulated-leg robots, but the real action is inside his head: pistons furiously pump up and down, while the head antennae spin — just like the movie inspiration. Nomura marketed Mechanized Robot for a number of years, producing a limited number of color variations. Note that reproductions exist, and are so marked inside the leg battery compartments. Also note the accompanying values are based on all-original toys (domes are often replaced), and mint-original box includes all original packaging insert materials. The wild marketplace success of Mechanized Robot flouts collector urban legend which claims MGM enjoined Nomura over Robby Space Patrol (1950s). All hail the cornerstone of space toys — Nomura's Mechanized Robot.

NOMURA
MOON SPACE SHIP
JAPAN • 1958

BUILDER:	NOMURA
RELEASED:	1958
OPERATION:	BATTERY

VALUES:

GOOD	**$2000**
EXCELLENT	**$3000**
MINT WITH ORIGINAL BOX	**$4500**

It's not clear what brought about the premature demise of Nomura's masterpiece, Robby Space Patrol (1950s). Its rarity today is the stuff of legend — legend that includes the premise MGM legally enjoined Nomura from further Robby Space Patrol imports. Whatever happened, the fact is Moon Space Ship is the progeny of Robby Space Patrol, and it exists in far greater quantities, having been available from Sears in 1958 for $3.79. Switched on, the toy mystery actions about, while transverse piston assemblies oscillate within the clear-plastic illuminated dome. Incredible stamping quality, striking lithography, a stylish color scheme, and good action make this a highly desirable toy. Interestingly, most if not all bear the "Linemar" circular logo on the rear panel, suggesting some or all of the run was imported by Marx's Japanese subsidiary. The third incarnation of Robby Space Patrol is the interminably named Robby Moon Patrol — Space Division No. 3. For striking design and great coloration, Moon Space Ship by Nomura is in a class by itself.

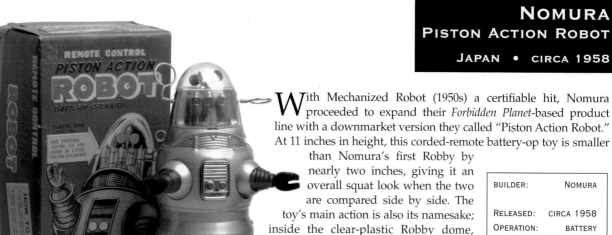

ROBERT JOHNSON / COMET TOYS USA IMAGE

NOMURA
PISTON ACTION ROBOT
JAPAN • CIRCA 1958

With Mechanized Robot (1950s) a certifiable hit, Nomura proceeded to expand their *Forbidden Planet*-based product line with a downmarket version they called "Piston Action Robot." At 11 inches in height, this corded-remote battery-op toy is smaller than Nomura's first Robby by nearly two inches, giving it an overall squat look when the two are compared side by side. The toy's main action is also its namesake; inside the clear-plastic Robby dome, small pistons churn up and down furiously during operation. The toy also boasts stiff-legged walking motion which is decidedly less impressive than that of Mechanized Robot. Still, the toy is a decent evocation of the overall Robby look. Its presence in fairly large quantities today suggests a multi-year run — yet another nail in the argumentative coffin for those who believe Nomura was enjoined by MGM from releasing Robby Space Patrol (1950s) due to copyright infringement. With so many Robby-derivative products from a single manufacturer, it's highly unlikely MGM's attorneys would have stopped with one infringing product. As a member of the Mechanized Robot-based family, Nomura's Piston Action Robot comes in a classic-period illustrated box that makes a terrific visual complement to the Mechanized Robot package.

BUILDER:	NOMURA
RELEASED:	CIRCA 1958
OPERATION:	BATTERY
VALUES:	
GOOD	$1100
EXCELLENT	$1500
MINT WITH ORIGINAL BOX	$3000

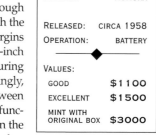

ROBERT JOHNSON / COMET TOYS USA IMAGE

NOMURA
PISTON ACTION ROBOT
JAPAN • CIRCA 1958

Nomura filled out its mid-priced Robby-style product range with alternate colors of Piston Action Robot. Then as now, multiple colors allow manufacturers to offer case lots of similar goods to wholesalers for easy break-up at the retailer level. In this way, cost savings are passed on through the various levels of distribution, with the ultimate goal of enhancing profit margins on each unit shipped. This gold version of the 11-inch Piston Action Robot was likely manufactured during the same timeframe as the silver edition. Interestingly, collectors ascribe little valuation difference between silver and gold versions. As expected, the toy is functionally identical in every way, and comes packed in the same, high-quality illlustration box that makes such a nice complement to that which houses Mechanized Robot. Silver or gold, the squatness of Piston Action Robot shines through.

BUILDER:	NOMURA
RELEASED:	CIRCA 1958
OPERATION:	BATTERY
VALUES:	
GOOD	$1100
EXCELLENT	$1500
MINT WITH ORIGINAL BOX	$3000

NOMURA

NOMURA

NOMURA
RADAR ROBOT

JAPAN • 1955

One of the many variants based on 1954's Zoomer the Robot (1950s), Radar Robot demonstrates how Nomura designers kept infusing new and fascinating thematic concepts into the basic Zoomer platform over the life of the product line. The basic toy is all here; straight-legged but articulated forward walking motion, bulb-illuminated eyes, and that trusty wrench in the right claw. Designers then added the still-technologically exotic blinking radar dish to the rear of the robot's back (total toy height: nine inches), and located two D-cells inside the iconic battery-control box.

The result: an even better toy than the original.

Two main packaging variants are known, but both rank among the best in Japanese illustration and design. Values represent complete toys with radar dishes and original battery boxes. When the best gets better, it must be Radar Robot by Nomura.

BUILDER:	NOMURA
RELEASED:	1955
OPERATION:	BATTERY

VALUES:

GOOD	$2000
EXCELLENT	$3000
MINT WITH ORIGINAL BOX	$4500

JAMES D. JULIA AUCTIONS IMAGES

NOMURA
RADAR ROBOT

JAPAN • CIRCA 1955

This version of Radar Robot is basically an alternate-color variation on the Zoomer platform (1950s), first released in 1954. Unlike its more sophisticated, battery-box namesake brother, this more humble, eight-inch tall Radar Robot carries its obligatory wrench, but moves visually upscale with bulb-eye illumination and a two-tone color scheme. Standard, straight-legged full articulation forward motion completes the battery-op features. As with Zoomer, a single battery is inserted through the robot's left torso side. Also like Zoomer, this Radar Robot boasts an early "label" box, where a standard base and lid are customized through a color label appliqué. And, as with Zoomer and even the main Radar variant, this Radar Robot's label art is striking and iconic, adding to the value of a mint-loose example by nearly twofold. Interestingly, this box variant is considered somewhat rare in the realm of Zoomer-related packaging. For Zoomer completists, the hunt may never truly be over — but with prey like this Radar Robot variant, it is all the more fascinating.

BUILDER:	NOMUA
RELEASED:	CIRCA 1955
OPERATION:	BATTERY

VALUES:

GOOD	$300
EXCELLENT	$1200
MINT WITH ORIGINAL BOX	$2200

JAMES D. JULIA AUCTIONS IMAGES

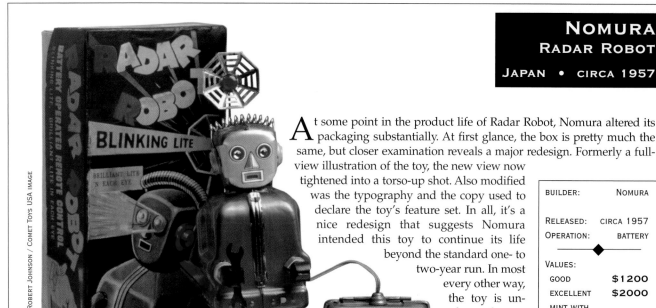

ROBERT JOHNSON / COMET TOYS USA IMAGE

NOMURA
RADAR ROBOT
JAPAN • CIRCA 1957

At some point in the product life of Radar Robot, Nomura altered its packaging substantially. At first glance, the box is pretty much the same, but closer examination reveals a major redesign. Formerly a full-view illustration of the toy, the new view now tightened into a torso-up shot. Also modified was the typography and the copy used to declare the toy's feature set. In all, it's a nice redesign that suggests Nomura intended this toy to continue its life beyond the standard one- to two-year run. In most every other way, the toy is unchanged: eyeball lightbulb feature, blinking satellite dish, and facial control box. For Zoomer (1950s) collectors, this Radar Package represents yet another example of how Nomura effectively dealt with an aging product — by this point, a nearly four-year-old toy.

BUILDER:	NOMURA
RELEASED:	CIRCA 1957
OPERATION:	BATTERY
VALUES:	
GOOD	$1200
EXCELLENT	$2000
MINT WITH ORIGINAL BOX	$3500

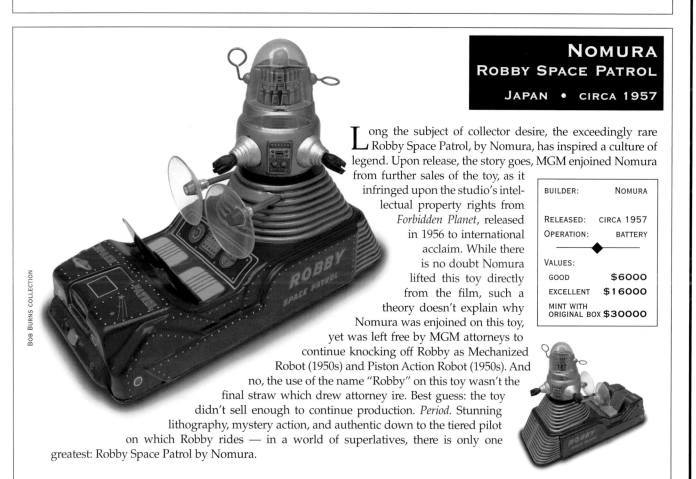

BOB BURNS COLLECTION

NOMURA
ROBBY SPACE PATROL
JAPAN • CIRCA 1957

Long the subject of collector desire, the exceedingly rare Robby Space Patrol, by Nomura, has inspired a culture of legend. Upon release, the story goes, MGM enjoined Nomura from further sales of the toy, as it infringed upon the studio's intellectual property rights from *Forbidden Planet*, released in 1956 to international acclaim. While there is no doubt Nomura lifted this toy directly from the film, such a theory doesn't explain why Nomura was enjoined on this toy, yet was left free by MGM attorneys to continue knocking off Robby as Mechanized Robot (1950s) and Piston Action Robot (1950s). And no, the use of the name "Robby" on this toy wasn't the final straw which drew attorney ire. Best guess: the toy didn't sell enough to continue production. *Period.* Stunning lithography, mystery action, and authentic down to the tiered pilot on which Robby rides — in a world of superlatives, there is only one greatest: Robby Space Patrol by Nomura.

BUILDER:	NOMURA
RELEASED:	CIRCA 1957
OPERATION:	BATTERY
VALUES:	
GOOD	$6000
EXCELLENT	$16000
MINT WITH ORIGINAL BOX	$30000

NOMURA

NOMURA
SPACE COMMANDO
JAPAN • CIRCA 1956

Nomura's family of wind-up astronauts from the mid-1950s timeframe is certainly a desirable lot. Even one of the more pedestrian members, the 11-inch Space Commando, circa 1956, brings a hefty value when found in mint-original box condition. These astronauts all feature mechanical walking; surprisingly detailed lithography for early-period toys; a helmeted, partial-face appearance; and the ubiquitous laser rifle, usually toted in the right hand. In fact, this rifle (and the toy's generally related look) have led some collectors to suggest familial relations between these Nomura toys and the Deep-Sea Diver variants of Naito Shoten. Some speculate Naito Shoten was an allied builder who supplied Nomura with design and assembly services. Though it's impossible to establish such a connection today, the fact is, many components between the two lines of toys appear to be identical. Given the byzantine nature of subcontracting during the golden age of Japanese tin-toy manufacture, just about anything is possible.

BUILDER:	NOMURA
RELEASED:	CIRCA 1956
OPERATION:	BATTERY
◆	
VALUES:	
GOOD	**$900**
EXCELLENT	**$1800**
MINT WITH ORIGINAL BOX	**$2800**

JAMES D. JULIA AUCTIONS IMAGES

NOMURA
SPACE PATROL CAR
JAPAN • CIRCA 1958

Nomura's Space Patrol Car is an interesting toy, indeed. Its early-1950s Ford styling boasts bullet-nose grilles, rounded fenders, and horizontal "eye" lights. As a battery-operated toy with mystery action and a firing-gun sequence, Space Patrol Car is helmed by a round-headed lithographic robot who bears an uncanny resemblance to the robot drivers of the two Space Robot vehicle toys of Yonezawa — this, despite clear Nomura provenance. Though both robots appear incredibly similar (note the chest-high grilles on both toys — identical lithography), there are enough visible differences to prevent a cross-pollination hypothesis on the part of both Nomura and Yonezawa.

Nonetheless, Space Patrol Car is a fascinating toy that boasts a racuous performance cycle certain to delight just about any child. As the toy mystery actions about the floor, the robot "fires" the hood-mounted laser cannon, seemingly at will, complete with flashing lights and accompanying sounds. A 10 on the entertainment-factor scale, Space Patrol Car is a middle-tier collectible: not inexpensive, but not overpriced either. Nomura was definitely up to something different with Space Patrol Car — it's just unclear what that plan was!

BUILDER:	NOMURA
RELEASED:	CIRCA 1958
OPERATION:	BATTERY
◆	
VALUES:	
GOOD	**$1200**
EXCELLENT	**$1800**
MINT WITH ORIGINAL BOX	**$2600**

KALMBACH IMAGE

NOMURA
SPACE PATROL CAR
JAPAN • CIRCA 1959

ROBERT JOHNSON / COMET TOYS USA IMAGE

Space Patrol Car is another Nomura real-life vehicle toy incorporating a sci-fi hook; the other being Atomic Fire Car (1950s). Even the platform is the same — a 10½-inch 1959 Ford Fairlane model. However, with Space Patrol Car, the "hook" isn't a futuristic fire-engine presentation, it's something more sinister: an astronaut with a hood-mounted cannon designed for one thing — wholesale mayhem. Space Patrol Car may be burdened with the done-to-death "Space Patrol" appellation, but it more than makes up for it with the detailed astronaut and gun subassemblies. The astronaut is almost from the Nomura/Naito Shoten (1950s) school of deep-sea-diving astronaut design, employing a full face mask and rounded helmet enclosure to obscure the identity of the person within. The gun is of classic angular design, with semi-realistic litho to convey the power. During operation, the mystery-action toy swerves about the floor, its gun blasting with rat-tat-tat sound and illuminated barrel flares. A classic hybrid, Space Patrol Car does a fine job of learning to live with its humble Ford underpinnings.

BUILDER:	NOMURA
RELEASED:	CIRCA 1959
OPERATION:	BATTERY

VALUES:

GOOD	$700
EXCELLENT	$1100
MINT WITH ORIGINAL BOX	$2000

NOMURA
U.S. AIR FORCE M-207 ROCKET
JAPAN • CIRCA 1959

BUILDER:	NOMURA
RELEASED:	CIRCA 1959
OPERATION:	FRICTION

VALUES:

GOOD	$85
EXCELLENT	$200
MINT WITH ORIGINAL BOX	$350

As the 1950s progressed, the U.S. Air Force's forward designs began to spread into the public consciousness. Indeed, famed government visionaries such as Werner Von Braun and Willy Ley actually cooperated with toy and model-kit manufacturers to bring authentic theoretical designs to the child market — part of the "let's build the future" philosophy predominant during the can-do 1950s. Nomura's US Air Force M-207 rocket is clearly indebted to these designs and this philosophical environment. Not a jet, and not a traditional vertical rocket, M-207 is a hybrid toy drawn from both toy-design camps. Friction powered with sparkling visible through the rear "exhaust" plastic lens, M-207 is roughly nine inches in length, with a third of that being consumed by its shock-absorbing plastic nose. A humble design that still evokes the American public's fascination with futurist design in all things airborne, M-207 is an eminently affordable late-1950s toy, perfect for any beginning collection or for adding completeness to a growing one.

M-207

U.S. AIR FORCE

NOMURA

NOMURA
X-RAY GUN
JAPAN • CIRCA 1955

Everybody knows about ray guns — from Daisy's iconic *Buck Rogers* sidearms (pre1940s) to the huge array of Japanese click-guns featuring sci-fi themes, toy hand-sized firearms are the dominant form. But what about larger weapons, the kind that need shoulder straps, or even tripods? Nomura tackled this challenge in the 1955 period with X-Ray Gun. Battery-operated X-Ray Gun is essentially a World War II-inspired automatic machine gun with sci-fi branding. Pull the trigger, and the gun issues a loud, staccato report, with the requisite flashing lights to infer escaping, lethal x-rays. A substantial toy, nearly 20 inches in length, its strongest suit is its fascinating package depicting a determined astronaut firing at incoming saucers. Designed with wraparound graphics on the full-color lid, X-Ray Gun jumps in value when accompanied by a crisp original box. Even so, this oddball member of the space-toy weapons category is an affordable item in good condition.

BUILDER:	NOMURA
RELEASED:	CIRCA 1955
OPERATION:	BATTERY
◆	
VALUES:	
GOOD	$350
EXCELLENT	$800
MINT WITH ORIGINAL BOX	$2100

NOMURA
ZOOMER THE ROBOT
JAPAN • CIRCA 1954

BUILDER:	NOMURA
RELEASED:	CIRCA 1954
OPERATION:	BATTERY
◆	
VALUES:	
GOOD	$250
EXCELLENT	$650
MINT WITH ORIGINAL BOX	$1800

One of Nomura's all-time bestselling toys, Zoomer the Robot spawned a huge family of variations and inspired an even greater assembly of knockoffs and inspirationally-influenced competitive models. The look is basic: an expressionless gaze; Cubist torso; coiled-wire-form head antenna; slow-speed, deliberate forward shuffle; claw hands; and the iconic wrench — what tin-toy godfather Teruhisa Kitahara believes symbolizes the potential a robot is capable of. As an early battery-op, Nomura's robot isn't the greatest performer, but his look overwhelms any underperforming mechanics. Interior illumination brings forth an eerie red glow from Zoomer's eyes during operation, as he walks forward, and his backpack antenna spins. Found in a number of colors, with silver-blue being among the most common, values do fluctuate depending on perceived color rarity. Inexpensive for an early and iconic piece, Zoomer is rather common in all condition grades. Note that a number of packaging variants also exist, though the main one — depicting Zoomer walking through an urban wasteland clearly influenced by Japan's wartime nuclear damage — is by far the most popular and enduring. For one of the most influential of all Japanese robots, Nomura's Zoomer can't be beat.

ROBERT JOHNSON / COMET TOYS USA IMAGE

This Zoomer variation, likely released within the same product year as the debut Zoomer, boasts Radar Robot-like (1950s) lightbulb eyeballs as well as a striking two-toned presentation. Unlike the more gaudy red-and-black hues of some Radar variants, the subdued silver-blue and silver components provide a classy, understated study in differentiation. Manufacturers like Nomura often employed multi-color variations to help provide variety to case lots sent to distributors; with variations like these, wholesalers could help ensure some degree of product exclusivity among various competing retail accounts.

BUILDER:	NOMURA
RELEASED:	CIRCA 1954
OPERATION:	BATTERY
◆	
VALUES:	
GOOD	**$650**
EXCELLENT	**$1000**
MINT WITH ORIGINAL BOX	**$2500**

Single-color variations are also quite common with Zoomers. As this striking silver example demonstrates, less flash is better with the deconstructed Modernist design used to create Zoomer. Nomura would release Zoomer variants in a stunning array of color variations, many of which bring meaningful premiums in contemporary valuations.

BUILDER:	NOMURA
RELEASED:	CIRCA 1954
OPERATION:	BATTERY
◆	
VALUES:	
GOOD	**$500**
EXCELLENT	**$900**
MINT WITH ORIGINAL BOX	**$2000**

ROBERT JOHNSON / COMET TOYS USA IMAGE

NOMURA

NOMURA-SHOWA
ROBOT TRACTOR
JAPAN • CIRCA 1957

In the world of tomorrow, futurists once proclaimed, every tedious task will be performed by robots. While members of contemporary society continue to await this day's arrival, toys like Robot Tractor by Nomura-Showa illustrate how the past envisioned toiling in the future. Little is known about Showa, other than the fact that their mark is found on a number of toys, and that they likely subcontracted to many firms like Nomura. Robot Tractor is a standard battery-op that owes its existence to Marvelous Mike (1950s). Switched on, the standard Caterpillar-style tractor moves forward, its pistons moving up and down within clear-plastic illuminated cylinders. In control is a stern-faced blockheaded robot, its claw hands grasping the tractor's control levers. Many examples today have reproduction treads, which depresses the accompanying values. A few color variations are known of this toy, but gray is the most common. Live the life of pampered luxury with your own fleet of Robot Tractors by Nomura-Showa.

BUILDER:	NOMURA SHOWA
RELEASED:	CIRCA 1957
OPERATION:	BATTERY
◆	
VALUES:	
GOOD	**$350**
EXCELLENT	**$700**
MINT WITH ORIGINAL BOX	**$1450**

NORTON-HONER
BUCK ROGERS SONIC RAY GUN
UNITED STATES • 1953

The postwar relaunch of the *Buck Rogers* franchise involved many things, including a revival of the prewar serials as television programming and a freshened comic strip. Naturally, the licensing machine was once again cranked up, with old standbys like Marx climbing aboard. New licensees also brought new ideas to the party, including the obscure firm of Norton-Honer. Their *Buck Rogers* Sonic Ray Gun is really nothing more than a pistol-shaped flashlight with a buzzer — but then, isn't that what a "sonic ray" is really all about? Styled to evoke the look and feel of a sci-fi weapon without actually resembling any of Buck's weapons, the Sonic Ray Gun lives up to the billing of being the "world's greatest signaling device" with a loud buzzer mechanism housed inside the plastic enclosure. At 7½ inches, it's not a small ray gun, either. Uncommon yet quite affordable, Norton-Honer's *Buck Rogers* Sonic Ray Gun is most avidly pursued by fans of the prewar sci-fi hero.

BUILDER:	NORTON-HONER
RELEASED:	1953
OPERATION:	BATTERY
◆	
VALUES:	
GOOD	**$200**
EXCELLENT	**$400**
MINT WITH ORIGINAL BOX	**$650**

KALMBACH IMAGES

OHTA
SPACE PATROL ROBBOT ON ROCKET (Z-MAN)
JAPAN • CIRCA 1959

As a small manufacturer, Ohta (known by their trademark "K") created a limited selection of space toys. Yet one of Ohta's only space toys is also one of the collecting community's favorite designs: Space Patrol Robbot (sic) on Rocket. Better known as Z-Man, Ohta's creation features the fabulous sociological marriage of a blockheaded robot and an intercontinental ballistic missile. Issued five years prior to 1964's *Dr. Strangelove*, Z-Man seems to have inspired — or at the very least, presaged — Slim Pickens' missile-riding scene from the Kubrick film. Grasping handlebars, Z-Man friction-pedals his way through space. Box art depicts Z-Man in a more heroic light: astride the ICBM, Z-Man rockets through space, passing Saturn with nary a glance. The tricycle effect of the real toy is somewhat less inspirational, but the impact remains — Z-Man is one of the best of its kind, and still relatively affordable compared to many of its contemporaries. Terrific original package art makes mint-original box the most desirable of all potential purchases.

BUILDER:	OHTA
RELEASED:	CIRCA 1959
OPERATION:	FRICTION
VALUES:	
GOOD	$450
EXCELLENT	$1200
MINT WITH ORIGINAL BOX	$1800

PAUL STONE
ROCKET RACE GAME
UNITED STATES • 1958

Yet another toy directly inspired by the Soviet launch of Sputnik in October 1957, Paul Stone's Rocket Race Game brings the space-race concept directly into the American living room. A basic game with a rather boring play pattern, Rocket Race Game is more noteworthy for its three-color cover and concentric-ring galaxy gameboard art than anything else. Not tremendously creative nor collectible, Rocket Race Game nonetheless can serve admirably as an interesting backdrop piece to other space toys on display. The lid is copyrighted "© 1958 Paul Stone." Most board games are found with missing components, and replacing original game tokens and other materials is nearly impossible.

BUILDER:	PAUL STONE
RELEASED:	1958
OPERATION:	STATIC
VALUES:	
GOOD	$100
EXCELLENT	$150
MINT WITH ORIGINAL BOX	$350

OHTA — PAUL STONE

PLAXALL
CAPTAIN VIDEO SPACE HELMET
UNITED STATES • CIRCA 1952

BUILDER:	PLAXALL
RELEASED:	CIRCA 1952
OPERATION:	STATIC

VALUES:	
GOOD	$800
EXCELLENT	$1200
MINT WITH ORIGINAL BOX	$2500

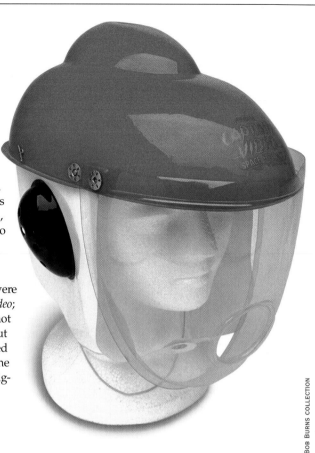

One of the coolest space toys based on one of the greatest television sci-fi shows nobody ever heard of — that's Plaxall's *Captain Video* space helmet. From 1949 through 1955, the DuMont Television Network aired *Captain Video* in daily strip format. Kids everywhere flocked to the program, with its cerebral bent (Captain Video was a futuristic genius, after all) and its decent-quality special effects and emphasis on brains over brawn. For reasons unclear at this time, few toys were ever licensed by DuMont for *Captain Video*; this Plaxall vacu-formed space helmet is not only fascinating for its relative rarity, but also for its fragility in the face of rugged child play. Rarely seen in its original box, the helmet's value jumps markedly when original packaging is present.

BOB BURNS COLLECTION

PRACTI-COLE PRODUCTS
TOM CORBETT SPACE CADET SPACE HELMET
UNITED STATES • CIRCA 1954

BUILDER:	PRACTI-COLE
RELEASED:	CIRCA 1954
OPERATION:	STATIC

VALUES:	
GOOD	$1000
EXCELLENT	$1800
MINT WITH ORIGINAL BOX	$2800

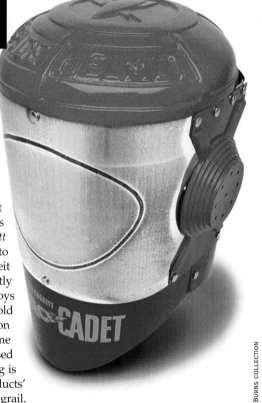

As the *Tom Corbett Space Cadet* program wound down its original run in the mid-1950s, a small, final rush of licensed product made it to market for one last capitalization on the tired license. This innovative Space Helmet by the oddly named Practi-Cole Products certainly pulled out all the stops for an also-ran license in the 1954 timeframe; its "reflective" visor screen is an early form of mirroring, allowing the viewer inside to peer outward, but obscuring others from seeing the helmet wearer's eyes. At nearly 12 inches in height, the *Tom Corbett Space Cadet* Space Helmet was big enough to accommodate even the oldest of fans, albeit somewhat claustrophobic. Made from mostly vacuformed plastic, it's unlikely many of these toys have survived. Considering even fewer were sold initially, owing to the product's late introduction relative to the license's lifecycle, this has become one very desirable and scarce *Tom Corbett*-licensed product — particularly when original packaging is present. For *Tom Corbett* fans, Practi-Cole Products' *Space Cadet* Space Helmet just may be the holy space grail.

BOB BURNS COLLECTION

PREMIER PRODUCTS
FLASH GORDON SOLAR COMMANDO
UNITED STATES • 1952

The reintroduction of *Flash Gordon* to a new generation in 1952 resulted in a wave of newly licensed product. 1930s-era serials were appearing on television for the first time, and their time-honored designs served as foundation for a new generation of toys. Premier Products' *Flash Gordon* Solar Commando is a classic example of a third-tier manufacturer riding the licensing wave. Their humble, single-shot molded-plastic toys captured some of the look and feel of the serial's spacecraft, but no matter: as a carded product, authenticity would always take a back seat to price point. Indeed, value was the name of the game for Premier Products — their *Flash Gordon* Solar Commando play pack includes three ships and two figures, plenty for any active childhood imagination. Loose, each item's value is negligible, so consider each value listed to include "on card" status, with mint-on-card as the ultimate find.

BUILDER:	PREMIER
RELEASED:	1952
OPERATION:	STATIC
VALUES:	
GOOD	**$200**
EXCELLENT	**$350**
MINT ON ORIGINAL CARD	**$650**

PYRO
X-300 SPACE CRUISER
UNITED STATES • CIRCA 1958

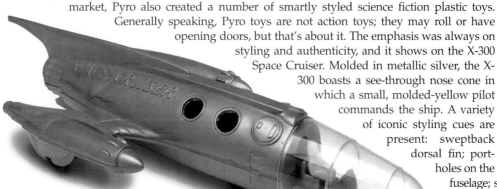

BOB BURNS COLLECTION

Pyro, of New Jersey, made its mark in postwar toymaking by marketing a huge array of mold-in-color plastic playthings from a variety of categories. Best known as a fierce competitor of Louis Marx & Co. for the add-on playset figure and accessory market, Pyro also created a number of smartly styled science fiction plastic toys. Generally speaking, Pyro toys are not action toys; they may roll or have opening doors, but that's about it. The emphasis was always on styling and authenticity, and it shows on the X-300 Space Cruiser. Molded in metallic silver, the X-300 boasts a see-through nose cone in which a small, molded-yellow pilot commands the ship. A variety of iconic styling cues are present: sweptback dorsal fin; portholes on the fuselage; short wingspan; and wingtip rocket motors. As a basic floor "push-it" toy, the Pyro X-300 doesn't scream exciting play patterns, but its value comes more from its styling and rugged good looks. Generally found among playset components, the X-300's values reflect a complete toy, including removable pilot figure and opening clear-plastic nose cone. The mint value reflects an X-300 still attached to its original card.

BUILDER:	PYRO
RELEASED:	CIRCA 1958
OPERATION:	STATIC
VALUES:	
GOOD	**$100**
EXCELLENT	**$175**
MINT ON ORIGINAL CARD	**$295**

RAY-O-VAC
SPACE PATROL ROCKET FLASHLIGHT
UNITED STATES • 1954

Question: when is a standard Ray-O-Vac flashlight much more than just a flashlight? Answer: when it's a *Commander Buzz Corry Space Patrol* Rocket Flashlight! This fascinating piece of purpose-built functionality was marketed in 1954 by Ray-O-Vac to capitalize on the popularity of ABC's *Space Patrol*, a daily serial which ran from 1950-55. Though numerous products were issued using the show's stylized logotype and "Official Buzz Corry" nomenclature, none demonstrate the stylish ingenuity that Ray-O-Vac's product does. Fashioned to resemble Buzz Corry's rocketship, the 12-inch flashlight stands on end, balanced by three directional "Jet Tube" fins which double as launchers for small cardboard "rocket" blow-darts. Switched on, the flashlight emits brilliant illumination through its clear nosecone. A long red-rubber tip is affixed to the nosecone's end, presumably to protect the clear plastic as well as accentuate the rocket look of the product. Sears marketed this product in their 1954 Wish Book for the original retail of $2.98. Not terribly expensive as far as space-toy collectibles go, Ray-O-Vac's *Space Patrol* Rocket Flashlight sheds meaningful light on the power of purpose-built licensed goods in a world of uncreative design.

BUILDER:	RAY-O-VAC
RELEASED:	1954
OPERATION:	BATTERY
VALUES:	
GOOD	$150
EXCELLENT	$300
MINT WITH ORIGINAL BOX	$550

BOB BURNS COLLECTION

REMCO
QX-2 WALKIE TALKIES
UNITED STATES • CIRCA 1958

American toymaker Remco is best remembered for its vast array of one-hit plastic-toy wonders spanning the mid-1950s through the mid-1970s. During the 1950s, they attempted to capitalize on the space craze with reformulated walkie-talkie products from their existing line. The QX-2 model from around 1958 represents their second-generation attempt at a space-toy communication product; their first being the Space Commander-branded toys, circa 1957. Like many American toys of the period, the packaging outsells the reality of the toy — a factor which only boosts a toy's appeal as a vintage collectible. Standard corded speaker-microphone units allow two children to speak "telephonically" to one another from the distance permitted by the included wire. Most impressive is the fold-top package, which converts into a window-standee display, revealing both the striking package art as well as the toys inside. Inexpensive and relatively available, Remco QX-2 Walkie Talkies are a great complement to any assembly of vintage sci-fi communications toys.

BUILDER:	REMCO
RELEASED:	CIRCA 1958
OPERATION:	BATTERY
VALUES:	
GOOD	$100
EXCELLENT	$200
MINT WITH ORIGINAL BOX	$550

BUILDER:	REMCO
RELEASED:	CIRCA 1957
OPERATION:	BATTERY
◆	
VALUES:	
GOOD	**$150**
EXCELLENT	**$300**
MINT WITH ORIGINAL BOX	**$650**

REMCO
SPACE COMMANDER WALKIE TALKIES
UNITED STATES • CIRCA 1957

As Remco's earliest foray into corded communication devices, Space Commander Walkie Talkies are somewhat unimpressive. After all, aren't "walkie talkies" wireless devices, enabling the users to travel great distances, free from the hassles of corded communication? Of course they are — but "corded communication device" simply doesn't have the verve of "walkie talkie," hence the somewhat misleading branding. Even so, Remco's toys worked as advertised, allowing kids to speak to one another through microphone-speaker assemblies housed in futuristic plastic handsets. The only limitations: the child's imagination — and the length of wire included with the set.

Terrific packaging sets Remco apart from contemporaries; this toy's child space explorer design leveraged a simple two-color print job into a striking piece of commercial art. Relatively inexpensive and available, Remco Space Commander Walkie Talkies would be eclipsed within a year by the rebranded QX-2 models (1950s), and ultimately by yet another generation of product before the corded communication device trend had run its course.

REMCO
SPACE GUN
UNITED STATES • CIRCA 1958

On the heels of their successful walkie-talkie ventures, Remco released their Electronic Space Gun using many of the same principles: killer packaging, basic play patterns, and plastic, plastic, plastic! As little more than a glorified flashlight, Electronic Space Gun boasts an underwhelming array of features: changeable-gel illumination accompanied by clicking sounds when the light switch/trigger is pulled. Not exciting enough for you? Then try the package's claims: "powerful color rays"; "high speed atom chamber"; "televideo sights". Made from mold-in-color plastic, Remco's Space Gun has rather

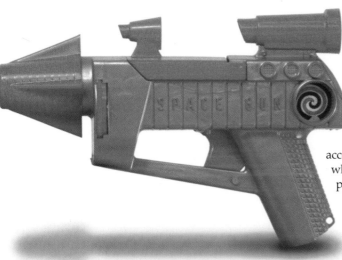

BUILDER:	REMCO
RELEASED:	CIRCA 1958
OPERATION:	BATTERY
◆	
VALUES:	
GOOD	**$150**
EXCELLENT	**$300**
MINT WITH ORIGINAL BOX	**$650**

pedestrian design, but comes packaged in a stellar box complete with child-at-play artwork, a planet-filled night sky, and a futuristic city. Buy it for the box, but even loose, Remco's Electronic Space Gun provides good contrast to some truly innovative toy ray gun designs of the same period — those created by Japanese tin-litho manufacturers.

REMCO

REMCO — SANYO

REMCO
WALKIE TALKIES
UNITED STATES • CIRCA 1959

Remco closed out their profitable 1950s-era run in the corded-communication category with "2-way electronic magnet powered" Walkie Talkies, circa 1959. Like the originals on which these toys are based, Remco's "walkie talkies" were really children's play telephones, outfitted with speaker-microphone assemblies housed inside sleek, futuristic plastic cases. The toys come packaged in a standee-style box, which folds up and back to reveal the toys through a glassine window. Perhaps most interesting is Remco's use of the term "2-way electronic magnet powered" — essentially a synonym for "telephone," as opposed to wireless walkie-talkie communication. For completists, all three Remco walkie-talkie sets are desirable, particularly when displayed in mint-original box condition.

BUILDER:	REMCO
RELEASED:	CIRCA 1959
OPERATION:	BATTERY
VALUES:	
GOOD	$100
EXCELLENT	$200
MINT WITH ORIGINAL BOX	$450

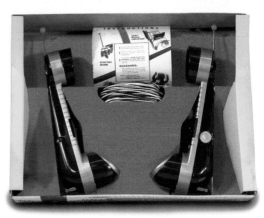

SANYO
EXPLORER
JAPAN • CIRCA 1952

Sometimes very innovative things come in small packages. The circa-1952 Explorer, by Sanyo, is a perfect example: at little more than four inches in length, friction-powered Explorer looks small and inconsequential, but that's where appearances can be deceiving. Stamped from a single piece of lithographed tin, Explorer is a humble toy, designed to compete on the lowest level of toy merchandising — penny toys. However, Sanyo's inclusion of friction drive, along with the striking lithographic art and curvaceous design, makes this far more than a disposable dimestore purchase.

A fair amount of Explorers have survived the intervening years, making the toy a reasonable buy, even when found in the desirable mint-original box condition. Despite the fact that little is known about Sanyo, their toys such as Explorer confirm their creative potential, even more than 40 years after the fact.

BUILDER:	SANYO
RELEASED:	CIRCA 1952
OPERATION:	FRICTION
VALUES:	
GOOD	$150
EXCELLENT	$265
MINT WITH ORIGINAL BOX	$450

BOB BURNS COLLECTION

SANYO
RACER

JAPAN • CIRCA 1956

Sanyo's Racer comes from the days when futuristic vehicle design still borrowed heavily from the trends of the day. Long, sweeping lines are complemented by rounded corners and body-length chrome trim. Glowing red paint is matched with rich cream, creating a classic two-tone scheme that's at home in any century. And to finish the design, a central dorsal fin, angled aft, inferring the tremendous speeds of which the vehicle is capable. Sanyo's evocative design suggests an early build; research indicates the Racer likely emerged around 1956. Its prodigious use of chrome, as well as the simple driver figure included in the central cockpit location, both suggest a pre-1960 build — a date after which plated parts in general became less common on most Japanese tin toys. Outfitted with friction drive, the nine-inch Racer (numbered "76" on the dorsal fin) belongs to the pantheon of futuristic vehicle toys, a product category that was highly popular during the era of Motoramas and Cars of Tomorrow.

BUILDER:	SANYO
RELEASED:	CIRCA 1956
OPERATION:	FRICTION
VALUES:	
GOOD	$350
EXCELLENT	$600
MINT WITH ORIGINAL BOX	$1800

SANYO
ROCKET JEEP

JAPAN • CIRCA 1958

During the 1950s, the under-$1 retail toy category was a burgeoning one, with a huge group of manufacturers vying for children's pocket-money purchases. Brands like Matchbox and Tootsietoy exposed the massive market for kid-driven purchasing, and Japanese toymakers followed suit. Of course, the Japanese had long been manufacturers of penny toys, but this slightly upscale shift towards the 49-, 59- and 69-cent purchases meant a repositioning of the formula. Thus, toys like Rocket Jeep emerged to meet both demand and price points, with good results. Considering that Sanyo's toy is little more than a lithographically re-designed friction-powered U.S. Army Jeep, it still merits collector attention today, primarily because of its fascinating use of rocket and outer-space imagery. Colorful yet quaint, the Sanyo Rocket Jeep is difficult to find in mint-original box condition, with upwardly mobile prices to match.

BUILDER:	SANYO
RELEASED:	CIRCA 1958
OPERATION:	FRICTION
VALUES:	
GOOD	$300
EXCELLENT	$500
MINT WITH ORIGINAL BOX	$1200

SANYO

SANYO
S-2 MAN MADE SATELLITE
JAPAN • CIRCA 1958

Talk about timely. When Sanyo released its S-2 Man Made Satellite in the 1958 timeframe, Sputnik II carrying Laika the Heroic Communist Dog had flared out barely eight months before, in November 1957.

BUILDER:	SANYO
RELEASED:	CIRCA 1958
OPERATION:	WIND-UP
VALUES:	
GOOD	$450
EXCELLENT	$900
MINT WITH ORIGINAL BOX	$2000

Clearly inspired by real-life Soviet space exploits, this scarce wind-up features authentic design cues, right down to Sputnik's multiple antenna projections and the silhouetted viewport depicting a dehydrated Laika obviously on the re-entry portion of the satellite's bell curve. Switched on, the satellite spins around in position, just as a real-life satellite would do. Rare packaging makes this Sanyo toy far more collectible when found in mint-boxed condition. Even at lower condition grades, the S-2 Man Made Satellite is a worthy toy that serves as a lasting symbol for its time and place of origin — not to mention a monument to thirsty dogs everywhere.

SAUNDERS
MARVELOUS MIKE
UNITED STATES • 1955

BUILDER:	SAUNDERS
RELEASED:	1955
OPERATION:	BATTERY
VALUES:	
GOOD	$200
EXCELLENT	$400
MINT WITH ORIGINAL BOX	$900

Frequently mistaken for a Japanese toy, Marvelous Mike is actually the output of Saunders Co., of Aurora, Illinois, and is certainly the inspiration for Robotrac Tractor (1950s) and similar toys. Riding atop his classic Caterpillar bulldozer, Mike operates the tractor with aplomb, shifting gears and reversing direction whenever an impedance is struck. At more than 14 inches in length, Marvelous Mike isn't a strong collectible, likely due to its size and the toy's high survival rate. Values listed require original rubber treads. Sears carried the toy in their 1955 catalog, retailing it for $8.95 — certainly a reflection of both Mike's functionality as well as his size. Interestingly, the toy is marked "Patented 1939, 1953," indicating Saunders may have presaged the entire automaton construction vehicle category by nearly 15 years. It's unclear whether the early patent covered a robotic driver or merely the mystery-action feature, but one thing's for sure: Marvelous Mike easily lives up to his grandiose billing.

JAMES D. JULIA AUCTIONS IMAGES

SNK
FLASHY JIM
JAPAN • CIRCA 1955

SNK is another in a long line of postwar Japanese toymakers whose history is now forgotten. Believed to be an acronym for "Sankei," the company's real name, SNK is best remembered for its line of blocky silver robots with entertaining names. This toy, for example, goes by the name Flashy Jim, and is believed to be from the post-Zoomer Cubist school of robot design which thrived around 1955. SNK's design is extremely evocative — iconic, almost — but because they weren't dedicated at marking their toys, many term the toy "unknown." Flashy Jim is the battery-op variant of the seven-inch family, with forward walking motion and illuminated eyes. Other members in the SNK robot family (Sparkling Mike and Robbie the Roving Robot, 1950s) differ in terms of operation as well as lithographic chest details. Original packaging sends mint-loose examples skyrocketing in value. A classic robot with an unforgetttable name — Flashy Jim by SNK.

BUILDER:	SNK
RELEASED:	CIRCA 1955
OPERATION:	BATTERY
VALUES:	
GOOD	**$400**
EXCELLENT	**$900**
MINT WITH ORIGINAL BOX	**$2100**

SNK

JAMES D. JULIA AUCTIONS IMAGES

SNK
ROBBIE THE ROVING ROBOT
JAPAN • CIRCA 1956

Yet another variant on the Flashy Jim family of block-headed robots is Robbie the Roving Robot. Manufactured by SNK in the 1956 timeframe, Robbie is a wind-up version of Flashy Jim. The seven-inch toy also features alternative lithographic details on its chest, as well as bright-red circular (versus diamond) kneecaps and red feet. Original packaging for Robbie the Roving Robot is noteworthy for more than just its rarity; it also is devoid of any corporate identity. As a result, for years Robbie has been termed an "unknown manufacturer" toy, despite the fact that the Flashy Jim variant's package bears the SNK logotype. A highly valuable toy in mint-original box condition, SNK's Robbie the Roving Robot demonstrates that sometimes, mechanical is better than battery-operated.

BUILDER:	SNK
RELEASED:	CIRCA 1956
OPERATION:	WIND-UP
VALUES:	
GOOD	**$1200**
EXCELLENT	**$2100**
MINT WITH ORIGINAL BOX	**$4500**

SNK
SPARKLING MIKE ROBOT
JAPAN • CIRCA 1957

It's hardly ironic that the most humble of the SNK robot family is also the most common. After all, oftentimes the most cost-reduced products sell the best, and that's likely the case with Sparkling Mike Robot. As the third release along the SNK timeline — the one that begins with Flashy Jim (1950s) — Sparkling Mike is believed to be a circa-1957 release. Like stablemate Robbie the Roving Robot, Mike is a seven-inch wind-up. Unlike Robbie, however, Mike features diamond-shaped kneecaps, blue feet, and a hole in his chest through which sparks fly during operation. Claw hands and the tiny diamond-shaped head antenna complete the SNK feature list. An inexpensive robot in good condition, Sparkling Mike Robot is one of those vintage robots that has been passed over for his more, well, "flashy" cousins. Too bad, because this toy is nearly as old, boasts an interesting backstory, and has a spectacular family tree. How many blockheaded automatons can make that claim? *Exactly.*

BUILDER:	SNK
RELEASED:	CIRCA 1957
OPERATION:	WIND-UP

◆

VALUES:	
GOOD	$350
EXCELLENT	$600
MINT WITH ORIGINAL BOX	$1200

SONSCO-?
SPACE MAN
JAPAN • CIRCA 1958

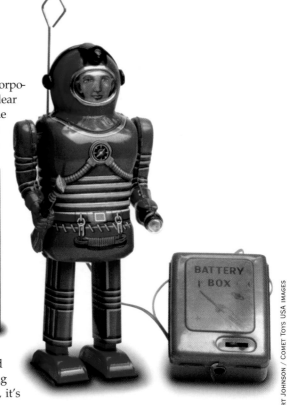

So little is known about Sonsco today that it's been suggested their corporate lifespan could have been measured in months, not years. It's clear they were a small-time distributor, possibly working out of Japan, the U.S., or both. They issued a very small number of toys, many of which were marketed directly by their builders. And then there's the enigmatic Space Man, believed to be circa 1958. Its lush lithography is matched only by its classic-period illustrated packaging. As a corded remote toy, Space Man patrols his environs with his tin-litho rifle in his right hand and an illuminated flashlight in his left. A helmet-mounted beacon also helps signal the way. Space Man's silver-blue look suggests Daiya, but is believed to be the product of Nomura. To be expected, toys like Space Man are scarce, and command tremendous respect (with the expected values) among knowledgeable space-toy collectors. For rarity or design importance, it's difficult to find equals to Sonsco's Space Man.

BUILDER:	SONSCO
RELEASED:	CIRCA 1958
OPERATION:	BATTERY

◆

VALUES:	
GOOD	$1500
EXCELLENT	$3000
MINT WITH ORIGINAL BOX	$7500

James D. Julia Auctions Images

Strenco
Robot ST1
West Germany • circa 1955

At the risk of sounding like a bad 1950s thriller, Who is Strenco and What's the Story with Robot ST1? Amazingly similar to Nomura's Zoomer the Robot (1950s), Robot ST1 is generally credited to little-known German toymaker, Strenco. Besides sharing the same basic form factor, ST1 and Zoomer also boast matching details like a coiled head antenna; forward-facing, unposeable hands; a slow, shuffling walk (ST1 is a mechanical toy, unlike Zoomer); and even a centrally located accent strip down the torso. Clearly a knockoff of Zoomer, the seven-inch ST1 is believed to have been released around 1955, as Zoomer was mopping up the small-robot segment of the toy market. Strenco also marketed an ST1 variant, which pushes a small baggage-style cart; this version sells for more than twice the mint-boxed value of the non-cart version. Though odd and not generally found, collectors don't assign over-the-top valuation to ST1, making it a somewhat affordable robot, and a great conversational complement to any Zoomer collection. It appears imitation really is the most sincere form of flattery — if you're Zoomer, that is.

BUILDER:	STRENCO
RELEASED:	CIRCA 1955
OPERATION:	WIND-UP
VALUES:	
GOOD	$600
EXCELLENT	$900
MINT WITH ORIGINAL BOX	$1800

Tri-Ang Minic
Push and Go Interplanetary Research Unit
United Kingdom • circa 1956

Though not known for its outer-space focus, British toymaker Tri-ang Minic did produce this fascinating Push and Go Interplanetary Research Unit "presentation set" during the 1956 time period. Tri-ang is regarded for its historic line of vehicle toys, in particular the prewar wind-up Minics made from enameled and lithographed tin. This set features primarily die-cast construction, along with Minic's "push and go" flywheel drive mechanism. The set includes 10 pieces, such as rockets, launch vehicles, and all types of support vehicles — clearly pulled from military-themed sets. Even so, Interplanetary Research does boast stunning packaging, from the gauzy "serving suggestion" lid art to the "wild blue yonder" background of the inner tray. As with any sort of assembly of product, packaging is the only real establishment of authenticity. Thus, this set's mint-original box value reflects the difficult-to-find nature of both the lid and tray, as well as underscoring the set's entire look and feel — or, as Tri-ang might put it, its *presentation.*

BUILDER:	TRI-ANG MINIC
RELEASED:	CIRCA 1956
OPERATION:	MECHANICAL
VALUES:	
GOOD	$400
EXCELLENT	$750
MINT WITH ORIGINAL BOX	$1600

Strenco — Tri-Ang Minic

U.S. PLASTICS

U.S. PLASTICS
SPACE PATROL BINOCULARS
UNITED STATES • CIRCA 1952

One of the early postwar sci-fi licensing successes was *Space Patrol*, which ran in various forms between 1950 and 1955. Headed up by the fictional Buzz Corry character, *Space Patrol* caught its stride by the 1952 timeframe, when most licensed product began to hit the toy market. This set of binoculars was offered as a premium through a forgotten (possibly food-related) direct-response scheme. Built from period thermoplastic and cardstock, its functionality is less impactful than the overall look and feel of the piece itself. Featuring the series' logotype and a standard vertical rocket icon, the binoculars produce a "faraway" perspective when viewed as designed — certainly the opposite of the desired effect, but fun for kids nonetheless. Note that mint condition does not include original packaging. For *Space Patrol* enthusiasts, however, this is certainly a desirable item that provides a terrific complement to more traditional toys.

BUILDER:	U.S. PLASTICS
RELEASED:	CIRCA 1952
OPERATION:	STATIC
VALUES:	
GOOD	$100
EXCELLENT	$160
MINT	$250

BOB BURNS COLLECTION

U.S. PLASTICS
SPACE PATROL GUN
UNITED STATES • CIRCA 1952

Early postwar thermoplastics represented a new wave of design in American toymaking — but with a catch: they weren't very resilient. In the hands of horseplaying kids, most plastic toys had mercifully short lifespans. Without a doubt, U.S. Plastics' *Space Patrol* guns met similar fates; their stylish molded design and smart, hot-stamped logotype were likely no match for the playground wars they inspired. Still, for fans of the 1950-55 radio and TV series *Space Patrol* starring fictional character Buzz Corry, this gun and its click-projectile play pattern no doubt delivered many hours of outer-space fun. Both red and green mold-in-color variants are known. Due to their somewhat unique design, it's possible these toy were actual re-creations of the sidearms used on the program. The guns are marked with relief lettering reading "U.S. Plastics" and "Pasadena, Calif." as well as the *Space Patrol* logotype hot-stamping.

BUILDER:	U.S. PLASTICS
RELEASED:	CIRCA 1952
OPERATION:	MECHANICAL
VALUES:	
GOOD	$100
EXCELLENT	$165
MINT WITH ORIGINAL BOX	$350

BOB BURNS COLLECTION

BUILDER:	UNKNOWN
RELEASED:	CIRCA 1957
OPERATION:	WIND-UP

◆

VALUES:	
GOOD	**$600**
EXCELLENT	**$1200**
MINT WITH ORIGINAL BOX	**$2500**

UNKNOWN
ROBOT BOAT NO. 7
JAPAN • CIRCA 1957

Robot Boat No. 7, by an unknown manufacturer, is a fabulous hybrid toy spanning the wind-up boat and robot segments of the 1957 period. Colorful lithographic design characterizes the boat, but it's the blockheaded robot at the helm which grabs the attention; expressionless, the grim automaton pilots the boat with claw hands and lightning-bolt chevrons on both arms. Two boat variants are known — this version as well as Robot Boat R-7 (1950s). Both are considered the product of the same manufacturer, as the robots and hull stampings are identical. Interestingly, the toy is marked "E.T.", which is believed to be a Japanese export concern — essentially the same as Linemar. The wind-up has a centrally mounted crank which powers up the flywheel-equipped propeller. Direction is established by manually setting the friction rudder at the boat's stern. Original packaging doubles the value between excellent and mint-original box. Shrouded in mystery, Robot Boat No. 7 is the kind of offbeat hybrid collectible that easily becomes the centerpiece of any collection.

UNKNOWN
ROBOT BOAT R-7
JAPAN • CIRCA 1959

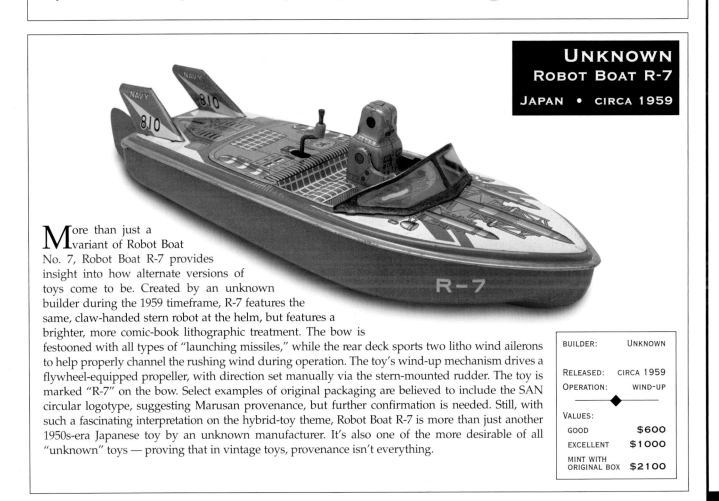

More than just a variant of Robot Boat No. 7, Robot Boat R-7 provides insight into how alternate versions of toys come to be. Created by an unknown builder during the 1959 timeframe, R-7 features the same, claw-handed stern robot at the helm, but features a brighter, more comic-book lithographic treatment. The bow is festooned with all types of "launching missiles," while the rear deck sports two litho wind ailerons to help properly channel the rushing wind during operation. The toy's wind-up mechanism drives a flywheel-equipped propeller, with direction set manually via the stern-mounted rudder. The toy is marked "R-7" on the bow. Select examples of original packaging are believed to include the SAN circular logotype, suggesting Marusan provenance, but further confirmation is needed. Still, with such a fascinating interpretation on the hybrid-toy theme, Robot Boat R-7 is more than just another 1950s-era Japanese toy by an unknown manufacturer. It's also one of the more desirable of all "unknown" toys — proving that in vintage toys, provenance isn't everything.

BUILDER:	UNKNOWN
RELEASED:	CIRCA 1959
OPERATION:	WIND-UP

◆

VALUES:	
GOOD	**$600**
EXCELLENT	**$1000**
MINT WITH ORIGINAL BOX	**$2100**

UNKNOWN

UNKNOWN
ROCKET RACE TO SATURN GAME
UNITED STATES • CIRCA 1958

The amazing thing about pop fads is the huge amount of detritus that spews forth from every sector wishing to cash in. Take Rocket Race to Saturn by an unknown American manufacturer. This board game is about as uninventive as they come — a dim path-style game that guarantees boredom before the first player reaches the finish. Pedestrian board game design is hardly the exclusive domain of space-toy themes, of course, but this particular one reeks of me-tooism. Even so, collectors pursue items such as this simply for their backdrop potential, which makes sense. At relatively affordable prices, even in mint-original box condition, toys like Rocket Race to Saturn may only continue to serve into the future as shelf decoration — but the world needs wallcoverings, too.

BUILDER:	UNKNOWN
RELEASED:	CIRCA 1958
OPERATION:	STATIC
VALUES:	
GOOD	$100
EXCELLENT	$250
MINT WITH ORIGINAL BOX	$450

UNKNOWN
STRATO BANK
UNITED STATES • CIRCA 1958

There's a certain inherent ingenuity in the design of mechanical banks — so much so that the earliest examples were often patented by their inventors to prevent intellectual piracy. The concept of saving money is a basic one, but combined with a mechanical-action reward, the experience becomes a pleasurable one for kids — one that encourages ongoing thrift. Strato Bank, by an unknown American manufacturer, takes this venerable savings concept to the space age with stylish success. The die-cast toy has a heavy, strong feel, and its action is straight from the old school of mechanical-bank design. Place the coin in the breech of the rocket, then pull that rocket back into its locked position. Press the actuator button on the rear of the large rocket, and the coin is launched directly into the awaiting planet. At eight inches, it's a substantial toy, and despite its entertaining play pattern, it's a difficult toy to find today, likely due to poor distribution upon initial release. For a space-age twist on an old-time play pattern, it's Strato Bank.

BUILDER:	UNKNOWN
RELEASED:	CIRCA 1958
OPERATION:	MECHANICAL
VALUES:	
GOOD	$55
EXCELLENT	$95
MINT WITH ORIGINAL BOX	$190

UNKNOWN

UNKNOWN

YONEZAWA
ATOM JET
JAPAN • CIRCA 1954

At 30 inches in length, only one word really describes Yonezawa's Atom Jet, and that's "big." Then again, "expensive" might also work. Pursued by both vehicle and space-toy enthusiasts, Atom Jet is an early toy from Yonezawa that captures the can-do, anything-is-possible mentality of the early 1950s. Yet despite its popularity, collectors have yet to determine the source of Y's inspiration. Perhaps it's a salute to the Bonneville land-speed record participants who were making news constantly throughout the early part of the decade. Maybe the design is nothing more than a derivation of auto show concept vehicles. Or it could simply be the work of exceedingly fertile Yonezawa imaginations. Either way, it's certainly the most sci-fi of

BUILDER:	YONEZAWA
RELEASED:	CIRCA 1954
OPERATION:	FRICTION
VALUES:	
GOOD	$2500
EXCELLENT	$6000
MINT WITH ORIGINAL BOX	$18000

vehicles, and perhaps the most valuable, as well. Outfitted with friction drive, Atom Jet features stunning, aircraft-like lithography, a central cockpit, and the stylized "Atom Jet" script on the central dorsal fin. Original packaging for Atom Jet — a plain cardboard box with a four-color custom label applied to the hinged lid — is virtually unheard of; its presence produces an explosive gain in pricing. Mint-original box values should include absolutely mint examples, with crisp corrugated packaging to match. For style, for rarity, and for impact in space-themed vehicle toys, Yonezawa's Atom Jet sets the standard that no plaything can match.

YONEZAWA
MOON ROCKET
JAPAN • CIRCA 1956

There's no doubt major American films like MGM's *Forbidden Planet* (1956) had tremendous impact on the Japanese toy industry; scores of thematically indebted toys flooded the market for years after that film's release. But what about smaller, less-remembered films? Films like George Pal's iconic *Destination Moon* (1950) and even the Velveeta-esque *Flight to Mars* (1951)? So, too, did these films make their mark, but in more subtle ways. Yonezawa's Moon Rocket (circa 1956) is one such toy whose creative intent is clearly based on designs manifested in films like *Destination Moon*. Using the vertical rocket form factor which would come to define Man's preferred method of future conveyance throughout the 1950s (that is, men use vertical rocketships, aliens use flattened flying saucers), Yonezawa designers unwittingly set their own precedent for successive rocket-toy releases. Moon Rocket, it would appear, is one of the first rocket toys to include the now-standard set of vertical rocket animation sequences: it rolls along the floor, then stops; it slowly rises into a vertical position using a camouflaged lift lever, then

BUILDER:	YONEZAWA
RELEASED:	CIRCA 1956
OPERATION:	BATTERY
VALUES:	
GOOD	$1500
EXCELLENT	$2500
MINT WITH ORIGINAL BOX	$5000

proceeds through a "launch sequence" — generally speaking, lots of flashing lights and sounds. Yonezawa also included a detailed, opening cockpit on this toy, complete with an illuminated "radar lunar scope" for determining the perfect landing location, no doubt. Not uncommon, but certainly not pedestrian, Moon Rocket by Yonezawa is not only one of the early vertical rocket toys, but also one of the most secondarily influential, as well.

KALMBACH IMAGE

YONEZAWA

YONEZAWA

YONEZAWA
ROBBY ROBOT
JAPAN • CIRCA 1958

Yonezawa's small astronaut/robot product line was a hardy one, a line which raised the time-honored tradition of subassembly reuse to a fine art. Products like Robby Robot (indebted in name to 1956's *Forbidden Planet*) and X-27 Explorer (1950s) would serve as the foundation for a number of successive Yonezawa releases, including such famous progeny as Roby and Conehead Robots of the early 1960s. It's easy to see why Y reused the components — functionality! This family of product, while obviously cost-reduced to meet certain price points, features solid performance, thanks to its tried-and-true walking mechanism. Though somewhat "cheap" by many contemporary products' standards (those wrench-like stamped-tin hands which dangle limply at the robot's side leave much to be desired), these toys nonetheless have risen to become one of the more desirable (if not famous) families of robot product from postwar Japan. Standing eight inches, Robby is from the vanguard of this family, with values to match its relative scarcity in the market today. Robby's youthful, almost childlike face inside the diving-bell helmet also serves as a reminder that no matter how valuable they become, these were kids' toys, first, foremost, and always.

BUILDER:	YONEZAWA
RELEASED:	CIRCA 1958
OPERATION:	WIND-UP
◆	
VALUES:	
GOOD	**$1200**
EXCELLENT	**$2100**
MINT WITH ORIGINAL BOX	**$4500**

JAMES D. JULIA AUCTIONS IMAGES

YONEZAWA
SPACE EXPLORER
JAPAN • CIRCA 1959

BUILDER:	YONEZAWA
RELEASED:	CIRCA 1959
OPERATION:	BATTERY
◆	
VALUES:	
GOOD	**$800**
EXCELLENT	**$1200**
MINT WITH ORIGINAL BOX	**$2200**

Back when television was young, manufacturers did what they could to camouflage the ungainly appliance. Most were designed to resemble living room furniture — some with pull-over screens to obscure the picture tube. So it's no surprise that when Yonezawa decided to combine the "TV spaceman" concept with that of "giant robot," they came up with Space Explorer, one of the first and greatest transformational toys. This circa-1959 battery-op begins its operational sequence as a small TV-like oblong cube, then telescopes outward, the camouflage screen lowering to reveal a menacing human within. The robot eccentric-wheel walks for a short distance, then telescopes inward again. *Incredible!* Not rare, but not common, Space Explorers are expensive repairs, making nonfunctionals dicey purchases. Three variations are known: gray, red, and a tooling-altered version with a secondary on-off switch. Incredibly, there are reports of Space Explorer having been cataloged as late as the mid-1960s, further underscoring the timeless design. Few toys can boast such a surprising "wow!" factor during operation, placing Yonezawa Space Explorer at the summit of toy design.

JAMES D. JULIA AUCTIONS IMAGE

YONEZAWA
SPACE EXPLORER
JAPAN • CIRCA 1959

As one of two major toys by the same manufacturer to sport identical names, and probably during the same year, Yonezawa's "other" Space Explorer doesn't seem to bear much kinship to its more famous cousin, the transfoming TV also called Space Explorer (1950s). In fact, this Space Explorer is essentially an electrical gauge that's been taken over by a teenage boy. Yonezawa's premise is plausible: the gauge "measures" the Astroteen's oxygen supply. Given the needle's tendency toward wild fluctuation, it's a miracle Astroteen can still smile, but smile he does — the art demonstrates classic Japanese "happy against all odds" imagery. Standing 9½ inches, Space Explorer is somewhat large for a wind-up toy, but the motor is strong and the toy lumbers along, swinging its arms during operation. Also included in the toy's feature set is sparkling. Perhaps due to its strangeness, Space Explorer brings good, but not monstrous, valuations in the contemporary collector environment. Yonezawa's Space Explorer is an impressive toy with positively industrial art direction.

BUILDER:	YONEZAWA
RELEASED:	CIRCA 1959
OPERATION:	WIND-UP
VALUES:	
GOOD	$600
EXCELLENT	$1200
MINT WITH ORIGINAL BOX	$2800

YONEZAWA
SPACE ROBOT CAR
JAPAN • CIRCA 1958

KALMBACH IMAGE

One of Yonezawa's most substantial space vehicles, Space Robot Car is more than nine inches of tin-lithographed space fun. Piloted by a dome-headed gold robot, the circa-1958 battery-op includes an impressive feature set: motion, spinning lights under its plastic dome, a robot whose head turns to "look" side to side, and rear-mounted guns. Interesting design elements include the large dome; the robot's overall lithographic design; and the fascinating use of litho artwork on the vehicle's "windshield," as if to infer reflection of a futuristic skyline surrounding the vehicle. Colorful artwork and lettering down each side of the vehicle complete the toy's visual presentation. Overall, Yonezawa's Space Robot Car is considered a very desirable example of vehicle-based space toy design.

BUILDER:	YONEZAWA
RELEASED:	CIRCA 1958
OPERATION:	BATTERY
VALUES:	
GOOD	$800
EXCELLENT	$1400
MINT WITH ORIGINAL BOX	$2500

YONEZAWA

YONEZAWA
SWINGING BABY ROBOT
JAPAN • CIRCA 1958

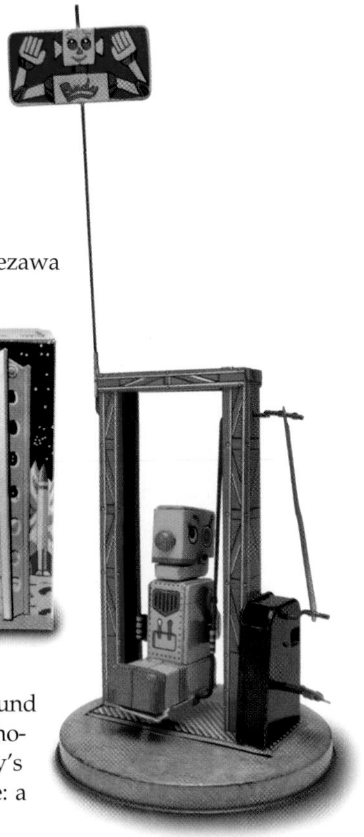

Who says robots and space toys have to be scary and full of foreboding? Not Yonezawa — their 1958-era Swinging Baby Robot is a classic study in simplicity and fun. A basic clockwork mechanism causes the block-headed baby robot to swing back and forth, much like a contemporary infant swing set. The colorful litho, "nah-nah" artwork on the swing's counterweight, and the happy look on the robot's face all suggest Yonezawa was trying to reach beyond their core boy market with this product. Based on relative scarcity, the "girl consumer" plan probably didn't work; plus, an alternative litho version suggests Y tinkered with the concept before abandoning it entirely. A wonderful toy, with terrific, life-like action, Swinging Baby Robot is often found without its counterweight (this example has a reproduction), and in two primary lithographic variations. Note Yonezawa's striking original packaging helps escalate the toy's value substantially. Swinging Baby Robot is an exception to a rarely challenged rule: a simple toy whose entertainment value exceeds its collectibility.

BUILDER:	YONEZAWA
RELEASED:	CIRCA 1958
OPERATION:	WIND-UP
VALUES:	
GOOD	$650
EXCELLENT	$1250
MINT WITH ORIGINAL BOX	$2100

PACKAGE IMAGE: ROBERT JOHNSON / COMET TOYS USA

YONEZAWA
X-27 EXPLORER
JAPAN • CIRCA 1958

One of the earliest members in Yonezawa's small astronaut/robot wind-up family is X-27 Explorer. This wind-up astronaut toy shares many components with its brethren, but is completely unique in overall impact. Much of this impression comes from four key components: the barrel chest; the bulging flexi-style arms; the mushroom-like head; and the bent TV-aerial antennae. The effect is alternately foreboding and goofy, probably just the impact Yonezawa designers sought. The toy shares its drive mechanism and legs with Robby Robot (1950s), as well as later products like Roby and Conehead Robots (1960s). A good performer, this toy elicits solid demand from collectors in any condition, with mint-original packaging examples having the greatest appeal. Worth owning just for the "Help! I'm trapped in a goofy space-suit!" expression on the astronaut's litho face, X-27 Explorer walks the line between hilarious and humbling. Just don't mention those antennae . . . .

BUILDER:	YONEZAWA
RELEASED:	CIRCA 1958
OPERATION:	WIND-UP
VALUES:	
GOOD	$1200
EXCELLENT	$2800
MINT WITH ORIGINAL BOX	$4500

JAMES D. JULIA AUCTIONS IMAGES

YONEZAWA

YOSHIYA
ACTION PLANET ROBOT
JAPAN • CIRCA 1958

Amid the rush to capitalize on the Robby the Robot craze inspired by MGM's 1956 classic, *Forbidden Planet*, came a flurry of Robby knockoffs from a wide variety of Japanese manufacturers. Though the best-known is Nomura's Mechanized Robot (1950s), others did a good job of replicating the seminal robot's design. Yoshiya's Action Planet Robot is one of the best to emerge from this gold rush, due largely to the toy's solid functionality and its approximate replication of Robby's good looks. Created from enameled tin, Action Planet Robot is an eight-inch wind-up, with forward walking motion and sparkling through both the chest and "mouth" area. Though smaller, and lacking the complex set of head-piston movements of the Nomura toy, Action Planet Robot does capture the form factor of the movie robot. An inexpensive toy in lesser grades, it's obvious Yoshiya marketed Planet Robot variants for a number of years, attesting to the large quantities available today, as well as production variations such as tin-claw hands (earlier) and molded-rubber ones (later). Note that a number of color variations are known across both the wind-up and battery-op versions, with black being the most common for wind-ups. For Robby enthusiasts, Action Planet Robot in any hue is a true must-have.

BUILDER:	YOSHIYA
RELEASED:	CIRCA 1958
OPERATION:	WIND-UP
VALUES:	
GOOD	$300
EXCELLENT	$600
MINT WITH ORIGINAL BOX	$1100

BOB BURNS COLLECTION

YOSHIYA
CHIEF ROBOTMAN
JAPAN • CIRCA 1959

It never ceases to amaze — the negative reaction that plastic can draw from select perspectives. And for what? It is simply because plastic had the misfortune to be the harbinger of dark days for the Japanese toymakers. Once they had "gone plastic," their toys — and their industry — were never the same. But rewind a handful of years, and there was a time when plastic was a medium of choice, particularly as an accent component on mostly-tin toys. Yoshiya's Chief Robotman is one such toy. Strategic use of plastics — particularly in the face and chest plate regions — adds what no lithography ever could. Of course, the toy's animation provides another reason for enduring popularity; mystery action is complemented by the robot's spinning antennae, swinging arms, flashing lights, and turning head. The largest of Yoshiya's skirted robots, the 11¾-inch automaton surfaced (often in modified form) as other toys: Cragstan Radical Robot, Mystery Moon Man, Chief Smoky, and Mighty Robot. Stylish design and relative scarcity make this an always-popular choice for seasoned and rookie collectors alike.

BUILDER:	YOSHIYA
RELEASED:	CIRCA 1959
OPERATION:	BATTERY
VALUES:	
GOOD	$800
EXCELLENT	$1200
MINT WITH ORIGINAL BOX	$2500

ROBERT JOHNSON / COMET TOYS USA IMAGE

YOSHIYA

YOSHIYA
CHIEF ROBOTMAN
JAPAN • CIRCA 1959

BUILDER:	YOSHIYA
RELEASED:	CIRCA 1959
OPERATION:	BATTERY
VALUES:	
GOOD	$800
EXCELLENT	$1200
MINT WITH ORIGINAL BOX	$2500

Yoshiya added to its overall product count in 1959 with multiple color variations on their 11¾-inch Chief Robotman product. This example boasts an interesting, vintage-at-birth cream face, with dark-gray metallic body. The effect is not only sharp on its own, but provides a terrific contrast to the appearance of the more standard white-faced, silver-bodied brother-in-tin. As to be expected, all actions remain the same: mystery action motion, swinging arms, illumination, twirling ear antennae, and turning head.

ROBERT JOHNSON / COMET TOYS USA IMAGE

YOSHIYA
MOON EXPLORER
JAPAN • CIRCA 1959

The post-Robby crush of robot-styled products influenced even humanoid toy design. Yoshiya's Moon Explorer is a good example; its sausage-link legs and splayed claw-hands and arm assemblies are directly borrowed from the industrial design of *Forbidden Planet*'s Robby the Robot. Though the 7½-inch toy purports to depict an astronaut, the only thing identifying a human presence is the small lithographed face behind the clear-plastic dome. Considered something of a rare toy, Moon Explorer features wind-up locomotion in the form of eccentric-wheel movement housed in the nonarticulated leg assembly. During operation, the toy rolls forward while the four-bladed head propeller spins. Both red and cobalt blue versions are known, as are a small number of packaging variants. Indeed, this one is considered most desirable because of the illustrations on all four lid sides. Note Yoshiya's depiction of the toy doing the R. Crumb "Keep on Truckin'" dance, despite the fixed-leg reality of the toy. A basic space toy with a strong scarcity factor, Yoshiya Moon Explorer is the Robby wannabe of astronaut wind-up toys.

BUILDER:	YOSHIYA
RELEASED:	CIRCA 1959
OPERATION:	WIND-UP
VALUES:	
GOOD	$800
EXCELLENT	$2000
MINT WITH ORIGINAL BOX	$3500

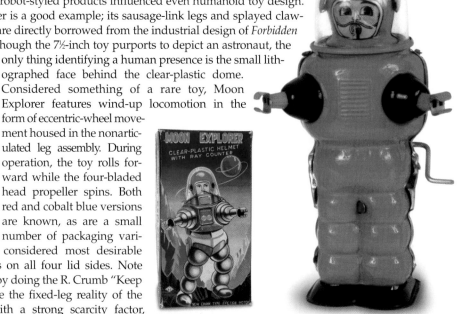

MOON EXPLORER
CLEAR-PLASTIC HELMET WITH RAY COUNTER

JAMES D. JULIA AUCTIONS IMAGES

YOSHIYA

YOSHIYA
MOON EXPLORER
JAPAN • CIRCA 1959

Yoshiya's Moon Explorer "cobalt blue" variation is something of an enigma. For starters, it's unclear as to whether this version was even marketed in the United States and Europe. The reasoning behind this lack of clarity: an incredibly short supply of the toys, compounded by the fact that the astronaut within reflects an Asian heritage, as opposed to the more doe-eyed universalist approach normally taken by Japanese toy designers. If only from an aesthetic perspective, this color variation is highly desirable; its richness and rarity make it a must-have for Yoshiya devotees, irrespective of its profound scarcity. Unlike the red version, which has contrast-color feet and arm projections simply to add to the look, the blue version is one solid color, except for the claw hand components. And its facial variation? Neither Yoshiya nor the astronaut in question was available for comment.

BUILDER:	YOSHIYA
RELEASED:	CIRCA 1959
OPERATION:	WIND-UP
VALUES:	
GOOD	$600
EXCELLENT	$1000
MINT WITH ORIGINAL BOX	$3000

ROBERT JOHNSON / COMET TOYS USA IMAGE

YOSHIYA
PLANET ROBOT
JAPAN • CIRCA 1958

As a battery-operated toy, Yoshiya's Planet Robot is far superior to its mechanical brother, Action Planet Robot (1950s). Not only is the action more fluid and entertaining, but the toy itself is more scarce than any of the mechanical variants known today. During operation, the eight-inch robot walks forward, its vertical head antenna turning, and interior illumination lighting both the "mouth" and chest red gels. In fact, a small diffuser inside the toy's head region actually moves, replicating the movie Robby's on-off "speaking" effect quite nicely. One-button control makes operating Planet Robot a snap. Though generally found in blue, other color variations are known, as well as running production changes such as metal vs. rubber claw hands. Still not as desirable as the more substantial and complex Mechanized Robot (1950s), Planet Robot remains a valuable vestige of the post-*Forbidden Planet* wave of knockoffs, particularly when found in mint-original package condition.

BUILDER:	YOSHIYA
RELEASED:	CIRCA 1958
OPERATION:	BATTERY
VALUES:	
GOOD	$600
EXCELLENT	$1100
MINT WITH ORIGINAL BOX	$1800

BOB BURNS COLLECTION

YOSHIYA

YOSHIYA

YOSHIYA
ROBBY

JAPAN • CIRCA 1958

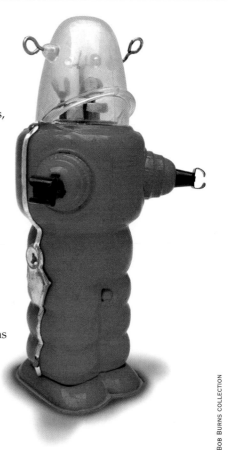

Around the time they were offering the Robby-inspired Planet Robot toys, Yoshiya also marketed this downmarket Robby variant for the even lower price-point consumers. Outfitted with a "wobble" drive mechanism, this humble seven-inch wind-up is clearly inspired by *Forbidden Planet*'s famous automaton, right down to the dome head, cylindrical torso, claw hands jutting outward at a 270-degree angle from one another, and bulbous, sausage-link legs. Because the toy uses an eccentric-wheel drive mechanism instead of functioning legs, it's likely Yoshiya positioned this toy as their most entry-level model. The toy also has rotating internal antennae within the clear-plastic dome. Note many examples have cracked or reproduction domes. A small number of color variants are also known.

BUILDER:	YOSHIYA
RELEASED:	CIRCA 1958
OPERATION:	WIND-UP

VALUES:

GOOD	$650
EXCELLENT	$900
MINT WITH ORIGINAL BOX	$1800

BOB BURNS COLLECTION

YOSHIYA
ROBOT DOG

JAPAN • CIRCA 1956

Even in the future, Man will need a sidekick. And what better pal to cavort around the cosmos with than Yoshiya's Robot Dog? Borrowing designs for robotic pets appearing in early issues of *Amazing Stories* and other sci-fi pulps, Yoshiya created a lasting icon for the fun side of space-toy collecting with the circa-1956 Robot Dog. A mechanical wind-up, the seven-inch Robot Dog ambles along, opening and closing his mouth, while his googly-eyes roll about. The spring-tail can be manually twitched, as can the dangling metal ears, to further enhance the robot's dog-like behavior. Yoshiya created a number of friction-powered Robot Dog variations, but made relatively lower numbers of wind-ups. In addition, the company marketed a battery-operated version, Magic Space Dog (known as "Girl Space Dog"). Note that Robot Dog is part of Yoshiya's "robot animal" series, which includes Space Elephant and Space Whale (1950s). Interestingly, Sears marketed a strikingly similar, eleven-inch toy called "Robot Dog" in their 1956 Wish Book. Close examination suggests *one* of these two companies knew of the other's product and knocked it off in short order. Who was first? Even in the future, it would seem, Man has to keep an eye out for his best friend.

BUILDER:	YOSHIYA
RELEASED:	CIRCA 1956
OPERATION:	WIND-UP

VALUES:

GOOD	$650
EXCELLENT	$1000
MINT WITH ORIGINAL BOX	$1800

YOSHIYA
SPACE TANK V-2
JAPAN • CIRCA 1958

Yoshiya was quite motivated during the 1958 timeframe — motivated, that is, to knock off *Forbidden Planet*'s Robby as many times as possible, in as many iterations as possible. This version, Space Tank V-2, demonstrates Yoshiya's uncanny ability to integrate the Robby archetype into just about any of their new or existing platforms. Though created from its own tooling, the robot is from Yoshiya's Planet Robot school of design, with black-gel chrome faceplate and simple claw hands. The tank tread and gearing mechanism is nicely replicated in lithography; the rear section of the tank features an illuminated "television screen" depicting outer space doings; and the front includes the World War II-evocative "V 2" designation, complemented by a partial atomic symbol. Mystery action carries this toy where it needs to go, with Robby facial illumination adding to the entertaining presentation. A desirable toy, Space Tank V-2 is Yoshiya's Robby knockoff program in full bloom.

KALMBACH IMAGE

BUILDER:	YOSHIYA
RELEASED:	CIRCA 1958
OPERATION:	BATTERY
VALUES:	
GOOD	$650
EXCELLENT	$1100
MINT WITH ORIGINAL BOX	$2400

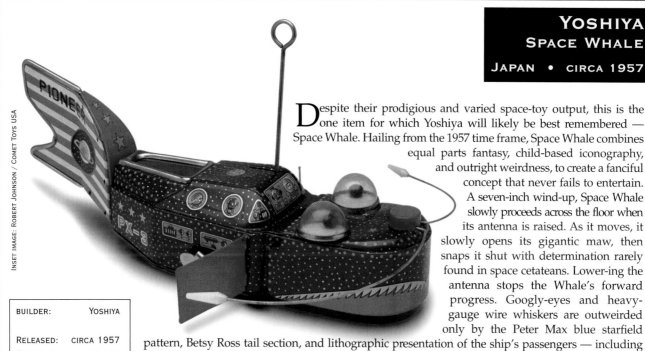

YOSHIYA
SPACE WHALE
JAPAN • CIRCA 1957

INSET IMAGE: ROBERT JOHNSON / COMET TOYS USA

Despite their prodigious and varied space-toy output, this is the one item for which Yoshiya will likely be best remembered — Space Whale. Hailing from the 1957 time frame, Space Whale combines equal parts fantasy, child-based iconography, and outright weirdness, to create a fanciful concept that never fails to entertain. A seven-inch wind-up, Space Whale slowly proceeds across the floor when its antenna is raised. As it moves, it slowly opens its gigantic maw, then snaps it shut with determination rarely found in space cetaceans. Lowering the antenna stops the Whale's forward progress. Googly-eyes and heavy-gauge wire whiskers are outweirded only by the Peter Max blue starfield pattern, Betsy Ross tail section, and lithographic presentation of the ship's passengers — including an odd blockheaded robot located in the copilot's seat. Not expensive, except when found in mint-original box condition, Space Whale is the leading member of Yoshiya's space animal product line, which also includes Space Elephant and the Robot Dog (1950s) variants. Strange, outlandish, and beautiful — Space Whale, by Yoshiya.

BUILDER:	YOSHIYA
RELEASED:	CIRCA 1957
OPERATION:	WIND-UP
VALUES:	
GOOD	$350
EXCELLENT	$600
MINT WITH ORIGINAL BOX	$1800

YOSHIYA

YOSHIYA

YOSHIYA
SPARKY ROBOT
JAPAN • CIRCA 1954

BUILDER:	YOSHIYA
RELEASED:	CIRCA 1954
OPERATION:	WIND-UP

VALUES:	
GOOD	$400
EXCELLENT	$800
MINT WITH ORIGINAL BOX	$1800

As one of Yoshiya's earliest space toys, wind-up Sparky Robot is essentially a knockoff of Nomura's Zoomer the Robot (1950s). The seven-inch wind-up sports a block head; round, hollow eyes, behind which sparkling occurs; expressionless mouth; square body with Zoomer-like tapering; and slow, deliberate forward-motion walking. Yoshiya's most original element is the automaton's round head antenna. Humble Sparky would lay the groundwork for later versions, some of which would attain great desirability within the space-toy collecting community, primarily for their packaging variations. Basic versions of Sparky make affordable additions to collections when found in good, loose condition, but values escalate predictably for mint-original box examples.

YOSHIYA
SPARKY ROBOT
JAPAN • CIRCA 1955

Sometimes you have to shrink to get noticed. That's just what Sparky Robot did in a successive production run — it dropped almost half an inch as it added prodigious amounts of color lithography. The result: a better toy that boasts better collectibility and perhaps even more respect. Often derided as a Zoomer (1950s) knockoff, Sparky Robot is just as its name implies — a wind-up that displays sparkling through its round, stamped-open eyes. The only original point of differentiation — the head antenna — doubles as an on-off switch for the toy. The boxy, tapered torso now includes Masudaya Non-Stop Robot-like (1950s) Cubist imagery that probably confused kids more than it sparked their imaginations. Nonetheless, the toy is valued surprisingly well today, with mint-original examples bringing meaningful values. Even with reduced stature, Yoshiya's Sparky Robot stands proud.

BUILDER:	YOSHIYA
RELEASED:	CIRCA 1955
OPERATION:	WIND-UP

VALUES:	
GOOD	$600
EXCELLENT	$1200
MINT WITH ORIGINAL BOX	$2400

YOSHIYA
SPARKY ROBOT
JAPAN • CIRCA 1959

As the Sparky Robot line matured, Yoshiya kept tinkering with the toy's formula to provide low-cost freshening. Apparently, it worked — revised, dramatic packaging and a more futuristic, plated-lithographic finish to the toy helped Yoshiya squeeze one more vital year out of this early platform. The toy is essentially identical to the previous year's model, except for its silver-plated look and revised lithography. Gone is the Cubist styling borrowed from Masudaya; in its place, more utilitarian drawings which don't threaten the viewer's sensibilities. The wind-up is still on-offed by the round head antenna, but the toy's legs and feet constitute new subassemblies — an odd tack for Yoshiya to take with this long-in-the-tooth toy (by circa 1959, anyway). Of greatest interest is the toy's package, which is often referred to as the "detective box," due to its inclusion of an armed *Perry Mason*-like figure who scopes out Sparky as the automaton wreaks havoc on its host city. Because of this fascinating — and highly desirable — package artwork, mint-boxed examples have exceedingly strong value for such a humble and technologically low-rent plaything.

BUILDER:	YOSHIYA
RELEASED:	CIRCA 1959
OPERATION:	WIND-UP

VALUES:

GOOD	**$800**
EXCELLENT	**$1400**
MINT WITH ORIGINAL BOX	**$3000**

JAMES D. JULIA AUCTIONS IMAGES

YOSHIYA

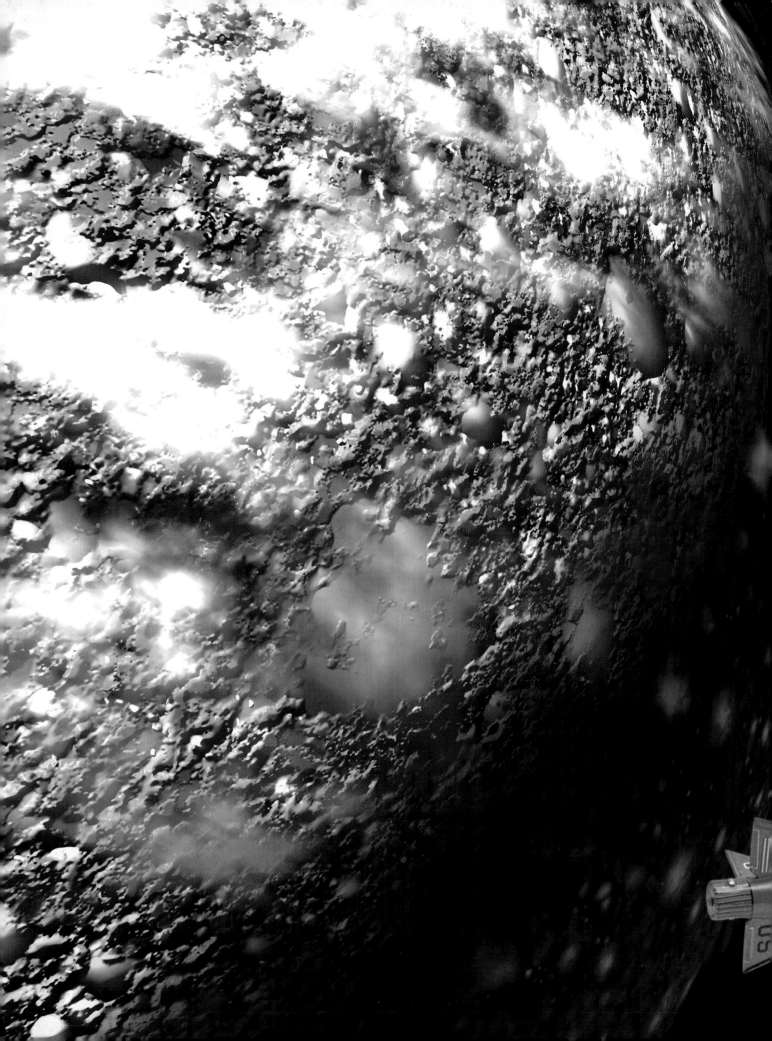

THE 1960s

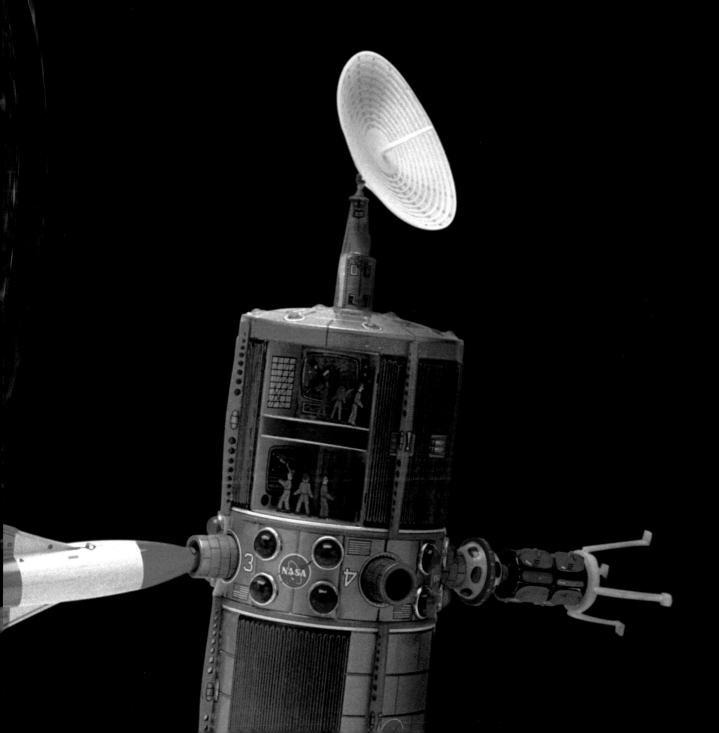

NEW SPACE REFUEL STATION

CIRCA 1961

BY WACO

JAPAN

THE 1960s

From a design point of view, the 1960s were a time when the fantasy of science fiction collided headlong with the reality of the American and Soviet space programs. No longer were spacecraft the exclusive design domain of creative thinkers at pulp magazines and toy companies. Suddenly, with the dawning of the Mercury space program, there were actual, true-to-life examples of space vehicles for children and toy designers to ponder.

This infusion of reality into space-toy design had profound impact on both child demand and the toys that emerged in response. Interest in fanciful designs waned; toys based on the Mercury, Gemini, and ultimately Apollo spacecraft supplanted whimsy with blueprinted reality. And all of this change took place amid the Tokyo toy industry's struggle with skyrocketing overhead costs.

Japan had dominated the 1950s robot and space toy category with innovation, creativity, and perhaps most important, low price points. Yet their success was also their undoing, because as the Japanese saw their standard of living grow, the costs associated with their successful industries also rose, reducing their marketplace competitiveness. In the end, it was a no-win situation: costs rose at a time when the export consumer was demanding more for less.

Most Japanese toymakers fought this losing battle well into the decade, but by the end of the 1960s, most had either vanished or constricted precipitiously. In fact, as the 1970s dawned, it was becoming difficult to find playthings on American toy shelves marked "Made in Japan."

The meteoric spectacle of success was almost over for Japan.
But not before a handful of stunning final efforts would emerge.

ALPS
FIREBIRD III

JAPAN • CIRCA 1962

BUILDER:	ALPS
RELEASED:	CIRCA 1962
OPERATION:	BATTERY
VALUES:	
GOOD	$550
EXCELLENT	$900
MINT WITH ORIGINAL BOX	$2100

The 1960s. It was the dawning of a new era, and the future seemed limitless. This unbounded optimism spilled into all facets of contemporary life, including toys. Using design concepts from world auto shows, Japanese toy manufacturers continued to hybridize their vehicle lines into space- and future-oriented products.

The results were mixed, just as the real-life concepts were, but the lasting impact remains. Alps' Firebird III is a perfect example of this: looking eerily reminiscent of late-1960s vehicles, this circa-1962 toy includes a long nose, hidden headlights, dual-cone cockpit, three dorsal fins, and a judiciously tapered rear clip. At the helm are two futuristic drivers. Mystery action directs the 13-inch battery-op; during operation, lights flash wildly as the car searches for an impedance from which to reverse. Original packaging for Firebird III is rarely seen, resulting in a doubling-plus for mint-boxed examples. From the perspective of today, Alps' Firebird III recalls yesterday while it suggests Tomorrow.

ALPS
MECHANICAL TELEVISION SPACEMAN

JAPAN • CIRCA 1965

BUILDER:	ALPS
RELEASED:	CIRCA 1965
OPERATION:	WIND-UP
VALUES:	
GOOD	$100
EXCELLENT	$200
MINT WITH ORIGINAL BOX	$350

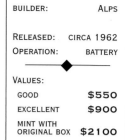

By the mid-1960s, the party was over for Japanese tin toy manufacturers. Rising wages and material costs were quickly making tin toys too expensive for their market position. Worse, lithographed tin was now viewed as passé, cheap, and even dangerous, from a product-safety standpoint. Many Toyko firms shifted to plastic toys or consumer electronics manufacture, or simply shut down. A few soldiered on, continuing to create tin-based playthings. One of these hardy firms was Alps, whose corporate history extended back to the early postwar period. Rather than switch, Alps narrowed its focus and in some ways enhanced the quality of its toys. Mechanical Television Spaceman is a good example: while functionally simple (a basic wind-up with eccentric-wheel walking motion), the toy boasts stunning lithography and the once-novel television animation feature. Though the toy does include plastic poseable arms and a plastic base, the look and feel of Mechanical Television Spaceman is from an earlier time, making it an affordable entry-level collectible today. Within a few years of this toy's release, however, Alps, too, would abandon toys for consumer and industrial electronics.

ALPS
SPACECRAFT "APOLLO"
JAPAN • CIRCA 1969

From our end-of-the-century perspective, it's difficult to recall the amazing engineering feats involved in the 1960s-era Apollo space program — but amazing they were. Surviving Japanese toymakers sought to shore up sagging demand by capitalizing on the American consumer's fascination with the space program and creating Apollo-themed toys, such as Spacecraft "Apollo," by Alps.

This battery-op mystery actions about the floor as both the nosecone and "motor" section illuminate, while the top-mounted lights revolve. A kind-of faithful rendition of the Command Module, Spacecraft "Apollo" has a reality-based artwork package typical for the period. The toy was reissued many times during the next handful of years; the version depicted here is the original 1969-era release.

BUILDER:	ALPS
RELEASED:	CIRCA 1969
OPERATION:	BATTERY
◆	
VALUES:	
GOOD	**$250**
EXCELLENT	**$350**
MINT WITH ORIGINAL BOX	**$550**

ALPS
SPACECRAFT RANGER
JAPAN • CIRCA 1969

So sad for Alps — no one told them that their hybrid product, Spacecraft Ranger, was doomed from the onset. Not only were fanciful space toys on the wane, but even realistic ones were looking long in the tooth after the July 1969 moon landing. Worse, Alps' toy isn't just a space toy — it's a hybrid that rides on a track, model railroad-style. And by 1969, toy trains were about as *dead* as dead can be.

Yet Alps plunged ahead, and as to be expected, the toy didn't survive marketplace pressures. Even so, Spacecraft Ranger is novel; Japanese toymakers had marketed miniature railroad toys for some time, but this was the first example of a hybrid train-flying saucer ever attempted. During operation, the saucer cruises around the integral track system, flashing its lights and making its space noise. Unlike model railroading, however, there weren't any water towers to visit, or stations for dropping off robot passengers, to enhance the play pattern. A short marketplace run didn't positively boost contemporary values; Spacecraft Rangers can be had for exceedingly affordable prices, and they make great holiday tree decorations, as well.

BUILDER:	ALPS
RELEASED:	CIRCA 1969
OPERATION:	BATTERY
◆	
VALUES:	
GOOD	**$200**
EXCELLENT	**$350**
MINT WITH ORIGINAL BOX	**$650**

ALPS

95

AMICO-MASUDAYA
SPACE SCOOTER
JAPAN • CIRCA 1964

Amico is a little-known importer whose products date mainly from the mid-1960s through the 1970s. Working with both major and minor Japanese (and later, Hong Kong) toymakers, Amico seemed to focus on the more goofy and child-like tin toys, as the hybrid-style Space Scooter (circa 1964) demonstrates. Built by Masudaya, the hybrid Space Scooter spans the space-toy and doll categories by using the child-astronaut and the Lambretta-like space scooter elements. Masudaya's child is of classic early-1960s Japanese character design: tin-litho body with some plastic componentry (in this case, the space helmet), capped off with a slightly oversized vinyl character head. The scooter's upper portion and main body design is litho tin, while the footboards, handle-bars, and wheels are plastic. During operation, the battery-op with "engine sound" scoots around, head- and taillights flashing, its direction dictated by mystery action. Masudaya likely marketed this toy on its own, as well; the head, in particular, seems like it was pulled straight from the parts bin. An inexpensive toy even in mint-original package condition, Space Scooter from Amico-Masudaya makes a fine addition to any late-period Japanese display.

MARKETER:	AMICO
BUILDER:	MASUDAYA
RELEASED:	CIRCA 1964
OPERATION:	BATTERY

◆

VALUES:	
GOOD	$200
EXCELLENT	$350
MINT WITH ORIGINAL BOX	$550

ANKER
CCCP SPACE VEHICLE
EAST GERMANY • CIRCA 1964

Once the pride of Communist East Germany, little is known today about Anker — apart from their fascinating array of toys. As one of the few toymakers left in East Germany after the postwar division, Anker had to uphold the Teutonic toymaking tradition under obviously strained conditions. Many of their toys were built for sale within the old Soviet bloc, such as this CCCP Space Vehicle from around 1964. Made primarily from tin, the eight-inch CCCP Space Vehicle features battery-powered operation and clearly odd styling. Perhaps Anker designers didn't have access to the same reference material as their Japanese and American counter-parts, for this "space vehicle" has all the verve of a streamlined Trabant. Given the smart design of Jupiter Space Rocket Launcher (1960s), could it be possible this lame design represented a subtle dig at their Soviet oppressors? No matter what, this is a scarce toy with lush package art, making it worthy of inclusion in any collection simply for conversational purposes alone. For collectors who prefer the truly *outré* — or the intentionally lame, as the preference may be — count on toys like Anker's CCCP Space Vehicle to fill the bill.

BUILDER:	ANKER
RELEASED:	CIRCA 1964
OPERATION:	BATTERY

◆

VALUES:	
GOOD	$600
EXCELLENT	$800
MINT WITH ORIGINAL BOX	$1400

ANKER
JUPITER SPACE ROCKET LAUNCHER
EAST GERMANY • CIRCA 1966

As an East German toymaker in the 1960s, Anker didn't have the same range of distribution and manufacturing options its Western counterparts enjoyed. Even so, the company managed a number of interesting space-themed toys, such as Jupiter Space Rocket Launcher from around 1966. The tank-based launcher appears ready for any environment, smartly styled to echo both Gerry Anderson (*Thunderbirds*) design as well as late-period Yonezawa and Nomura space tank-based vehicle toys. Mostly a plastic toy, Jupiter Space Rocket Launcher features a poseable rocket boom, a functional firing mechanism (watch those eyes!), plus battery-operated tread action. Scarce, yet inexpensive because of its late date of manufacture and its relatively unknown status, Jupiter Space Rocket Launcher is right at home next to many of its Japanese contemporaries.

BUILDER:	ANKER
RELEASED:	CIRCA 1966
OPERATION:	BATTERY
VALUES:	
GOOD	$200
EXCELLENT	$400
MINT WITH ORIGINAL BOX	$1200

ASAHI
PROP FLYING ROBOT CAR
JAPAN • CIRCA 1961

KALMBACH IMAGE

Around 1961, Asahi reissued its classic Space Patrol in a rear-mounted propeller package and called it Prop Flying Robot Car. The red tones add to the impact of Asahi's evocative Mercedes-Benz racer design. The propeller assembly itself is a curious thing, obviously grafted onto the original Benz slope-back, using parts likely borrowed from aircraft toys elsewhere in the Asahi line. During operation, the friction toy grumbles its way across the floor, while the propeller turns. Original packaging adds a nice boost to values, as the box depicts the car flying across a lunar landscape, set against a midnight-blue outer-space sky.

BUILDER:	ASAHI
RELEASED:	CIRCA 1961
OPERATION:	FRICTION
VALUES:	
GOOD	$800
EXCELLENT	$2000
MINT WITH ORIGINAL BOX	$3000

ANKER — ASAHI

ASAHI
SPACE CAPSULE CARROUSEL
JAPAN • CIRCA 1964

Toy carousels have been around since the late 1800s. Japanese toymakers joined the party in the 1950s, building a wide variety of carousels using tried-and-true themes. But Asahi (ATC) went *way* over the top with Space Capsule Carrousel. Asahi modified a standard carousel toy to include three miniature Gemini space capsules, each decorated with a name of a Gemini astronaut: John Glenn, Walter [Wally] Schirra, and Allen Shepherd. During operation, this fantastic piece of science whimsy revolves, causing each capsule's nose propeller to spin as the capsules themselves centrifugally fly outward. Asahi's package adds substantially to the toy's value. It depicts a lunar landscape dotted with carnival equipment, while a Gemini capsule streaks overhead. Truly weird and definitely wonderful, Asahi Space Capsule Carrousel shows just how far toy manufacturers will go to capitalize on a bankable current event.

BUILDER:	ASAHI
RELEASED:	CIRCA 1964
OPERATION:	WIND-UP

VALUES:

GOOD	**$1000**
EXCELLENT	**$1800**
MINT WITH ORIGINAL BOX	**$2800**

ASTRO MANUFACTURING CO.
SPINAROUND PLAN-IT COIN BANK
JAPAN • CIRCA 1962

Since the mid-nineteenth century debut of cast-iron mechanical banks, toy makers have used animation as a reward for child thrift. The dawning of the space age may have transformed kiddie bank design, but it still required animation to cajole nickels and dimes from kids' hands. Astro Manufacturing Co.'s Spinaround Plan-It coin bank (circa 1962) provides just the sort of novel animation to make savings fun. Drop a coin into the cast-metal 8½-inch bank, and it begins to spin. Once spinning ceases, kids can marvel at the solar-system relief map on the saucer section. Even the toy's name plays on its flying saucer design, while stressing frugality and fiscal preparedness. A fringe hybrid toy, Astro's Plan-It coin bank is an interesting icon from the dawning of the financial space age.

A MINIATURE SOLAR SYSTEM IN ACTION!

Spinaround **PLAN-IT** COIN BANK

BUILDER:	ASTRO MFG.
RELEASED:	CIRCA 1962
OPERATION:	WIND-UP

VALUES:

GOOD	**$200**
EXCELLENT	**$400**
MINT WITH ORIGINAL BOX	**$650**

BANDAI
SPACE PATROL CAR
JAPAN • CIRCA 1969

The merging of show cars with the U.S. space program is likely responsible for Bandai's Space Patrol Car of the 1969 time period. The stylized vehicle appears to be a thematic conglomeration of auto-show concepts, Mattel Hot Wheels, and to some extent, a prescient interpretation of 1970s-era Corvette design elements — in all, an interesting (if impractical) vehicle. But what's impractical on Earth is perfectly suited to outer space, so Bandai added two Apollo-style space-suited astronauts to pilot the vehicle. The result is a Bandaized version of what would ultimately become NASA's moon buggy. Is it a case of reality imitating toys, or merely happenstance? Space Patrol Car is a classic late-period battery-op,

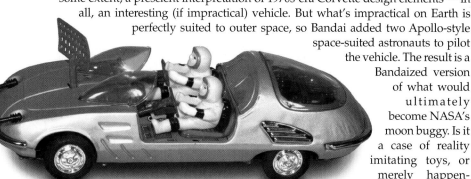

with mystery action, flashing lights, rotating hood-mounted antenna, nose cannon, and more. Packaging helps the value of this piece; its artwork reveals Bandai's late-1960s marketing strategy of using doe-eyed, *anime*-style children on side panels to attract young buyers perusing crowded toy-store shelves.

BUILDER:	BANDAI
RELEASED:	CIRCA 1969
OPERATION:	BATTERY
VALUES:	
GOOD	$400
EXCELLENT	$800
MINT WITH ORIGINAL BOX	$1800

BANDAI
TETSUJIN-26 SKY ROCKET
JAPAN • CIRCA 1966

From an American's perspective, it's difficult to grasp the impact the Tetsujin-26 character has made on the past 30 years of Japanese culture. As Gigantor here in the United States, Tetsujin-26 had a short first-run in syndicated animation, followed by a decade of reruns and the inevitable plunge into obscurity. In Japan, however, the character is still held in great regard, which explains even the most tenuous of toy licenses like Tetsujin-26 Sky Rocket, by Bandai. During the original animated program, Gigantor would often be depicted as flying alongside aircraft containing his child controller, Jimmy. And when injured or returning from battle, Tetsujin-26 could be seen holding onto aircraft, almost as if to infer robotic fatigue. Evidently this is what the Bandai toy is depicting when it includes a splayed view of Gigantor just aft of the cockpit. Bandai's packaging features a beautiful, near-realistic illustration of a pilot looking out toward the sky, up at . . . something. But what? Values are generally in the lower range, though original packaging adds handsomely to mint-loose values. For Tetsujin-26 fans, this toy is probably as close to the oddball Holy Grail as it comes.

BUILDER:	BANDAI
RELEASED:	CIRCA 1966
OPERATION:	FRICTION
VALUES:	
GOOD	$450
EXCELLENT	$900
MINT WITH ORIGINAL BOX	$1800

BANDAI

CENTURY 21 — CRAGSTAN-DAIYA

CENTURY 21 TOYS
PROJECT SWORD MOON RANGER

HONG KONG • 1967

A funny thing happened on the way to creating a line of toys for Gerry Anderson's British TV series, *Project Sword* — the show didn't get picked up. A Hong Kong-based company named Century 21 Toys — likely a spinoff of Anderson's own production company — nonetheless pressed ahead with the toys, marketing them for what appears to be two years, beginning in 1967, the intended debut season for the failed program.

The 8½-inch Moon Ranger was evidently to be one of the major vehicles in the program, as this is the most common toy from the range. A battery-op, it moves foward using its tank treads, lifting and lowering its bulldozer blade while its rear-mounted antenna rotates.

Almost entirely made of plastic, Moon Ranger comes in a nicely illustrated box that's both European and Oriental in its package design. Due to plastic construction and general obscurity, *Project Sword* Moon Ranger is a low-valued toy. For Gerry Anderson fans, it's a reminder of their creative genius' unfulfilled vision — but to everyone else, it's an interesting plastic space item.

BUILDER:	CENTURY 21
RELEASED:	1967
OPERATION:	BATTERY
VALUES:	
GOOD	$100
EXCELLENT	$200
MINT WITH ORIGINAL BOX	$450

CRAGSTAN-DAIYA
ASTRONAUT

JAPAN • CIRCA 1961

One of the more famous of all Cragstan-imported space-toy products is the Astronaut, by Daiya. This barrel-chested explorer features terrific action and exquisite lithography, and because it exists in fairly large numbers today, is both highly regarded and generally available to many collecting budgets.

During operation, the 11-inch battery-op walks forward with determined locomotion. At a certain point in the operational cycle, the figure stops, raises his jackhammer "gun", and begins a firing sequence, consisting of flashing gun lights and a loud *rat-tat-tat* from within the astronaut's chest cavity. Once complete, the Astronaut lowers the gun and again walks forward. Throughout the entire sequence, the head-mounted plated antenna dish spins. Cragstan-Daiya Astronaut is known in three versions: blue, green, and red, each with minor lithographic differences. (Green is considered the most rare.) Rosko sold the blue version as Space Conqueror (1960s). Sears sold the "X-70" shoulder-patch version in its 1961 Wish Book for the original retail price of $3.79. No matter which version or which package, the Daiya Astronaut is simply one of the best-action and nicest-lithography astronaut toys of any era.

MARKETER:	CRAGSTAN
BUILDER:	DAIYA
RELEASED:	CIRCA 1961
OPERATION:	BATTERY
VALUES:	
GOOD	$800
EXCELLENT	$1200
MINT WITH ORIGINAL BOX	$2500

DETAIL AND PACKAGE IMAGES: ROBERT JOHNSON / COMET TOYS USA

CRAGSTAN-DAIYA
ASTRONAUT
JAPAN • CIRCA 1962

Daiya's "other" astronaut is the round-chested Cragstan Astronaut, from the 1962 period. Roughly contemporaneous with the more famous and desirable of the Cragstan-Daiya Astronauts (1960s), this Astronaut boasts colorful lithography and good actions as well as an impressive 15-inch stature. Despite all this, the toy isn't accorded the same marketplace valuation of its battery-op brother. During operation, the Astronaut walks forward, then stops and raises its gun to fire, producing a *rat-tat-tat* sound with an illuminated gun barrel. A large *Cragstan Astronaut* logotype adorns the toy's waistline, while oxygen tanks on the figure's back conceal the toy's D cells. Color variations are known, as are two packaging variants. Sears carried the Astronaut in its 1962 Wish Book for the steep price of $5.95 — a warning sign of growing retail inflationary pressures on Japanese toys. For action, litho, and bigtime stature, nothing beats the Cragstan-Daiya Astronaut.

MARKETER:	CRAGSTAN
BUILDER:	DAIYA
RELEASED:	CIRCA 1962
OPERATION:	BATTERY

VALUES:	
GOOD	$600
EXCELLENT	$800
MINT WITH ORIGINAL BOX	$1500

CRAGSTAN-YONEZAWA
CRAGSTAN ROBOT
JAPAN • CIRCA 1962

Yonezawa's 12-inch Mr. Robot (1960s) platform, which debuted in approximately 1960 as the Cragstan-branded toy, lived a long and mechanically fruitful life as many different toys. This example, Cragstan Robot, is nearly identical to the original, but boasts altered decoration and packaging. Hailing from about 1962, this reissue has a metallic silver body, and retains Mr. Robot's comical bump-and-go mystery action, swinging arms, spring-loaded mechanical brain, and cranial illumination. Perhaps the best part of Cragstan Robot is the package, which depicts the toy through realistic art, set against a desolate lunar landscape with Saturn floating in the night sky. Yonezawa would build a number of other versions using the Mr. Robot tools, including Modern Robot, Talking Robot, and Directional Robot (all 1960s), before retiring the platform at mid-decade. For variation collectors, it's tough to beat the extended-family reunion presented by Yonezawa's Mr. Robot line.

MARKETER:	CRAGSTAN
BUILDER:	YONEZAWA
RELEASED:	CIRCA 1962
OPERATION:	BATTERY

VALUES:	
GOOD	$800
EXCELLENT	$1500
MINT WITH ORIGINAL BOX	$2600

ROBERT JOHNSON / COMET TOYS USA IMAGES

CRAGSTAN-YONEZAWA
M-27 MOON DETECTOR
JAPAN • CIRCA 1964

As a late toy, the Cragstan M-27 Moon Explorer (1960s) of 1963 represented a great, and perhaps final, space-vehicle leap for builder Yonezawa. The "walking" lunar vehicle boasted a number of actions and animations, making it popular and innovative enough to be included in the 1963 Sears Wish Book. Naturally, Yonezawa and American marketing partner Cragstan needed a follow-up for the next selling season, resulting in the M-27 Moon Detector. Though less sophisticated, the eight-inch toy still retains much of the original's innovative look and feel, and doubtless provided kid owners many hours of playtime fun. Primary changes include discarding the walking feature of the original, opting for a more dependable, cost-reduced tank-tread form of locomotion. Also new are the poseable, illuminated "detector" antennae projecting from the vehicle's forward section. Revised lithography in a dark-blue format adds to visual differentiation. Relatively common, this toy sold well during its run. Note that the somewhat lackluster packaging doesn't add appreciably to the value of an otherwise mint toy.

MARKETER:	CRAGSTAN
BUILDER:	YONEZAWA
RELEASED:	CIRCA 1964
OPERATION:	BATTERY

VALUES:	
GOOD	$500
EXCELLENT	$900
MINT WITH ORIGINAL BOX	$1600

KALMBACH IMAGE

CRAGSTAN-YONEZAWA
M-27 MOON EXPLORER
JAPAN • 1963

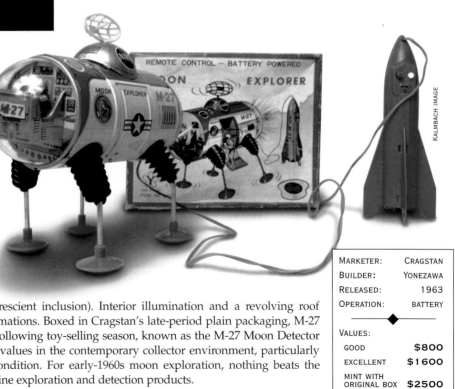

Cragstan-Yonezawa's M-27 Moon Explorer of 1963 is one of the great late-period playthings. Its innovative "walking" locomotion, combined with its additional array of entertaining actions, suggests a toy from an earlier time. And yet, here it is. A corded-remote battery-op, eight-inch M-27 employs an ingenious internal mechanism to create the look of elevated, all-terrain walking. Press another button, and the access door opens, revealing a "floating" astronaut who slowly glides out, shooting the lunar terrain with his handheld television camera (in itself, something of a prescient inclusion). Interior illumination and a revolving roof antenna provide the multimedia animations. Boxed in Cragstan's late-period plain packaging, M-27 spawned a cost-reduced cousin the following toy-selling season, known as the M-27 Moon Detector (1960s). Moon Explorer brings solid values in the contemporary collector environment, particularly when found in mint-original box condition. For early-1960s moon exploration, nothing beats the Cragstan-Yonezawa M-27 family of fine exploration and detection products.

KALMBACH IMAGE

MARKETER:	CRAGSTAN
BUILDER:	YONEZAWA
RELEASED:	1963
OPERATION:	BATTERY

VALUES:	
GOOD	$800
EXCELLENT	$1600
MINT WITH ORIGINAL BOX	$2500

JAMES D. JULIA AUCTIONS IMAGE

CRAGSTAN-YONEZAWA
MR. ATOMIC
JAPAN • 1962

Although undeniably unique, Mr. Atomic is one of those rare, ultra-high-end space toys to actually decline in value in recent years. The reasons: a quick run-up in value due to spectacular early-1990s auction results, and a Korean reproduction in 1994. Indeed, there was a time when people paid $30,000 for truly mint-boxed Mr. Atomics. Not today — values have settled in for the long haul, with the market having absorbed the repros. But back to the original: marketed by legendary New York distributor Cragstan, and built by Yonezawa, 9¼-inch Mr. Atomic mystery-actions his way around, tap-tapping his feet and swinging his claw-handed arms while his electronic brain (16 miniature lamps) flash in rhythmic fashion. Valued for scarcity and that bullet-shaped industrial design, Mr. Atomic is a rarity of robot design — no head, all torso. (Or is it *all head, no torso*?) Original packaging is very difficult to find, hence the premium. Two main variations are known; original silver and presumed-later metallic blue. Sears marketed Mr. Atomic in its 1962 Wish Book for $6.95. If ever a toy symbolized the "swords into plowshares" maxim — that is to say, bullets into computers — Mr. Atomic is it. Long may he compute, even if his value has diminished.

MARKETER:	CRAGSTAN
BUILDER:	YONEZAWA
RELEASED:	1962
OPERATION:	BATTERY

◆

VALUES:	
GOOD	$4500
EXCELLENT	$8000
MINT WITH ORIGINAL BOX	$20000

CRAGSTAN-YONEZAWA
MR. ROBOT
JAPAN • CIRCA 1960

Masudaya had the Gang of Five. Ideal had Robert Robot. Marx had Father and Son. And Cragstan had Yonezawa's Mr. Robot. The defining element between them? *Skirting*, that dive-to-the-ground design school of locomotion which allows toy manufacturers to create movement in a humanoid figure without having to articulate actual legs. And Mr. Robot lives up to the standards of his skirted brethren. He boasts a clean, enameled finish, stylish chestplate, dome head housing an obviously superior spring-loaded brain, and wrench-like hands. During operation, the 12-inch Mr. Robot mystery-actions about, swinging his arms while his eyes glow in eerie iridescence. Interestingly, Mr. Robots are often found with original packaging, so the mint-boxed premium isn't as profound. Mint values demand all cardboard inserts. Mr. Robot sired many offspring, including Modern Robot (1960s), Jupiter Robot, Directional Robot (1960s), and Talking Robot (1960s). View post-industrial design through the prism that is Mr. Robot by Yonezawa.

MARKETER:	CRAGSTAN
BUILDER:	YONEZAWA
RELEASED:	CIRCA 1960
OPERATION:	BATTERY

◆

VALUES:	
GOOD	$800
EXCELLENT	$1600
MINT WITH ORIGINAL BOX	$2300

CRAGSTAN-YONEZAWA

CRAGSTAN-YONEZAWA
MR. ROBOT
JAPAN • CIRCA 1961

Cragstan marketed this interesting color variation as an easy way of filling out its Mr. Robot line. The predominantly white toy has a clean-room feel, as though the automaton should be creating semiconductors instead

of using them in his spring-loaded cranial cavity. As to be expected, the white Mr. Robot variation is found in far less quantities today, resulting in higher valuation by the contemporary collecting environment. Note original packaging is identical between both the white and red versions, while the toy's

chestplates are unique to each iteration. After this small exercise in deco-variation marketing, Cragstan and Yonezawa would release a number of successive models based on this platform, including Jupiter Robot, Modern Robot (1960s), Cragstan Robot (1960s), Talking Robot (1960s), and Directional Robot (1960s) — each with its own compelling take on the successful skirted platform.

MARKETER:	CRAGSTAN
BUILDER:	YONEZAWA
RELEASED:	CIRCA 1961
OPERATION:	BATTERY

VALUES:
GOOD	$1500
EXCELLENT	$2800
MINT WITH ORIGINAL BOX	$4500

ROBERT JOHNSON / COMET TOYS USA IMAGES

CRAGSTAN-YONEZAWA
TALKING ROBOT
JAPAN • CIRCA 1963

One of the final toys to be built on the successful and long-lived 12-inch Mr. Robot platform is Talking Robot. Marketed by Cragstan and built by Tokyo toy powerhouse Yonezawa, Talking Robot is more than just an exercise in parts-bin diving; it's a unique toy that — in the parlance of today's business environment — leverages the key attributes of other successful platforms. An obfuscatory way of saying it's a hodge-podge of parts from

other toys, Talking Robot uses a revised Mr. Robot (1960s) body stamping, Mr. Mercury (1960s) head, and an off-the-shelf talker from the Yonezawa bin. As noted on the box, Talking Robot has a "battery powered voice" but is a "friction powered robot." Talking Robot uses only a single D cell to power its talking mechanism; this allows the toy to sit in place and chatter away. Talking Robot "broadcasts four different messages, loud and clear." A limited-release toy, Talking Robot isn't as common as others in his family. The package has striking depictions of the robot in a lunar waste-land. For fans of the Mr. Robot family of product, examples like Talking Robot are true must-haves.

MARKETER:	CRAGSTAN
BUILDER:	YONEZAWA
RELEASED:	CIRCA 1963
OPERATION:	BATTERY

VALUES:
GOOD	$700
EXCELLENT	$1200
MINT WITH ORIGINAL BOX	$2000

ROBERT JOHNSON / COMET TOYS USA IMAGE

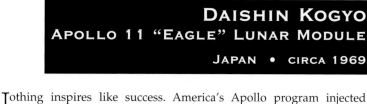

DAISHIN KOGYO
APOLLO 11 "EAGLE" LUNAR MODULE
JAPAN • CIRCA 1969

Nothing inspires like success. America's Apollo program injected thematic life and direction into the moribund Japanese tin-toy manufacturing sector. On the decline for a handful of years, the industry's survivors immediately set about re-creating authentic renditions of Apollo spacecraft. While Apollo was no magic bullet for reversing their decline — as exporters to the American market, Japanese toymakers would essentially vanish in a few short years — builders like Daishin Kogyo (DSK) did manage to capitalize one final time before the end. DSK's Apollo 11 "Eagle" Lunar Module is a faithful re-creation of the American craft, with interesting battery-operated animations like mystery action, lights, twirling antennae, and emerging astronauts ready to take one giant leap for Mankind. Extensive use of plastic components — typical for late-period Japanese space toys — keeps this product from attaining higher value, making it a good candidate for new or growing collections. Though little is known about Daishin Kogyo, their legacy lives on through their Apollo-era toys.

BUILDER:	DAISHIN KOGYO
RELEASED:	CIRCA 1969
OPERATION:	BATTERY
VALUES:	
GOOD	$300
EXCELLENT	$500
MINT WITH ORIGINAL BOX	$750

DAISHIN KOGYO
STRANGE EXPLORER
JAPAN • CIRCA 1962

What's old is often new again — if one waits long enough. Nearly 25 years had intervened between the debut of the Marx Superman Turnover Tank in 1940 and Daishin Kogyo's Strange Explorer, but the concept is identical. During operation, both toys proceed forward, then appear to be "lifted" up and turned over by powerful beings which emerge from beneath the tank. In DSK's case, that "powerful being" is a giant space gorilla, menacing enough to cause any space tank to turn up and over in fear. At eight inches in length, Strange Explorer isn't a small toy, but given its lackluster lithography and one-note play pattern, it's unlikely this toy became many kids' favorite. Collectors agree; despite a somewhat difficult nature to locate, Strange Explorer has relatively low value today. Still, as a visual juxtaposition to the Marx Superman Turnover Tank, it's just the thing.

BUILDER:	DAISHIN KOGYO
RELEASED:	CIRCA 1962
OPERATION:	BATTERY
VALUES:	
GOOD	$350
EXCELLENT	$600
MINT WITH ORIGINAL BOX	$1200

DAISHIN KOGYO

ROBERT JOHNSON / COMET TOYS USA IMAGE

DAIYA
ASTRONAUT
JAPAN • CIRCA 1963

Like most builders for Cragstan, Daiya didn't wait around for reorders from its import-distribution partner — they marketed nearly identical versions of Cragstan-branded toys under their own name. Astronaut is a classic example. This revised-litho version of 15-inch Cragstan Astronaut (1960s) is the same barrel-chested explorer, right down to the Asian visage hidden behind a ventilation face-mask. Actions are identical to its Cragstan brother: "walks — stops — raises gun — fires with flashing lights rata-tat sound." The major change: the toy's basic lithographic design. Interestingly, the toy's package is nearly identical as well, speaking both to the manufacturer's emphasis on cost savings, as well as the interchangeable nature of toys and branding during this period. Indeed, Cragstan's version of the toy was on sale only a year earlier, in Sears' 1962 Wish Book, for the not-inconsequential sum of $5.95. As the price suggests, retail pressures were already beginning to mount for Japanese toymakers by 1963. Desirable, yet not uncommon, Daiya Astronaut makes a fine complement to its Cragstan stablemate in any collection of variations.

BUILDER:	DAIYA
RELEASED:	CIRCA 1963
OPERATION:	BATTERY
VALUES:	
GOOD	$1000
EXCELLENT	$2000
MINT WITH ORIGINAL BOX	$4500

DAIYA
DOCKING ROCKET
JAPAN • CIRCA 1969

BUILDER:	DAIYA
RELEASED:	CIRCA 1969
OPERATION:	BATTERY
VALUES:	
GOOD	$250
EXCELLENT	$350
MINT WITH ORIGINAL BOX	$550

The Apollo craze of the late 1960s was good for all surviving Japanese toymakers, including Daiya. This toy, Docking Rocket from around 1969, shows how even late-period toys can still be somewhat innovative when saddled with an undue amount of cheesy plastic componentry. During operation, the 16-inch representation of the Command and Lunar Modules separate, then "redock" using a clutch-equipped winch inside the larger unit. The toy also features blinking lights, a revolving antenna, and forward motion. Most notable is the lavishly illustrated package, which depicts "the toy" (sort of) in space, orbiting the moon. Because of its late dating and heavy use of plastic, Daiya's Docking Rocket is an extremely affordable battery-op, perfect for adding to Apollo-era representations of Japanese toymaking.

DAIYA

DAIYA
LOOPING SPACE TANK
JAPAN • CIRCA 1962

Based on a standard military-tank toy, Looping Space Tank by Daiya does just that — it turns over during operation thanks to a hidden "up and over" arm located on the toy's chassis. When operating in right-side-up orientation, the 8¾-inch Looping Space Tank also includes a kaleidoscope color display under the plastic dome, as well as *rat-tat-tat* sound from the forward-facing cannon. Close comparison of the domes on this toy and Yonezawa's Space Robot Car (1960s) suggest a common parts supplier — or Daiya's involvement in the earlier Yonezawa space vehicle's production. Either way, it's this kind of shared componentry that helps establish both provenance and timeline with many little-known toys. The package includes a great scene of a space gorilla threatening the vehicle as it patrols a lunar surface. A similiar theme is found on Daishin Kogyo's Strange Explorer (1960s), though unlike that toy, no examples of space-gorilla lift mechanisms have been reported on Looping Space Tank. Generally inexpensive, Looping Space Tank is a basic battery-op that provides good entertainment at reasonable values.

BUILDER:	DAIYA
RELEASED:	CIRCA 1962
OPERATION:	BATTERY
VALUES:	
GOOD	**$400**
EXCELLENT	**$800**
MINT WITH ORIGINAL BOX	**$1450**

DUX
ASTROMAN
WEST GERMANY • CIRCA 1962

It's interesting that Germany, home of Bauhaus design, didn't produce more space toys and robots. After all, this school literally provided the foundation for much of the look used by Japanese and American space-toy makers. But one German toymaker did bring the clean simplicity and functionality of Bauhaus design to robots: Astroman, by Dux. Known for construction sets, Dux veered *way* off course with the circa-1962 Astroman. For starters, the 12-inch toy is sheathed in translucent green styrene, allowing the child to peer inside and view the toy's complex inner workings., much like an Apple iMac is today. (Coincidence?) As a competitor to Yonezawa's Mr. Mercury (1960s), the toy boasts an intricate set of operations. Using a corded remote control, a child can make Astroman walk forward or reverse, bend over, grasp or release objects, and raise or lower objects held between its foam-padded hands. A valuable toy, Dux Astroman is a complex plaything; avoid nonoperables. Repro antennae exist. See-through ingenuity — Dux Astroman.

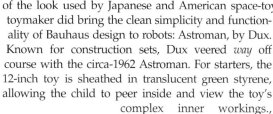

BUILDER:	DUX
RELEASED:	CIRCA 1962
OPERATION:	BATTERY
VALUES:	
GOOD	**$1000**
EXCELLENT	**$1800**
MINT WITH ORIGINAL BOX	**$2600**

DAIYA — DUX

HAJI
FLYING SAUCER 8
JAPAN • CIRCA 1962

Small-time manufacturer Haji is best known for its vehicle toys — in particular, its emphasis on cars pulling travel trailers. Their Space Trooper (1950s) was an initial and stunning entry into the category, but most Haji space-toy output would wait until the 1960s, with toys like Flying Saucer 8. Commanded by two tin-litho astronauts, Flying Saucer 8 is friction powered, like most Haji vehicle toys. Push it along the floor and its internal flint mechanism produces sparking from the rear. Bold lithography, using declarative primary colors (typical for the early 1960s period), helps distinguish the toy from the hordes of tin-litho competitors. The package art is stylized and evocative, adding a sense of action and speed to what is otherwise a push-it-around floor toy. Affordable and generally available on the open market, Haji's Flying Saucer 8 is a good acquisition for the entry-level collector.

BUILDER:	HAJI
RELEASED:	CIRCA 1962
OPERATION:	FRICTION
VALUES:	
GOOD	$150
EXCELLENT	$225
MINT WITH ORIGINAL BOX	$350

HORIKAWA
ASTRONAUT
JAPAN • CIRCA 1962

The Horikawa family of battery-operated astronauts and robots/Martians began around 1958 (Robot, 1950s), but grew explosively during the 1960s. Beyond the sheer play-value of the toys, it's difficult to pinpoint exactly why Horikawa continued to thrive while others withered. What is known is that Horikawa marketed a huge array of toys built around this basic platform, and continued to do so well into the 1980s. This example, an Astronaut from about 1962, sports most of the early-generation Horikawa features: metal components throughout, as well as the human face peering through the blocky "space helmet" head. During operation, the 11-inch toy walks forward, then stops and fires guns hidden behind the face-design double torso doors. (Horikawa fitted many differing door designs, from model to model, throughout the years.) Huge marketplace success means Horikawa robots are generally very affordable, making variation collecting both practical and entertaining.

BUILDER:	HORIKAWA
RELEASED:	CIRCA 1962
OPERATION:	BATTERY
VALUES:	
GOOD	$200
EXCELLENT	$400
MINT WITH ORIGINAL BOX	$650

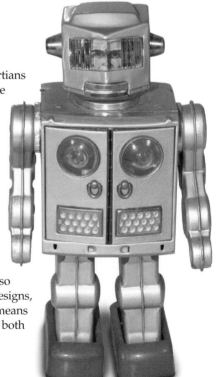

HORIKAWA
ASTRONAUT
JAPAN • CIRCA 1963

This version of Horikawa's 11-inch journeyman Astronaut battery-op hails from around 1963, and sports a new door covering theme: high technology. This particular combination — high-tech doors, gray finish, and human face behind the plastic shield — would reoccur under similar branding throughout the 1960s. Of course, later runs suffer from cost reduction, affecting both the perceived and actual quality of the later pieces. First-generation Astronauts (this toy represents the last of the group) are very nearly all tin; the second versions use plastic feet; Version Three has plastic feet and arms; and the final versions have plastic feet, arms, and legs. Like virtually all Horikawa Astronauts, this one has the Big Surprise: cannon hidden within the chest which burst forth when the toy's chest doors swing open, firing mercilessly at unsuspecting enemies. A good value with a great play pattern, Horikawa Astronaut makes a smart first purchase.

BUILDER:	HORIKAWA
RELEASED:	CIRCA 1963
OPERATION:	BATTERY
VALUES:	
GOOD	$200
EXCELLENT	$350
MINT WITH ORIGINAL BOX	$550

HORIKAWA
ATTACK ROBOT
JAPAN • CIRCA 1962

Horikawa rolled out a variation on their 11-inch Robot around 1962 with the aggressively named Attack Robot. Essentially the same toy with modified branding and packaging, Attack Robot walks, stops, and fires its camouflaged chest cannon like all its product family members. What's different is found in aesthetics: new high-tech litho designs on the chest-fire doors suggest a combination of mechanized dread and technology, while the two-tone metallic-flake paint scheme adds to the visual oomph of the toy. Note the main visual difference between Horikawa Astronauts and Robots is the head; Robots have the "fly eye" perforated-tin salt shaker effect, while Astronauts are human faces peering through plastic faceshields. Early two-tone Attack Robots bring a slight premium, and look menacingly terrific when presented against a unicolor panoramic assembly of Robots and Astronauts.

BUILDER:	HORIKAWA
RELEASED:	CIRCA 1962
OPERATION:	BATTERY
VALUES:	
GOOD	$350
EXCELLENT	$450
MINT WITH ORIGINAL BOX	$750

HORIKAWA
ATTACK ROBOT
JAPAN • CIRCA 1964

Though the two-toned Attack Robots are more popular with collectors and eyeballs alike, it's the single-colored variants which comprise the infantry of this battle-hardened lot. Indeed, this example from around 1964 is typical of Horikawa's approach: mostly metal, solid performance, and fun features like their trademark camouflaged chest-firing guns. A quick shorthand for Horikawa robots involves looking at the toy's head and face. If there's a human peering from behind a plastic panel, it's an Astronaut. If one is confronted by a fly-like visage sporting two decidedly salt-shakery eyes, it's a Robot of some Attack variation or another. Affordable and fun for variation hunting, Horikawa's Attack Robots are interesting takes on their standard line of 11-inch automata.

BUILDER:	HORIKAWA
RELEASED:	CIRCA 1964
OPERATION:	BATTERY
VALUES:	
GOOD	**$200**
EXCELLENT	**$400**
MINT WITH ORIGINAL BOX	**$650**

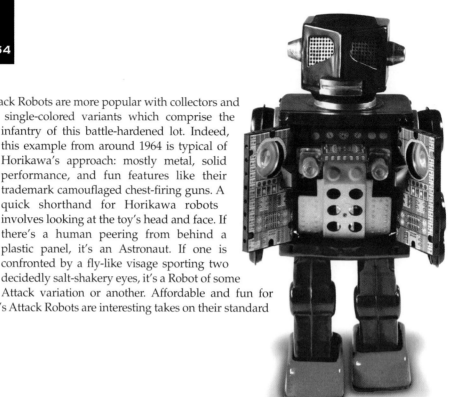

HORIKAWA
ATTACKING MARTIAN
JAPAN • CIRCA 1964

Around 1964, as the life began to ebb from their Attack Robot line, Horikawa put a spin on the theme with the Attacking Martian family of 11-inch product. Fundamentally identical to its Robot forebears, Attacking Martian boasts revised chest-panel artwork as well as updated chest-firing innards. In addition, designers changed small elements like the ears (formerly conical, now cylindrical) and revised the toy's legs, eliminating the knock-knees in favor of a more straight-legged approach. Packaging is always middle-classed with Horikawa — while not pedestrian, the art and typography aren't exactly over the top, either. This version features the low/wide angle perspective which would dominate the depiction of Horikawa automata in later years.

BUILDER:	HORIKAWA
RELEASED:	CIRCA 1964
OPERATION:	BATTERY
VALUES:	
GOOD	**$250**
EXCELLENT	**$450**
MINT WITH ORIGINAL BOX	**$650**

HORIKAWA
BATTLE ROBOT
JAPAN • CIRCA 1962

ost Horikawa 11-inch automata come in two basic varieties: Astronauts and Robot/Martians. But there is a third family member that, like Shemp of The Three Stooges, demands attention and respect. This could only mean Battle Robot, the blockheaded sibling whose saucer eyes and expressionless mouth make it seem like Zoomer's (1950s) psychotic, glue-sniffing older brother. Ironically, Battle Robot is also the toy that most Americans recognize, thanks to its recent reproduction and inclusion in Duracell battery commercials. Battle Robot dates to 1962, when it boasted nearly all-metal construction, gauge-and-dial lithography on the chest doors, and that patented Horikawa camouflaged chest-fire gunnery. The main point of differentiation, of course, is the head: round-eyed, blockheaded, and domed-and-antennaed ears. As with all Horikawa toys, cost reduction would influence successive issues of Battle Robots; feet, arms, and ultimately legs and heads would be converted to plastic. In general, they're slightly more desirable than the average Astronaut or Robot/Martian due to less availability. Duracell commercial fame aside, Battle Robots truly are the forgotten Shemps of Automata.

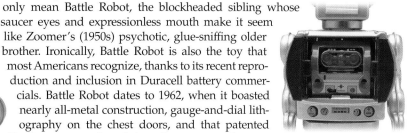

BUILDER:	HORIKAWA
RELEASED:	CIRCA 1962
OPERATION:	BATTERY

VALUES:	
GOOD	$300
EXCELLENT	$450
MINT WITH ORIGINAL BOX	$800

HORIKAWA
CAPSULE MERCURY
JAPAN • 1962

True-to-life manned space flight in the early 1960s helped create an entirely new category of space-themed playthings: reality-based toys. An early example of this is Horikawa's Capsule Mercury, an interesting evocation of the orbiter/reentry vehicle piloted by Mercury astronauts like John Glenn. As a 10-inch friction toy, it was loaded with features. Just listen to Sears' 1962 Wish Book description (original retail: $1.95): "Push capsule to start it rolling; everything's A-OK when siren screams . . . sparks fly from exhaust . . . friction motor 'roars.' Astronaut

BUILDER:	HORIKAWA
RELEASED:	1962
OPERATION:	FRICTION

VALUES:	
GOOD	$200
EXCELLENT	$350
MINT WITH ORIGINAL BOX	$550

inside 'floats in space.'" Horikawa marketed a John Glenn-based variation of Capsule Mercury, likely within six to eight months of the first toy's release, called Friendship 7. The key difference between the two is the actual Friendship 7 logotype in place of the lower "jagged" window. Amazingly, this toy and the Friendship 7 variant are both reasonably priced collectibles. That's okay — low values represent opportunity for enlarging reality-based toy assemblies at affordable values.

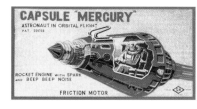

CAPSULE "MERCURY"
ASTRONAUT IN ORBITAL FLIGHT
PAT. 209733
ROCKET ENGINE WITH SPARK AND BEEP BEEP NOISE
FRICTION MOTOR

HORIKAWA

HORIKAWA ENGINE ROBOT

JAPAN • CIRCA 1968

An interesting variation, based on components from the Horikawa Astronaut and Robot families of product, is the battery-operated Engine Robot. Slightly smaller, at nine inches, and hailing from around 1968, Engine Robot uses the fly-eyed robot head from the 11-inch toy, as well as similar legs and feet assemblies (on this model, feet, arms, and gears are all plastic). Where it diverges, of course, is in the torso, in which Horikawa has integrated a fun and fascinating presentation of the Industrial Age in action. Four variously sized gears rotate during operation as lights blink inside. Engine Robot is a smaller-format version of larger High-Wheel Robots; both products feature see-through "electronic rooms" (as the packaging calls it) with spinning gears. Great as a complement or contrast to standard Horikawa Robots, Astronauts, and Martians, Engine Robot has its own legion of gear-meshing fans, in spite of (or perhaps due to) the low values this family of product manages to attract in the contemporary collecting environment.

BUILDER:	HORIKAWA
RELEASED:	CIRCA 1968
OPERATION:	BATTERY
VALUES:	
GOOD	$300
EXCELLENT	$450
MINT WITH ORIGINAL BOX	$550

HORIKAWA FIGHTING ROBOT

JAPAN • CIRCA 1962

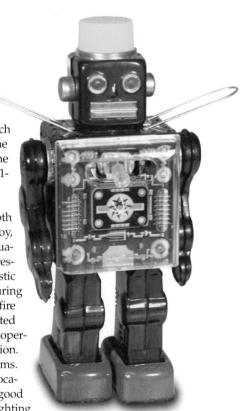

Even as masters of repackaging, Horikawa knew that it couldn't continually reissue its Astronaut/Robot platform and still enjoy solid sales. Thus, in the early 1962 period, Horikawa began marketing an 11½-inch variation which combines the best elements from multiple platforms: the clear-plastic torso of the High Wheel and Engine Robots (1960s), and the chest-firing action of 11-inch Astronaut/Robots. And because this is Horikawa, there are not one, but two, versions available (Robot and Space Man), giving kids both a hero and an adversary during playtime. This toy, Fighting Robot, is the automaton side of the equation: its blockheaded format features an expressionless face along with a large, translucent plastic dome, under which illumination projects during operation. Building on their successful chest-fire feature, Fighting Robot boasts a chest-mounted cannon which blasts at regular intervals during operation, panning the gun from side to side in classic pull-and-spray fashion. Throughout the sequence, the robot walks forward and swings its arms. Inexplicable (yet poseable) hoop-wireforms project from the robot's neck location. A fun toy with terrific action, Fighting Robot is generally available in good condition for terrific values — and makes a great complement to any Fighting Space Man, by design.

BUILDER:	HORIKAWA
RELEASED:	CIRCA 1962
OPERATION:	BATTERY
VALUES:	
GOOD	$400
EXCELLENT	$550
MINT WITH ORIGINAL BOX	$800

HORIKAWA
FIGHTING SPACE MAN
JAPAN • CIRCA 1962

To battle the evil Fighting Robots (1960s) of the world, Horikawa also marketed a human-face version of the toy, branding it Fighting Space Man. Outfitted with identical actions — forward walking, illuminated head dome, cyclical chest firing from the sweeping cannon — Fighting Space Man allowed Horikawa to economize during production by building two toys instead of one. As this toy debuted still relatively early in the Horikawa pantheon, it boasts loads of metal componentry, some of which would later be migrated to plastic in an on-going Horikawa effort to reduce cost and enhance per-unit margin. The clear-plastic torso covering also suggests a familial relation to the High Wheel and Engine Robots (1960s). Generally inexpensive, Fighting Space Men found mint in original packaging escalate, but are still relatively affordable.

BUILDER:	HORIKAWA
RELEASED:	CIRCA 1962
OPERATION:	BATTERY
VALUES:	
GOOD	$450
EXCELLENT	$600
MINT WITH ORIGINAL BOX	$900

HORIKAWA
MR. ZEROX
JAPAN • CIRCA 1968

As a sub-brand toy in the huge Horikawa family, one might think the 9½-inch Mr. Zerox has little in common with its better-known peers. To some extent, that's true, but there's also a lot the reprographically named Mr. Zerox shares with its Horikawa brethren. For example, there's the fly-eyed Robot (1960s) head, and the ubiquitous chest-fire mechanism — although on this toy, there's no need for camouflage. (Mr. Zerox, it would seem, is from the attack-first school of robot diplomacy.) In creating Mr. Zerox's torso, it appears Horikawa went rifling through the parts bin, using an existing chest-fire assembly and a Video Robot (1960s) torso stamping. Incidentally, though Xerox, the reprographic manu-facturer, adopted its name in the mid-1960s, the circa-1968 Mr. Zerox seems unimpressed by its corporately famous homonymic cousin — right down to the misplaced comma following the "Mister" contraction. Inexpensive and generally available, Mr. Zerox provides yet more symbolism to the massive production output of the brand called SH — Japan's Horikawa.

BUILDER:	HORIKAWA
RELEASED:	CIRCA 1968
OPERATION:	BATTERY
VALUES:	
GOOD	$250
EXCELLENT	$325
MINT WITH ORIGINAL BOX	$450

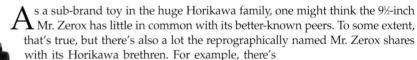

HORIKAWA
NEW SPACE CAPSULE
JAPAN • CIRCA 1964

Horikawa was one of the first Japanese manufacturers to plunge headlong into the segment of reality-based space toys with their Capsule Mercury in 1962. By 1964, with the American space program heating up and manifesting all sorts of new industrial designs, Horikawa was ready with its third Gemini design — the appropriately named New Space Capsule. A good evocation of the Gemini capsules being used by NASA at the time, New Space Capsule boasts an interesting set of battery-operated actions. As with most battery toys, it has its own means of propulsion (mystery action), complemented by an interesting reveal sequence: at a certain point in the performance, the toy stops and peels open its "access panels" to reveal the inside of the cockpit, astronaut included. Throughout, lights flash and a clicking noise ("space noise") ensues. Horikawa would go on to refine this formula in successive product releases throughout the 1960s.

BUILDER:	HORIKAWA
RELEASED:	CIRCA 1964
OPERATION:	BATTERY
VALUES:	
GOOD	$300
EXCELLENT	$400
MINT WITH ORIGINAL BOX	$650

HORIKAWA
NEW SPACE STATION
JAPAN • CIRCA 1964

As luck would have it, Horikawa's revision of the landmark toy Space Station (1950s) wasn't really a revision at all, but rather a mild cost reduction effort. Horikawa's Willy Ley design was still as fresh as it had been upon its release in 1958, but marketplace pressures were affecting companies like Horikawa (SH). Among the changes: the five-window format is reduced to four; its tin-litho base component is now plastic; and its central dish antenna updated into a panel array. Yet the magic remains: little figures vibrate inside the bays; lights blink, and the toy clicks like Sputnik; it mystery actions about the floor; and more. Viewed alongside its original incarnation, the message is clear: the end of quality Japanese tin-toy manufacture had arrived. Still considered highly valuable, this toy commands attention from every level of collector — a testament to its enduringly prescient design and sheer creative impact on period toymaking.

BUILDER:	HORIKAWA
RELEASED:	CIRCA 1964
OPERATION:	BATTERY
VALUES:	
GOOD	$1000
EXCELLENT	$1600
MINT WITH ORIGINAL BOX	$2800

HORIKAWA
RADAR-SCOPE SPACE SCOUT
JAPAN • CIRCA 1964

Compared to most of Horikawa's automata, Radar-Scope Space Scout is practically a dove-coddling pacifist. Lacking the chest-fire weaponry found on virtually all of its Astronaut and Robot/Martian brethren, the circa-1964 battery-op instead features a small, Alps-like television screen, through which a backlit series of soothing space-themed images projects during operation. The 9½-inch toy sports a Robot (1950s, 1960s) head, mostly metallic content, and the traditional space-travel program backlit-illuminated on the robot's torso TV screen. Though not an expensive toy in today's collecting environment, Horikawa's Radar-Scope Space Scout is a marginally uncommon variation on a well-established theme.

BUILDER:	HORIKAWA
RELEASED:	CIRCA 1964
OPERATION:	BATTERY
VALUES:	
GOOD	**$250**
EXCELLENT	**$400**
MINT WITH ORIGINAL BOX	**$650**

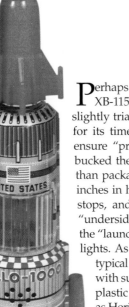

HORIKAWA
ROCKET XB-115
JAPAN • CIRCA 1966

Perhaps the most fascinating element of Horikawa's Rocket XB-115 isn't the toy itself, but the toy's packaging. Using a slightly triangular format, the toy's box is simply avant garde for its time — a period when boxes had to be uniform to ensure "proper, even display" on retailers' shelves. XB-115 bucked the trend, but that's where its rebellion ended; other than packaging, XB-115 is a basic vertical rocketship toy 12½ inches in height. Switched on, the toy rolls around the floor, stops, and deploys its hidden lifting lever from the toy's "underside." This lifts the toy to a vertical orientation. Finally, the "launch sequence" commences, amid much clicking of noise and flashing of lights. As a bonus, XB-115 includes a rotating nose cone. Overall, the toy is typical for its mid-1960s origin: a combination of lithographed tin, designed with subdued, metallic blue hues for enhanced realism, and mold-in-color plastic components. Fairly common, and not avidly pursued, toys such as Horikawa's Rocket XB-115 represent bargain values in today's collecting environment, particularly when found in mint-original box condition.

BUILDER:	HORIKAWA
RELEASED:	CIRCA 1966
OPERATION:	BATTERY
VALUES:	
GOOD	**$150**
EXCELLENT	**$250**
MINT WITH ORIGINAL BOX	**$550**

HORIKAWA

HORIKAWA

HORIKAWA
SHOOT DOWN FLOATING SATELLITE TARGET GAME
JAPAN • CIRCA 1962

By 1962, the global social impact of Sputnik was but a distant memory. In October 1957, the term "satellite" had a bright, shiny meaning, but in '62 it meant Plymouth sedans. Even so, there's nothing quite like an old-fashioned, Sputnik-era thrill of shooting down floating satellites. That's just what Horikawa marketers had in mind when they relaunched the circa-1958 classic, Shoot Down Floating Satellite Target Game. Essentially identical to the original, the game sticks with the tortured name, but features all-new packaging showcasing the refined space sensibilities of the Kennedy era. Ditching the original illustration of an adult astronaut on a lunar surface, the new package lid depicts a youth wearing a bubble helmet, standing before the game itself, his dart pistol raised high in anticipatory delight. Perfect for backdrops as well as its own display — Horikawa's Shoot Down Floating Satellite Target Game.

BUILDER:	HORIKAWA
RELEASED:	CIRCA 1962
OPERATION:	◆
VALUES:	
GOOD	$200
EXCELLENT	$350
MINT WITH ORIGINAL BOX	$500

HORIKAWA
SILVER RAY SECRET WEAPON SPACE SCOUT
JAPAN • CIRCA 1962

Here's another example of Horikawa's innovative approach to product differentiation. As it was, Horikawa only had a handful of robot platforms — but their distributors wanted at least 50 different products each season. What to do? Easy: strategic part-swapping and a judicious amount of new tooling. And that's just what happened with the 1962-era release of Silver Ray Secret Weapon Space Scout.

BUILDER:	HORIKAWA
RELEASED:	CIRCA 1962
OPERATION:	BATTERY
VALUES:	
GOOD	$400
EXCELLENT	$800
MINT WITH ORIGINAL BOX	$1800

Just in case that name didn't grab you the first time, there's a little matter of this toy's clear indebtedness to the James Bond 007 rage of the period. At a time when Bond's nifty gadgets were inspiring all kinds of licensed (and pirated) toy products, Horikawa wanted a piece of the action. What better way to hybridize the concept than by integrating a flashing "secret agent" miniature camera into the chest of their nine-inch robot platform — a camera that transforms into the deadly chest-fire weapon typical of Horikawa robots? (Answer: *there is no better way*.) Also noteworthy is Horikawa's use of vacuum-plated "chrome" finishing, a look rarely found on robots from this period. (The 1970s and '80s are another matter.) Considered scarce, particularly in top condition, Silver Ray Secret Weapon Space Scout is more than just an unfortunately name-burdened toy — it's also a classic hybrid product that managed to coattail the secret agent craze of the day.

HORIKAWA
SPACE ASTRONAUT
JAPAN • CIRCA 1969

As the 1960s progressed, the market began telling Horikawa that it wasn't going to keep consuming toys named Astronaut and Robot/Martian. Horikawa's solution: an entirely new item, with an entirely new (or newly assembled) name — Space Astronaut. Of course, this name change was accompanied by basically the same toy, with a newly enhanced level of plastic componentry. Like its earlier Horikawa Astronaut brethren, this toy features the human face behind the plastic shield. The toy also sports a camouflaged chest-fire mechanism that, by this time, had come to define Horikawa products. And of course, the toy included the standard walking and arm-swinging of so many earlier versions. To contemporary thinking, toys like Space Astronaut are more symbolic of their time than perhaps originally intended, but no matter. For completist Horikawa collections, Space Astronaut is a must-have, and for so many reasons — beginning with the letter A (for "anachronism").

BUILDER:	HORIKAWA
RELEASED:	CIRCA 1969
OPERATION:	BATTERY
VALUES:	
GOOD	$200
EXCELLENT	$350
MINT WITH ORIGINAL BOX	$550

HORIKAWA
SPACE CAPSULE
JAPAN • CIRCA 1963

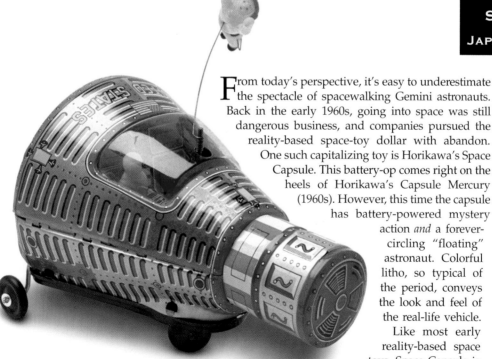

From today's perspective, it's easy to underestimate the spectacle of spacewalking Gemini astronauts. Back in the early 1960s, going into space was still dangerous business, and companies pursued the reality-based space-toy dollar with abandon. One such capitalizing toy is Horikawa's Space Capsule. This battery-op comes right on the heels of Horikawa's Capsule Mercury (1960s). However, this time the capsule has battery-powered mystery action *and* a forever-circling "floating" astronaut. Colorful litho, so typical of the period, conveys the look and feel of the real-life vehicle. Like most early reality-based space toys, Space Capsule is affordable, although mint-original boxed values do exhibit escalation. Horikawa would expand its capsule line throughout the 1960s with successor products like New Space Capsule (1960s) and Super Space Capsule (1960s) — all of which contribute to fine progressive-release displays, as well.

BUILDER:	HORIKAWA
RELEASED:	CIRCA 1963
OPERATION:	BATTERY
VALUES:	
GOOD	$350
EXCELLENT	$550
MINT WITH ORIGINAL BOX	$900

HORIKAWA

HORIKAWA

HORIKAWA
SUPER MOON EXPLORER
JAPAN • CIRCA 1969

By 1969, it was clear the basic "Super Astronaut" designation just wouldn't cut it any longer for Horikawa. A new and better name was needed, hence the rollout of the revised battery-operated toy known as Super Moon Explorer, featuring the recently introduced "Rotate-O-Matic" swiveling

BUILDER:	HORIKAWA
RELEASED:	CIRCA 1969
OPERATION:	BATTERY
VALUES:	
GOOD	$175
EXCELLENT	$275
MINT WITH ORIGINAL BOX	$350

torso effect. Despite this tremendous animation (which causes the toy's upper portion to rotate wildly while blasting its chest-fire cannon), Horikawa's mingling of plastic with tin componentry reflects its time of issuance. That's even more the case with this example of Super Moon Explorer, circa 1969. Plastic feet and arms surround an otherwise tin product. Also, the toy's packaging curiously omits the standard "SH" diamond logo of Horikawa in favor of a small white star, encompassing the letters "HK," inside a round, process-blue field. Though the toy is still marked "Japan," it's been believed Horikawa began to migrate some production of these toys to facilities in lower-overhead Hong Kong. Perhaps the mark reflects this transition. Whatever the case, Super Moon Explorer symbolizes the changing nature of toymaking in the late 1960s, for better or in this case, for worse.

HORIKAWA
SUPER SPACE CAPSULE
JAPAN • CIRCA 1968

The last, great manifestation of Horikawa's reality-based approach to space toys culminated in the release of Super Space Capsule around 1968. This solid, substantial, battery-operated toy measures in at nearly nine inches and boasts a range of interesting actions that belie its late introduction

BUILDER:	HORIKAWA
RELEASED:	CIRCA 1968
OPERATION:	BATTERY
VALUES:	
GOOD	$200
EXCELLENT	$350
MINT WITH ORIGINAL BOX	$550

date. During operation, the toy mystery actions about the floor, then stops, its nosecone blinking. Two panels peel open, revealing a blinking "engine" section and a molded-white plastic astronaut adjacent to a molded-gray TV camera and illuminated screen. Once open, the capsule initiates classic Horikawa Rotate-O-Matic action. Realistic litho accurately captures the sculpted exterior of period NASA capsules. Values are low, making Super Space Capsule not only a great icon for its time, but also a great bargain, particularly in mint-original package condition.

HORIKAWA
VIDEO ROBOT
JAPAN • CIRCA 1969

Long before the era of Mitsubishi big-screen televisions, Horikawa had Video Robot, a simple automaton whose sole purpose is to, as the packaging proclaims, "walk forward [and] catches scene of the moon on big screen." This basic toy incorporates the standard backlit animated projection feature to good effect, displaying a film-strip of far-off planets and spacecraft. Built using a serious amount of plastic componentry (feet, legs, arms, and a good portion of the torso section), Video Robot is a classic late-period (circa 1969) automaton.

Even its packaging, with a Consumer Products Safety Commission-mandated age-appropriate caution warning, reflects its time of creation. At nine inches in height, Video Robot hails from Horikawa's slightly-smaller family of automata, most of which incorporate components from their larger, 11-inch brothers. This toy, for example, still boasts a tin, fly-eyed Robot (1960s) head. For those on a budget, or those wishing to fill collection gaps at affordable values, late-period animated toys like Horikawa's Video Robot are just the big-screen ticket.

BUILDER:	HORIKAWA
RELEASED:	CIRCA 1969
OPERATION:	BATTERY
◆	
VALUES:	
GOOD	**$250**
EXCELLENT	**$350**
MINT WITH ORIGINAL BOX	**$450**

IBIS
BUCK ROGERS ANTHOLOGY
UNITED STATES • 1968

Though it's difficult to recall from the perspective of today's retro-centric pop culture, the 1960s was a period of great nostalgia for earlier times. Social and political upheavals compelled Americans to look back to a simpler era, inspiring all sorts of reissues and repackages of content from the earlier part of the century. Accompanying the many Charlie Chaplin retrospectives and 1920s-era Jazz Age music revivals was a resurgence of interest in early science fiction, partly as camp, partly as genuine appreciation for what had come before. And what better icon to re-explore than *Buck Rogers*, that early pioneer in space-toy collectibles? This anthology of *Buck Rogers* comic strips, many not seen for more than 30 years, was published in 1968 by IBIS, evidently a repackager of vintage content during the period. Collectors today regard this book with curiosity, as it not only sheds light on the early days of the Buck and Wilma characters, but also provides terrific background art against which the *Buck Rogers* toys of the 1930s can be placed. Moderately priced, the IBIS *Buck Rogers* Anthology costs less than most contemporary wallpaper, and it looks better, too.

BUILDER:	IBIS
RELEASED:	1968
OPERATION:	STATIC
◆	
VALUES:	
GOOD	**$25**
EXCELLENT	**$55**
MINT WITH ORIGINAL BOX	**$110**

HORIKAWA — IBIS

ICHIKO — IDEAL

ICHIKO
SPACE EXPLORER
JAPAN • CIRCA 1969

As a small-time Toyko toy manufacturer, Ichiko didn't make a tremendous mark on the robot and space category. Better known for its battery-operated vehicle and character toys, Ichiko obviously found the lure of the 1960s space-toy craze difficult to resist, leading to Space Explorer circa 1969. This flying saucer-based battery-op mystery actions about the floor, then stops and rises on its three plastic legs, while the "light panels" illuminate in a circular manner. (Packaging calls it "turning around the light.") Dating this toy is easy; not only does litho display late-period blues, but the package depicts an Eagle landing on the Moon. Surprisingly metallic for such a late piece, it's disappointing Ichiko didn't attempt more space toys.

BUILDER:	ICHIKO
RELEASED:	CIRCA 1969
OPERATION:	BATTERY
VALUES:	
GOOD	$250
EXCELLENT	$350
MINT WITH ORIGINAL BOX	$500

IDEAL
MR. MACHINE
UNITED STATES • 1962

It's ironic that the best-remembered robot toy isn't one valued by enthusiasts today: Ideal's gimmicky Mr. Machine. The plastic automaton became famous, not through impressive actions or long-lived play value, but because of Ideal's strategic use of saturation television advertising on children's strip programming, beginning in 1960. TV advertising helped lengthen the toy's life; at least two major versions are known — the first with metal gears and key, the second (depicted here) employing plastic for those parts. During operation, the wind-up cruises along, its arms swinging, bell ringing, siren sounding every 10 seconds, and a head with an opening and closing mouth. At 18 inches in height, this toy was certainly an impressive thing to watch in action (a single wind produces about a minute of play), but Ideal didn't stop there. Designers created Mr. Machine to double as a take-apart toy as well, integrating numeric and geometric patterning to assist in reassembly. Sears carried Mr. Machine in their 1960 Wish Book for the pricey sum of $8.77 — no doubt a reflection of the high marketing costs associated with the toy. Not surprisingly, the highly visible Mr. Machine provided clear influence to a number of Japanese toys, including Asahi's Mr. Robot (also known as Wheel Robot) and SY's Mego Man. Ideal even knocked itself off: Sears' 1961 Wish Book includes Mr. Machine Game, complete with a miniature version of the automaton. Accompanying values reflect the second version of Mr. Machine from 1962. Mint-original package values are generally very high for Mr. Machine, as most children immediately discarded the oversized box.

BUILDER:	IDEAL
RELEASED:	1962
OPERATION:	WIND-UP
VALUES:	
GOOD	$100
EXCELLENT	$200
MINT WITH ORIGINAL BOX	$900

IDEAL
ROBOT COMMANDO
UNITED STATES • 1961

Taking cues from their Japanese counterparts, Ideal brought Robot Commando to market in 1961 to do battle not only with imagined adversaries, but with the firm's overseas competition as well. Obvious indebtedness to Masudaya is visible in the design of Robot Commando; the "obeying spoken commands" emulates the Sonicon sound-control features of some Masudaya products, while the interactive nature of the toy seems patterned in particular on the large Masudaya skirted Target Robot (1950s). Whatever the source of inspiration, it's clear Ideal didn't do as well with Robot Commando as they did with Mr. Machine (1960s); this toy was marketed for but a few years, then dropped. Its all-plastic construction and 19-inch height make it a substantial toy, one whose box is rarely found today due to quick trashing by child owners. The corded remote-control battery toy's operations include rolling forward, reverse, left, and right; firing rockets; throwing missiles using its arms; and obeying "spoken commands," though the effectiveness of this functionality is usually in question. Most Robot Commandos found today lack their shoulder pads (like this example) as well as the easily-lost missiles and rockets. Not as desirable as Mr. Machine, Robot Commando still demonstrates that there's no such thing as a good idea not worth stealing.

BUILDER:	IDEAL
RELEASED:	1961
OPERATION:	BATTERY
VALUES:	
GOOD	**$250**
EXCELLENT	**$350**
MINT WITH ORIGINAL BOX	**$650**

KFZ
APOLLO FLYING SAUCER NR. 562
WEST GERMANY • CIRCA 1968

Though not major players in the space toy craze of the 1950s and '60s, German toymakers did market their share of interesting and iconic playthings. KFZ's Apollo Flying Saucer Nr. 562 is a representative example of period German toymaking: colorful litho, friction action, and decidedly retro styling that suggests a toy from a decade earlier. The use of the "Apollo" name helps date the toy to the 1968 timeframe, but the look and feel of the toy itself suggests an Asahi or even Haji flying saucer. The dome sports colorful art of the cosmos, while jutting outward from the top of the saucer deck are two wireform antennae (the package depicts three, which may be the original format). As a friction toy, Apollo Flying Saucer doesn't win any major animation awards, but it does what any consumer would expect from a small (six-inch diameter) tin-litho toy. Exceedingly affordable in today's collector environment, KFZ's toy adds variety to any assembly of classic flying saucer toys.

BUILDER:	KFZ
RELEASED:	CIRCA 1968
OPERATION:	FRICTION
VALUES:	
GOOD	**$85**
EXCELLENT	**$125**
MINT WITH ORIGINAL BOX	**$250**

IDEAL — KFZ

LINEMAR-YONEZAWA (vertical side text)

LINEMAR-YONEZAWA
(EASEL-BACK) ROBOT
JAPAN • CIRCA 1962

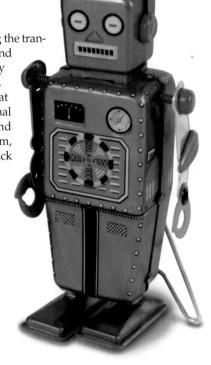

Yonezawa's Easel-back Robots (1950s) were a fairly long-lived lot, spanning the transition from the 1950s to the '60s with their inimitable large-format style and battery-operated action. So called because of their interesting (and visually distracting) use of an easel-style wireform to enhance stability during walking, the eleven-inch Easel-back sports classic styling and dependable action for what is essentially a basic-action toy. As with the original version, this toy was built by Yonezawa and marketed by Louis Marx & Co.'s import arm, Linemar, around 1962. The key difference is the lack of the clear-plastic space bubble helmet found on the initial version (1950s). Marx would begin phasing out the Linemar organization later in the decade, just as their Hong Kong subsidiaries were coming on line. ("Linemar" was a rearranging of a more famous Marx house brand, Marlines, generally used with its electric trains and vehicle toys.) It's very likely this 1962-era production was the final run for all Yonezawa Easel-back Robots, bringing a family of interesting and quizzically designed product to a close.

MARKETER:	LINEMAR
BUILDER:	YONEZAWA
RELEASED:	CIRCA 1962
OPERATION:	BATTERY

VALUES:	
GOOD	$250
EXCELLENT	$450
MINT WITH ORIGINAL BOX	$700

JAMES D. JULIA AUCTIONS IMAGES

LINEMAR-YONEZAWA
MR. MERCURY
JAPAN • 1962

As the second version of Mr. Mercury, the Yonezawa-built battery-op loses the original's (Yonezawa, 1960s) plastic arms and coal miner-vibe helmet lamp in favor of a more sedate and traditionally tin presentation. According to Japanese tin-toy historians, the changes were effected due to recommendations by Linemar, the Louis Marx & Co. import subsidiary that had selected this toy for inclusion in their 1962-63 product line. Evidently Linemar felt the tin-armed look would be more saleable, thus the running-change revision. The other main change is a new, litho-only chest nameplate (no more plastic-relief lettering). Of course, there was no need to fiddle with the toy's stupendous play pattern. Like the paddle-armed version, this Mr. Mercury features the same dandy actions: forward and backward walking motion; raising and lowering of arms; bending and straightening at the toy's "waistline;" and grasping and releasing objects within the toy's hands. And he still includes that supercool head-as-miniature-control-room feature which underscores the inferred enormity of the toy. For truly arresting visuals, fans would have to wait for Y's third version, the gold Mr. Mercury of 1963-64, also released by Linemar (1960s). But as a middle child, blue Mr. Mercury holds its own among its mechanical brothers in tin-and-plastic arms.

MARKETER:	LINEMAR
BUILDER:	YONEZAWA
RELEASED:	1962
OPERATION:	BATTERY

VALUES:	
GOOD	$800
EXCELLENT	$1400
MINT WITH ORIGINAL BOX	$2500

LINEMAR-YONEZAWA
MR. MERCURY
JAPAN • 1963

No matter what anyone says, Sears catalogs don't lie. As the Mr. Mercury line was researched, it became apparent conventional wisdom for the three variations' release schedule was challenged by documentation in the Sears Wish Books of the early 1960s. In short, collector legend has been completely opposite the reality: instead of the gold version first, followed by blue, and then by blue with paddle arms, the Wish Books depicts paddle arms for sale in 1961 and '62, and gold in 1963 and '64. Consultations with Japanese vintage-toy historians in possession of original Yonezawa documentation confirms the Sears timeline; Yonezawa indeed marketed the paddle-arm Mr. Mercury first, in 1961 (1960s), as a Y toy. Linemar then carried the final two versions, under their branding, in 1962-63 for the blue metal-arm version, and 1963-64 for the gold version. Of course, the toy's terrific actions remain the same across all releases. Still unconvinced? Then consider the toys' chest cavity litho plates. The first two versions, by the revised timeline, depict innards with glowing vacuum tubes. The third/gold version sports revised art showing a Wollensak reel-to-reel tape recorder. Is it likely Yonezawa would have gone from a tape recorder to vacuum tubes as it *updated* the toy? In a word, no.

MARKETER:	LINEMAR
BUILDER:	YONEZAWA
RELEASED:	1963
OPERATION:	BATTERY

VALUES:	
GOOD	$800
EXCELLENT	$1400
MINT WITH ORIGINAL BOX	$2500

LOUIS MARX & CO.
CAPE CANAVERAL PLAYSET
UNITED STATES • CIRCA 1962

The word "playset" wouldn't really exist if not for Louis Marx & Co. Not only did they create the modern playset (buildings, accessories, and loads of figures), but they refined it to an art form before their corporate clock was finally punched by Quaker Oats in the mid-1970s. Part of that refining came through successive releases of the same playset concept — for example, Cape Canaveral. At the dawn of the modern American space era, around 1960, Marx first released Cape Canaveral to a ready audience. Crammed with virtually every reality-based sci-fi concept ever tooled into plastic by a single company, Cape Canaveral was a huge hit, from both creative and value-focused perspectives. Cape Canaveral's progression through the 1960s witnessed the expected (and generally unfavorable) component changes, but the set always stayed true to Marx's basic concept of what a slightly futuristic American spaceport should be like. Of course, based on Marx's substantial long-term return on the Cape Canaveral line, it's clear that most Americans agreed with that vision. All values are based on the presence of original packaging; "mint" includes never-assembled tin-litho buildings.

BUILDER:	MARX
RELEASED:	CIRCA 1962
OPERATION:	STATIC

VALUES:	
GOOD	$200
EXCELLENT	$400
MINT WITH ORIGINAL BOX	$1000

LINEMAR-YONEZAWA — MARX

MARX

LOUIS MARX & CO.
HI-BOUNCER MOON SCOUT
JAPAN • CIRCA 1968

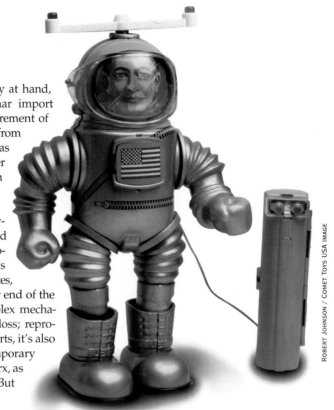

ROBERT JOHNSON / COMET TOYS USA IMAGE

With the economic implosion of the Japanese toy industry at hand, Louis Marx & Co., around 1968, folded their Linemar import subsidiary into the American corporation, resulting in the retirement of that notable brand. From this point onward, imported toys from Japan as well as Hong Kong would fall under the Marx banner, as the 1968-era release of Hi-Bouncer Moon Scout demonstrates. Based on the earlier Colonel Hap Hazard toy, the 11½-inch Hi-Bouncer Moon Scout is essentially the same battery-op, except that it now sports a corded remote control and has revised decoration. During operation, the toy's head-mounted helicopter blade rotates, with two miniature lamps on either end of the blade fully illuminated. This complex mechanism was prone to breakage and loss; reproductions do exist. As this toy represents the second of two imports, it's also the less-common toy, leading to higher valuations in the contemporary marketplace. Interestingly, it's unclear who built this toy for Marx, as packaging and the toy itself are devoid of any builder's mark. But Hi-Bouncer's smirk speaks volumes.

BUILDER:	MARX
RELEASED:	CIRCA 1968
OPERATION:	BATTERY
VALUES:	
GOOD	$1100
EXCELLENT	$2000
MINT WITH ORIGINAL BOX	$3500

LOUIS MARX & CO.
ROCK 'EM SOCK 'EM ROBOTS
UNITED STATES • CIRCA 1968

ANDREW BAKO COLLECTION

There's nothing quite like the magic of knocking an opponent's block off — when playing Rock 'Em Sock 'Em Robots, of course. This ingenious toy combines the interactive play patterns of early tin sporting toys with the resilience of plastic and the exciting horror of boxing — in short, a true candidate for the All-Star Toy Hall of Fame. Rock 'Em Sock 'Em Robots features two battle-hardened automata, both of whom throw lefts and rights directly to the opponent's "block" (as Marx period TV commercials put it). Whenever a direct hit is made, the receiving-end robot head goes skyward, accompanied by a screeching sound effect. Incredible sellers during their time (early 1960s through the late 1970s) Rock 'Em Sock 'Em Robots come in three versions: the original; the second version (depicted and valued here); and the third version, from the Quaker Oats era (1970s). Original valuations: $100 good, $200 excellent, $350 mint-original box. Few things in life, let alone toys, provide as much visceral satisfaction as Marx's battling automata. Live the experience today.

BUILDER:	MARX
RELEASED:	CIRCA 1968
OPERATION:	MECHANICAL
VALUES:	
GOOD	$65
EXCELLENT	$125
MINT WITH ORIGINAL BOX	$200

LOUIS MARX & CO.
WHISTLING SPACE TOP SET
JAPAN • CIRCA 1968

After the demise of Linemar, Marx continued to import numerous toys from Japan, marketing them under their own brand. This toy, Whistling Space Top Set, is from that post-Linemar line. Though it resembles a toy from much earlier, best estimates place the Marx Whistling Space Top Set at around 1968. Its low-budget approach to both toy and package design underscores not only the toy's late date of manufacture, but also the state of creativity at this price point. As the toy's name suggests, the tops produce a whistling sound when they're whirring about. Top-winding is provided by the battery-powered winder. Top lithography is colorful and definitely late-Japanese in style. It's believed this toy was marketed earlier under another brand, and that its design and packaging date back even further.

BUILDER:	MARX
RELEASED:	CIRCA 1968
OPERATION:	BATTERY
VALUES:	
GOOD	$150
EXCELLENT	$250
MINT WITH ORIGINAL BOX	$550

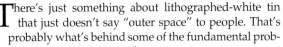

MASUDAYA
APOLLO SPACECRAFT
JAPAN • CIRCA 1966

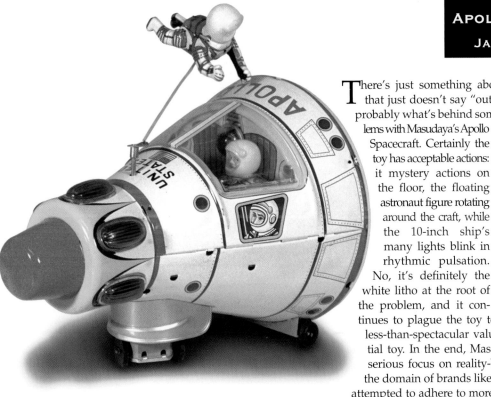

There's just something about lithographed-white tin that just doesn't say "outer space" to people. That's probably what's behind some of the fundamental problems with Masudaya's Apollo Spacecraft. Certainly the toy has acceptable actions: it mystery actions on the floor, the floating astronaut figure rotating around the craft, while the 10-inch ship's many lights blink in rhythmic pulsation. No, it's definitely the white litho at the root of the problem, and it continues to plague the toy to this very day, producing less-than-spectacular valuations for such a substantial toy. In the end, Masudaya wasn't known for a serious focus on reality-based space toys; that was the domain of brands like Horikawa, whose capsules attempted to adhere to more traditional decoration and design standards.

BUILDER:	MASUDAYA
RELEASED:	CIRCA 1966
OPERATION:	BATTERY
VALUES:	
GOOD	$450
EXCELLENT	$800
MINT WITH ORIGINAL BOX	$1600

MASUDAYA

MASUDAYA
CAPSULE 6
JAPAN • CIRCA 1960

ROBERT JOHNSON / COMET TOYS USA IMAGE

The pre-Mercury period in American space history is an interesting one. This was the time in which the best and the brightest were determining exactly how to make space vehicles viable and safe for the astronauts they'd be carrying. The public wouldn't get a taste for NASA's designs until late 1961 and early 1962, when the first Mercury capsules were put on public display.

Prior to this, of course, the designs of the future were an exercise in complete subjectivity, as Capsule 6, by Masudaya, demonstrates. This circa-1960 toy actually has more in common with the armor-shell concepts first pioneered by turn-of-the-century filmmaker Georges Méliès than the succeeding designs of NASA's Mercury and Gemini capsules. The tin-litho battery-op features standard mystery action, flashing lights, and its most notable element, a visible cockpit housing a tin-litho astronaut. Masudaya's packaging for Capsule 6 is particularly striking, making good use of primary-color capsule artwork rendered realistically against a stylized lunar background. A scarce toy, Capsule 6 commands serious attention from collectors today, both for its uncommon nature as well as its pre-NASA view of the future.

BUILDER:	MASUDAYA
RELEASED:	CIRCA 1960
OPERATION:	BATTERY
VALUES:	
GOOD	**$700**
EXCELLENT	**$1100**
MINT WITH ORIGINAL BOX	**$1500**

MASUDAYA
GLOBE WITH ORBITING SATELLITES
JAPAN • CIRCA 1960

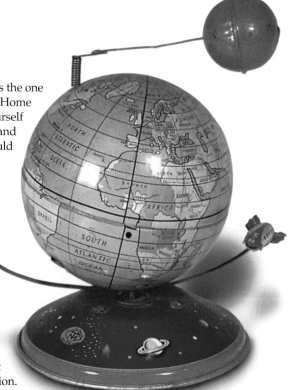

Located just off the toy aisle in any period department store was the one area no self-respecting kid went — the educational toy aisle. Home to pencil pots, chemistry sets, and science projects like build-it-yourself Fulton Steamboats, it was an aisle to avoid like bowl haircuts and pocket protectors. But that's sad, because it's also where kids would have discovered a terrific Mercury-era toy like Masudaya's Globe with Orbiting Satellites. This five-inch mechanical wind-up uses off-the-shelf kiddie globe tooling while capitalizing on the then-current fascination with artificial satellites circling the Earth. Wound and switched on, the globe spins in slow motion, while the Moon and spacecraft satellites begin their equally-scaled circumnavigations of our world. Masudaya's toy likely sold only to the most punitive of parents, so god willing, it can only be found on occasion. And with relatively affordable values in the contemporary collecting environment, it's safe once again to explore the universe without having to step into the educational-toy aisle, ever.

BUILDER:	MASUDAYA
RELEASED:	CIRCA 1960
OPERATION:	WIND-UP
VALUES:	
GOOD	**$300**
EXCELLENT	**$500**
MINT WITH ORIGINAL BOX	**$900**

MASUDAYA
LUNAR EXPEDITION
JAPAN • CIRCA 1964

Lunar Expedition by Masudaya is a fascinating toy that combines the emotional majesty of lithographed tin with the purposeful utility of injection-molded plastic. A classic mid-1960s product, 12-inch Lunar Expedition is a near-future sci-fi toy that comes from the reality hallway in the school of fantastic toy design. During operation, the battery-operated toy moves in any of a number of directions, controlled by an H-pattern "shifter" located on the rear of the toy. Just choose the direction desired, and the Lunar Expedition heads out, its treads churning the dust of a desolate moon. A clear-plastic cockpit dome reveals molded-plastic figures at the helm, while the mainly tin-litho body sports ultra-realistic lithography for an almost scientific look and feel. Even the toy's packaging is photo-realistic in its depiction of the toy blowing through lunar dunes. An odd plaything that's only occasionally seen on the open market, Lunar Expedition brings solid values, particularly when found in mint-original packaging condition. See into the not-so-distant future with Lunar Expedition by Masudaya.

BUILDER:	MASUDAYA
RELEASED:	CIRCA 1964
OPERATION:	BATTERY
VALUES:	
GOOD	$800
EXCELLENT	$1600
MINT WITH ORIGINAL BOX	$2500

MASUDAYA
NON-FALL MOON ROCKET
JAPAN • CIRCA 1962

Masudaya hit its space-toy design stride with the stylized teardrop form factor. First manifested on Non-Fall Moon Rocket, this teardrop design would mature into many different and exciting toys, ranging from Planet Explorer (1960s) to Super Sonic Moon Ship (1960s) to the granddaddy of them all, Sonicon Rocket (1960s). But it all started right here, with Non-Fall Moon Rocket's all-head, no-tail shape. Up front is the clear-domed cockpit housing a vinyl-headed astronaut figure. Outside, where sloping fins and plunging colors seem more at home in 1967 than 1962, there's a second astronaut astride a periscope-based stalk which rotates during operation, affording the explorer a full 360-degree view of the surrounding terrain. Mystery action gets this 9½-inch toy around the floor, complemented by flashing lights along the toy's side and in its cockpit. A generally affordable item, Non-Fall Moon Rocket offers a tremendous opportunity to assemble the entire range of Masudaya teardrop space vehicles for a value-focused price.

BUILDER:	MASUDAYA
RELEASED:	CIRCA 1962
OPERATION:	BATTERY
VALUES:	
GOOD	$300
EXCELLENT	$450
MINT WITH ORIGINAL BOX	$650

MASUDAYA
NON-STOP SPACE SURVEY X-09
JAPAN • CIRCA 1962

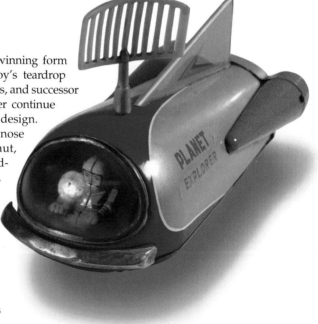

Non-Stop Space Survey X-09 certainly deserves better, but let's face it — it's a flying bedpan. Using a variation on Masudaya's teardrop school of design, X-09 mystery actions about the floor, its lights blinking and loud clicking emanating from within. Looking sharp in a trendy two-tone scheme of blue and Crimson Tide maroon, the toy is quite simply a floating set of design contradictions. Surprisingly, X-09 is a commonplace toy, with prices that reflect that level of availability. Go anywhere, be prepared — you're flying Masudaya's Non-Stop Space Survey X-09.

BUILDER:	MASUDAYA
RELEASED:	CIRCA 1962
OPERATION:	BATTERY
VALUES:	
GOOD	**$150**
EXCELLENT	**$350**
MINT WITH ORIGINAL BOX	**$550**

MASUDAYA
PLANET EXPLORER
JAPAN • CIRCA 1964

Masudaya wasted little time in capitalizing on the winning form factor of Non-Fall Moon Rocket (1960s). That toy's teardrop design was perfect for spaceship concepts in the early 1960s, and successor playthings like Planet Explorer continue to exploit that pioneering design. Planet Explorer features a nose cockpit carrying an astronaut, sweptback lines, illuminated-red taillights, mystery action, and that curious antenna, which seems to have come directly from scooping duties at the Masudaya family's cat litter box. Examples found in mint-original box condition bring a solid value, but interestingly, lesser-condition loose examples are quite affordable, making an assembly of numerous Masudaya teardrop space toys a realistic endeavor.

BUILDER:	MASUDAYA
RELEASED:	CIRCA 1964
OPERATION:	BATTERY
VALUES:	
GOOD	**$450**
EXCELLENT	**$600**
MINT WITH ORIGINAL BOX	**$1000**

MASUDAYA
R-35 ROBOT
JAPAN • CIRCA 1962

Humble little R-35 — so simple, basic, and unassuming, it's almost like a toy from the early 1950s. Yet this eight-inch automaton emerged late in the space-toy game, around 1962, placing it near the end of golden-age Masudaya toys. Numerous elements suggest an earlier introduction: the use of actual light bulbs for eyes; a round, canister-like head which recalls designs like Alps' Mr. Robot (1950s); and the waddle-walk mechanism. Switched on, R-35 waddles forward or reverse, its bulb eyes shining their eerily dim glow. The control box is one of the more nifty ones known, depicting three R-35s striding toward an unknown destination, their eyes conically lighting the way. An interesting side note is the stylized "ROBOT" lettering on R-35's chest; it's a striking adaptation of A.C. Gilbert Company's logotype, and it appears on both Golden and Lantern Robot packaging, oddly (1950s). Loose R-35s are affordable, making them good buys for both new collectors and those looking to pursue variations or upgrades. Experience the magic of early robot design with Masudaya's R-35 Robot.

BUILDER:	MASUDAYA
RELEASED:	CIRCA 1962
OPERATION:	BATTERY
◆	
VALUES:	
GOOD	**$450**
EXCELLENT	**$700**
MINT WITH ORIGINAL BOX	**$1600**

MASUDAYA
SONICON ROCKET
JAPAN • CIRCA 1963

BUILDER:	MASUDAYA
RELEASED:	CIRCA 1963
OPERATION:	BATTERY
◆	
VALUES:	
GOOD	**$500**
EXCELLENT	**$1200**
MINT WITH ORIGINAL BOX	**$2500**

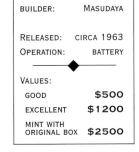

More than just the builder of the legendary Gang of Five, Masudaya is also distinguished for its Radicon (radio control) and Sonicon (sonic control) lines of toys. To facilitate sound control, Sonicon Rocket comes complete with a plastic whistle (in its own terrific box) which, when blown near the switched-on Rocket, will cause it to immediately alter its mystery-action direction. Humble by modern standards, this was a major feat in 1963. Sonicon repairs can be costly, so be wary of inoperables, except as shelf warmers. Mint-original box values demand the presence of all components (dish, whistle) and internal packaging and instructions. At least one parquet-patterned Sonicon Rocket variant is known, as well as non-Sonicon toys based on the same stampings, like Super Sonic Moon Ship (1960s).

MASUDAYA

MASUDAYA
SPACE CAPSULE WITH FLOATING ASTRONAUT
JAPAN • CIRCA 1969

Though not as prodigious as Horikawa or Yoshiya, Masudaya did manage a few reality-based toys during the 1960s. Their emphasis had always been on the more fanciful and outrageous, but as fortunes for such toys began to wane, Masudaya looked to NASA for inspiration. Space Capsule with Floating Astronaut mixes the reality of NASA designs with some tried-and-true toy play patterns, with fair success. Switched on, the nine-inch battery-op mystery-actions about while capsule and taillights flash. The toy's bonus is the "floating astronaut" who hovers above the Command Module's entry port. The packaging's illustration depicts the action almost like a skysurfing astronaut being towed behind the craft. Lithographed in late-period silver-blues, the toy is fun and interesting to view, both in action and as a static piece. Plus, pedestrian packaging makes even mint-original boxed examples approachable. For reality-based space toys by Masudaya, Space Capsule with Floating Astronaut is as good as they come.

BUILDER:	MASUDAYA
RELEASED:	CIRCA 1969
OPERATION:	BATTERY
VALUES:	
GOOD	$200
EXCELLENT	$350
MINT WITH ORIGINAL BOX	$550

MASUDAYA
SPACE PATROL
JAPAN • CIRCA 1961

Perhaps even more iconic than menacing battery-operated robots are Japan's big-headed, celluloid/vinyl kiddie toys. These bizarre, entertaining approximations of humanity adorned a huge variety of toys from the golden age of Japanese tin, covering all categories. Though most space toys escaped Big-Headism, Masudaya's Space Patrol wasn't so lucky. This friction motorcycle toy includes a big-headed vinyl kid wearing gas station attendant coveralls and a Gemini-era, zero-atmosphere helmet. Amazingly, this creatively challenged toy also happens to be famously desirable, with mint-original box examples commanding highly respectable values in today's collecting environment. There is, without question, no accounting for taste — but there is for scarcity.

BUILDER:	MASUDAYA
RELEASED:	CIRCA 1961
OPERATION:	FRICTION
VALUES:	
GOOD	$1200
EXCELLENT	$1800
MINT WITH ORIGINAL BOX	$2600

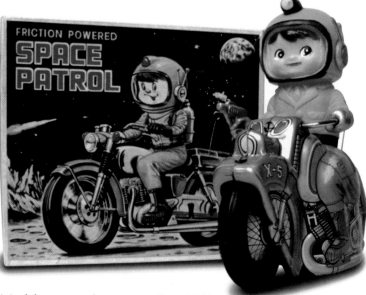

FRICTION POWERED
SPACE PATROL

KALMBACH IMAGE

MASUDAYA
SPACE TANK
JAPAN • CIRCA 1962

Masudaya got a lot of mileage from their space tank platform. This example, marketed simply as Space Tank, around 1962, has ties dating back to 1959, when it first emerged as the scintillatingly named Lighted Space Vehicle (1950s). Space Tank still has the original's main elements (centrally domed control center, wireform spring "light bumpers" at the rear, and mystery action) while adding new ones (turning antenna dish, freshened lithography). As a low price-point toy, Masudaya likely did very well with toys like Space Tank, as they exist today in fairly large quantities. Even so, Space Tank remains desirable, and not just because its antenna is shared by other Masudaya toys like Sonicon Rocket (1960s). Given its late manufacturing date and high metal-component value, Masudaya's Space Tank makes a terrific, quality-feel addition to tank-based assemblages, and for very little investment.

BUILDER:	MASUDAYA
RELEASED:	CIRCA 1962
OPERATION:	BATTERY
VALUES:	
GOOD	$250
EXCELLENT	$450
MINT WITH ORIGINAL BOX	$750

MASUDAYA
SPACE TANK M-41
JAPAN • CIRCA 1964

BUILDER:	MASUDAYA
RELEASED:	CIRCA 1964
OPERATION:	BATTERY
VALUES:	
GOOD	$150
EXCELLENT	$300
MINT WITH ORIGINAL BOX	$550

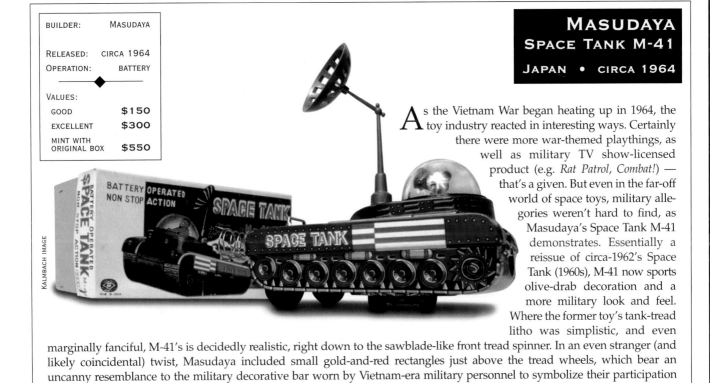

KALMBACH IMAGE

As the Vietnam War began heating up in 1964, the toy industry reacted in interesting ways. Certainly there were more war-themed playthings, as well as military TV show-licensed product (e.g. *Rat Patrol*, *Combat!*) — that's a given. But even in the far-off world of space toys, military allegories weren't hard to find, as Masudaya's Space Tank M-41 demonstrates. Essentially a reissue of circa-1962's Space Tank (1960s), M-41 now sports olive-drab decoration and a more military look and feel. Where the former toy's tank-tread litho was simplistic, and even marginally fanciful, M-41's is decidedly realistic, right down to the sawblade-like front tread spinner. In an even stranger (and likely coincidental) twist, Masudaya included small gold-and-red rectangles just above the tread wheels, which bear an uncanny resemblance to the military decorative bar worn by Vietnam-era military personnel to symbolize their participation in the conflict. Of course, though this design element's inclusion is most certainly coincidental, it does thematically underscore the toy-design transition taking place in the mid-1960s: out with the fanciful, in with the realistic — even when it comes to outer-space vehicle design. An affordable toy, Space Tank M-41 and its tooling relatives make a particularly insightful survey of toy evolution spanning the late 1950s to the mid-1960s.

MASUDAYA (vertical, left margin)

MASUDAYA
SUPER SONIC MOON SHIP
JAPAN • CIRCA 1963

Though technologically innovative, it's unclear what level of success Masudaya enjoyed with its Sonicon line. Not believed to exist in huge quantities, Sonicon Rocket (1960s) commands good (but not stellar) values today. One thing, however, is clear: Masudaya wasted little time bringing Sonicon Rocket-based toys to market. This example, Super Sonic Moon Ship, is essentially the same toy, albeit

BUILDER:	MASUDAYA
RELEASED:	CIRCA 1963
OPERATION:	BATTERY
VALUES:	
GOOD	$600
EXCELLENT	$900
MINT WITH ORIGINAL BOX	$1800

lacking the Sonicon's sound-control innards. The 14-inch battery-op is powered by mystery action, causing it to "hover" around a child's floor until an impedance is struck, resulting in a change of direction. Revised lithography, interior illumination, and curiously redesigned rear fins complete the package. Not massively common, Super Sonic Moon Ship is nonetheless a relatively "available" toy that can be found in a small handful of color and lithography variations.

MASUDAYA
TV SPACE PATROL
JAPAN • CIRCA 1962

The 1960s were the heyday of pro auto customizers. Names like George Barris, Von Dutch, and Ed "Big Daddy" Roth all contributed to the notion that cars didn't have to follow Detroit design trends. Partly inspired by, and partly a reaction to, the "show cars" of the late 1950s, auto customization took on a life of its own as the 1960s matured, many making their way to TV and into eternal public consciousness. How eternal? One word: *Batmobile.* Japan's toymakers had long been producing fanciful cars, but for the most part, tin auto toys followed the real-world's lead, as in the case of Masudaya's TV Space Patrol. This circa-1962 vehicle has clear indebtedness to the Lincoln Futura showcar of the late 1950s, as well as the pioneering, pre-Batmobile designs of George Barris. A substantial toy, nearly 14 inches in length, TV Space Patrol sports a TV camera-wielding driver inside the bubble cockpit who constantly surveys the landscape in 360 degrees during friction-powered operation. Interesting lithographic touches include the two-toned scheme, "ladder" for climbing into the cockpit (no doubt for the vertically challenged), and the inexplicable inclusion of the NATO herald on both doors. Oversized wheels and Moon-style hubcaps complete the vehicular presentation. It's likely this vehicle platform was used by Masudaya on alternative-branded versions, but this remains unclear.

KALMBACH IMAGE

BUILDER:	MASUDAYA
RELEASED:	CIRCA 1962
OPERATION:	FRICTION
VALUES:	
GOOD	$800
EXCELLENT	$1400
MINT WITH ORIGINAL BOX	$2100

The only good thing about being a toy on the downside of a long-running trend is that lack of creative accountability is pretty much a given. It certainly benefitted the UFOX05, or "X05," as it's more economically known. This Masudaya late-1960s toy owes more to Peter Max and psychedelic wallpaper design than it does classic space toys from the 1950s, but as a relic of its time, X05 is a winner, albeit a none-too-desirable one. The nine-inch diameter battery-op boasts mystery action and flashing lights as it hovers about a child's floor space, looking for impedances to bump. Located in the central control dome is a standard tin-litho astronaut figure, no doubt just as flabbergasted as most with the spacecraft's finish. The baby-blue disc is crowded with Peter Max-like starfields, while bold typographical arrows perforate the color maelstrom with Pop Art acuity and aplomb. The box is definitely mod: the apparent blueness of outerspace is punctuated by Twentieth Century Fox-like searchlight beams. Even Masudaya's marketers got into the spirit of the Sixties with the package's tag line: "For the children of the world from Masudaya of Japan." Far out, man!

BUILDER:	MASUDAYA
RELEASED:	CIRCA 1967
OPERATION:	BATTERY
VALUES:	
GOOD	$100
EXCELLENT	$200
MINT WITH ORIGINAL BOX	$350

In a decade characterized by horrendous takes on the classic flying saucer theme, there are some notable exceptions. Generally speaking, they hail from the early 1960s, feature interesting pilots, and still convey a sense of seriousness in their lithographic design. Masudaya's X8 Space Explorer Ship is just such an example. The nine-inch battery-op includes the obligatory central control dome, inside which a small, vinyl-headed astronaut figure runs the show. As with most Japanese vinyl toy heads, this one is cursed with Cute Face Syndrome. Switched on, X8 mystery-actions about the floor while projecting an animated light display through the upper-hull lenses. Surrounding the light display is purposeful lithographic art, detailing such saucer staples as exhaust ports, pressurized tanks, and entry ports. Due largely to the toy's early date of creation and its sharp lithography and animated lighting, X8 Space Explorer Ship enjoys stronger-than-average valuation in the contemporary collector environment. This platform would later play host to many horrible flying-saucer toys, sadly.

BUILDER:	MASUDAYA
RELEASED:	CIRCA 1961
OPERATION:	BATTERY
VALUES:	
GOOD	$350
EXCELLENT	$550
MINT WITH ORIGINAL BOX	$750

MASUDAYA

MASUO
JUPITER ROCKET
JAPAN • CIRCA 1960

There's an unexpected benefit to being a marketplace bottomfeeder — all that low creative flying allows one's products to avoid the vagaries of shifting contemporary tastes, leading to long runs for generally undeserving products. That's the case with Masuo's Jupiter Rocket. Starting as a pedestrian wind-up when released in the previous decade (1950s), the toy was positively long in the tooth by 1960. Yet a rock-bottom retail price, and simple yet effective play pattern allowed Masuo to keep the dogs of creativity at abeyance for a few more years. As before, the toy is keywound, then released, where it careens across the floor. When it strikes an impedance with its "patented" spring-loaded nosecone, the rocket proceeds with a horizontal-to-vertical transition made possible by an internal lift-arm mechanism. Revised, yet unmistakably recycled, litho art graces the fuselage. With low values, Jupiter Rocket is a great new-collector purchase, as well as the object of variation hunters who dwell deep below the currents of mainstream toy manufacture.

BUILDER:	MASUO
RELEASED:	CIRCA 1960
OPERATION:	WIND-UP
VALUES:	
GOOD	$125
EXCELLENT	$200
MINT WITH ORIGINAL BOX	$450

MEGO-YONEZAWA
MERCURY X-1 SPACE SAUCER
JAPAN • CIRCA 1964

Why be kind? It's clear Mercury X-1 Space Saucer is the result of a closed-eye spree through Yonezawa's parts bins one late night in 1964. Most obviously borrowed are the two "fins" (jet-airplane elevators) on either side of the cockpit, and the blue-plastic "exhaust" taken from one of Y's rocketship toys. Features include mystery action, flashing lights, revolving antenna (missing here), and "space noise." Perhaps the only original element is the translucent blue cockpit canopy. Little is known about Mego; it was likely a low-rent Cragstan competitor (unrelated to the Mego of the 1970s). In spite of the toy's complete lack of creative intent, Mercury X-1 does bring higher-than-average values. There's collectibility in them thar recycled parts, no doubt.

MARKETER:	MEGO
BUILDER:	YONEZAWA
RELEASED:	CIRCA 1964
OPERATION:	BATTERY
VALUES:	
GOOD	$350
EXCELLENT	$500
MINT WITH ORIGINAL BOX	$800

Identifying "lost" toymakers is an ongoing part of Japanese toy collecting. One such builder is N, whose logotype features a Mt. Fuji-like peak, an upward arrow within the peak, and the letter "N." Many collectors ascribe the mark to Noguchi, though positive confirmation of this awaits. Also suggested is N being a bottomfeeding sub-brand of Nomura (T-N), or a relation of SY (1960s).

Whoever they were, N is responsible for a handful of 1960s and '70s-era toys, most of which employ the distinctively ungainly "paddle foot" walking mechanism. Perhaps the most successful/common of all N toys is Mighty Robot, from around 1969. During operation, the wind-up toy moves forward as eccentrically mounted paddles churn. The toy also includes sparkling through the chest-mounted red gel. Classic-style lithographic body design is topped by an insipid, smiling visage in an obvious bid to appeal to the youngest of robot-oriented tastes. Inexpensive, even mint-original box examples are within the reach of most. Though N's identity remains shrouded, their barrel-chested paddle-walkers are still a distinctive symbol for the very, very late period of Japanese postwar tin toy manufacture.

BUILDER:	N
RELEASED:	CIRCA 1969
OPERATION:	WIND-UP
VALUES:	
GOOD	**$100**
EXCELLENT	**$150**
MINT WITH ORIGINAL BOX	**$250**

Z

BUILDER:	N
RELEASED:	CIRCA 1966
OPERATION:	WIND-UP
VALUES:	
GOOD	**$75**
EXCELLENT	**$150**
MINT WITH ORIGINAL BOX	**$500**

N
ROBOT-7
JAPAN • CIRCA 1966

The Japanese toy industry shrank precipitously during the mid-1960s, an inevitable response to soaring labor and material costs. While many began integrating plastic componentry into formerly all-metal designs, others moved to cost-reduced subassemblies — particularly a toy's means of locomotion. For N, builders of Robot-7, everything was fine: their paddle-walk movement was inexpensive and dependable. Wind the mechanical Robot-7, and its dome-shaped visage waddles forward, arms swinging, the colorful oscilloscope lithography blaring the toy's advance with technological precision. Colorfully decorated and interestingly shaped, Robot-7 is one of those rare late toys that command strong collector affinity today, perhaps due as much to its design as to its scarcity. Even in depressed times, creativity always overcomes the most oppressive of manufacturing and design maladies, as Robot-7 so deftly illustrates.

N
WIND UP WALKING ROBOT
JAPAN • CIRCA 1965

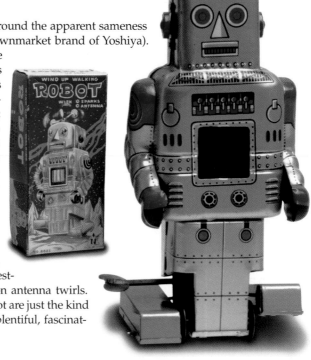

Part of the ongoing "Who was N?" mystery revolves around the apparent sameness of toys from N and SY (who some believe to be a downmarket brand of Yoshiya). Wind Up Walking Robot is one such example; many have accorded this toy with SY heritage, despite the fact that its package, as can be seen here, is marked with N's Mt. Fuji logo-type. Theories: SY built for N; N built for SY; N was a sub-brand of Nomura; N was SY's (and thus, Yoshiya's) sub-brand; N was its own entity, better known as Noguchi; and the list goes on. Whatever the heritage, it's obvious N built many variants on this paddle-walk platform. The wind-up moves forward using the paddle-footed walking mechanism, while a flint assembly creates sparkling through the chest-mounted red gel. Throughout, the robot's weather-station antenna twirls. Not terribly expensive, N toys like Wind Up Walking Robot are just the kind of product for new and growing collections: somewhat plentiful, fascinatingly varied, and fun to watch in action.

BUILDER:	N
RELEASED:	CIRCA 1965
OPERATION:	WIND-UP
◆	
VALUES:	
GOOD	$300
EXCELLENT	$700
MINT WITH ORIGINAL BOX	$1200

ROBERT JOHNSON / COMET TOYS USA IMAGES

NOMURA
APOLLO-Z CAPSULE
JAPAN • CIRCA 1969

Nomura's contribution to the late-1960s Apollo product rush is Apollo-Z Capsule, an interesting and semi-realistic (if unremarkable) toy. All the basics are here: flashing lights, mystery action, and "space noise." In fact, there's little to really define this toy as Nomura, beyond the trademarked use of the hyphenated-Z suffix found on so many T-N toys, including Robotank-Z (1960s). At 12 inches in length, this is a substantial plaything that leverages the period's "silver-blue" litho look to convey cool, calculating realism. Apollo-Z is one of many period playthings to be based, not on the lunar lander, but on the Command Module which orbited the moon. Once the astronauts had returned from the surface, they'd re-enter the earth's atmosphere in the Command Module's fore section — the re-entry vehicle (or "space capsule"). Collected by enthusiasts of late-period realism, Nomura's Apollo-Z is one of the last of its kind: a dignified (boring) space toy design that captures the real-life thrills and daring exploits of a lost time.

BUILDER:	NOMURA
RELEASED:	CIRCA 1969
OPERATION:	BATTERY
◆	
VALUES:	
GOOD	$200
EXCELLENT	$300
MINT WITH ORIGINAL BOX	$550

NOMURA
PLANET-Y SPACE STATION
JAPAN • CIRCA 1969

A s the reissue of Space Commander (1960s), Planet-Y Space Station is remarkable for one thing: it's practically unchanged from the original, right down to the SPACE STATION lettering on its outer ring. Though the toy didn't receive much freshening, it's still an admirable late-period effort by Nomura, who by this time was down-playing space toys.

Planet-Y operates using mystery action, and also includes flashing lights and something Nomura called "screen action." The only main differences between the two toys are found on the packaging. Apart from the obvious name change, Nomura also restyled the toy's cover art, with typography that suggests an influence by the *Planet of the Apes* logotype. Collectors see little difference between either version of this toy, with values that reflect such a perspective. Space Commander or Planet-Y — either way, it's a two-item variation collection for those on a budget.

BUILDER:	NOMURA
RELEASED:	CIRCA 1969
OPERATION:	BATTERY

VALUES:	
GOOD	$300
EXCELLENT	$500
MINT WITH ORIGINAL BOX	$750

NOMURA
ROBOTANK-Z
JAPAN • CIRCA 1966

N omura's Robotank-Z is an intriguing toy indeed. Borne of the Cubist school of automaton design, Robotank-Z is an intensely squat obelisk on tank treads. (The ancient Egyptians never had it so good.) The 10½-inch battery-op mystery-actions about the floor, its arms swinging and the illuminated "brain" whirling about in the clear cranium. The toy will then stop movement, and begin firing two illuminated clear-plasic cannon located just above the treads. After this Horikawa-like sequence, the toy once again heads out searching for adversaries as yet undiscovered. There are examples of Japanese domestic-market Robotank-Zs which include a speech mechanism — and naturally, they speak *Japanese*. American versions lack this feature, but the toy is nonetheless a fun and interesting variation on the square-format automaton. Also known is an alternative version with dark-gray litho-graphy; this version is also believed to have been used for the Japan-market Robotank-Z.

BUILDER:	NOMURA
RELEASED:	CIRCA 1966
OPERATION:	BATTERY

VALUES:	
GOOD	$600
EXCELLENT	$900
MINT WITH ORIGINAL BOX	$1600

NOMURA

NOMURA

NOMURA
SKY PATROL
JAPAN • CIRCA 1962

Sky Patrol by Nomura represents the end of an era — an era in which goofiness, high-concept style, and attention to lithographic detail ruled the day. Nomura had the concept, then stepped it up by adding stylized taillights (mounted on tailfins, no less), a hel-meted kid, and had the kid swivel-blast a machine gun gleefully (note the maniacally insipid vinyl-headed expression). Designers fin-ished the toy with accurate, detailed, and muted lithog-raphy and chrome trim. Put it all together, and it's a truly fanciful space-themed battery-op that isn't afraid to put a doll front-and-center. (After all, the doll *is* armed.) Sky Patrol employs mystery action and produces flashing lights and *rat-tat-tat* gun effects as doll-boy swivels. Strange, fun, thematically exuberant — Nomura Sky Patrol.

BUILDER:	NOMURA
RELEASED:	CIRCA 1962
OPERATION:	BATTERY

VALUES:	
GOOD	$800
EXCELLENT	$1400
MINT WITH ORIGINAL BOX	$2200

NOMURA
SPACE COMMANDER
JAPAN • CIRCA 1967

Space Commander by Nomura is a late-period toy that still retains the metallic charm of earlier times. Almost entirely tin-litho, Space Commander exhibits the mid-1960s trend towards subdued hues and artwork, where the emphasis is on realism, not flights of fancy. During operation, Space Commander mystery actions around the floor, searching for objects to bump into. All the while, the toy projects sequential-circular lighting around the eight top-mounted plastic lenses. Inside the central control dome, a minia-ture astronaut pilots the craft, while two adjacent wireform-spring antennae flap in the silent winds of space. Nomura would reissue Space Commander around 1969 as Planet-Y Space Station (1960s).

BUILDER:	NOMURA
RELEASED:	CIRCA 1967
OPERATION:	BATTERY

VALUES:	
GOOD	$300
EXCELLENT	$500
MINT WITH ORIGINAL BOX	$750

NOMURA
SPACE ROCKET SOLAR-X 7
JAPAN • CIRCA 1966

By the mid-1960s, every Japanese toymaker remotely interested in reality-based playthings was building a Saturn V-inspired toy. Nomura had their share, but the most successful platform was the Solar-X rocket. This battery-powered vertical rocket was like most of its competitors; it runs along the floor on wheels, then suddenly rises to a vertical position, using a camouflaged lift-arm assembly on the chassis underside. Once upright, the rocket proceeds through a "countdown," which features the "stowing" of the rocket's wings. The operational sequence culminates with the toy resuming its horizontal orientation. Released amid a flurry of vertical rockets, Solar-X is atypical, however, in that Nomura marketed two distinct versions of the toy, likely within one year of each other. The presumed first issue is this toy, Solar-X 7, resplendent in silver with red and yellow accents and capped with ICBM checkerboard patterning and a red-plastic nosecone which illuminates nicely. Solar-X 7's package depicts the rocket in flight, soaring skyward at a bit of an angle with its powerful exhaust plume dominating the lower portion of the image. The second version, Solar-X 8, would differ in terms of both litho and package design — an interesting fact, given that by the mid-1960s, most Japanese toymakers were content to reissue or even downgrade quality just to maintain price points and marketshare.

BUILDER:	NOMURA
RELEASED:	CIRCA 1966
OPERATION:	BATTERY

VALUES:	
GOOD	$200
EXCELLENT	$300
MINT WITH ORIGINAL BOX	$550

NOMURA
SPACE ROCKET SOLAR-X 8
JAPAN • CIRCA 1967

The second iteration of Space Rocket Solar-X carried more than just the "8" digit to distinguish it from its predecessor. It also boasts all-new lithography and packaging, suggesting Nomura wanted more than just a reissue's standard return on (non)investment. Where Solar-X 7 had more lithographic connectivity to the space toys of the early 1960s, Solar-X 8 is firmly rooted in the design ethos of late-period Japanese toy-making. The revised rocket sports the ultra-cool hues of silver-blue, but its actions remain the same; it cruises the floor on wheels, its wings extended outward, then stops, stows the wings, and lifts itself into an upright position for a noisy, illuminated count-down sequence. In general, the Solar-X 8 version is considered slightly more scarce than the original 7.

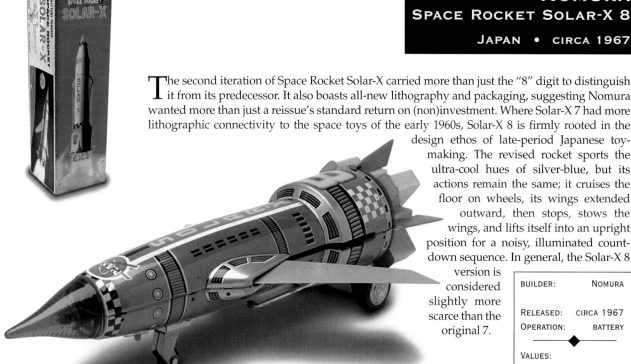

BUILDER:	NOMURA
RELEASED:	CIRCA 1967
OPERATION:	BATTERY

VALUES:	
GOOD	$200
EXCELLENT	$300
MINT WITH ORIGINAL BOX	$650

NOMURA

NOMURA
SPACE SHIP SS-18
JAPAN • CIRCA 1966

When Nomura's body of work is considered, rarely are low-end toys discussed. For the most part, it's because they're small in size, have lackluster performance, and are generally forgotten by the mainstream collecting community. One such example is Space Ship SS-18, a Nomura "penny toy" that likely was sold in bulk master packs for dimestores and other low-end retailers. Despite its humble origins, SS-18 has fascinating lithographic art, as well as friction drive and an interesting plastic canopy. Note that this canopy is generally found broken or missing today — and even when found in complete condition, count on fogging to obscure the lithographed interior detail from view. Space Ship SS-18 may have started life as a humble penny toy, but its general scarcity today accords it marketplace respect in the form of solid values. Though likely sold bulk, it's believed this toy did come in a two- or three-color box, so mint-original package samples should be detectable. Start low, finish high — that's the story of toys like Nomura's Space Ship SS-18.

BUILDER:	NOMURA
RELEASED:	CIRCA 1966
OPERATION:	FRICTION

VALUES:	
GOOD	**$200**
EXCELLENT	**$350**
MINT WITH ORIGINAL BOX	**$550**

PN
LUNAR ORBITER
WEST GERMANY • CIRCA 1969

Plastic space toys flooded the market prior to the July 1969 Apollo 11 moon landing. Toys from all corners of the globe swamped American retailers, as children and parents prepared to celebrate the great technological achievement with some down-home American-style consumerism. Lunar Orbiter from little-known German toymaker PN is one such toy: *cheap plastic* in the worst sense of the term, and devoid of any merit beyond its semi-realistic package depiction of the lunar surface. Essentially a 12-inch diameter version of the gyro-helicopter toys that had been on the market since the 1950s, the toy soars skyward when released from its launcher. Packaged in a box whose art was probably influenced by Kubrick's *2001: A Space Odyssey*, Lunar Orbiter is one of those toys that probably got used a handful of times before it either broke or became irretrievably lodged in a neighbor's tree. Valued mainly for the aforementioned packaging, Lunar Orbiter by PN proves the marketplace adage that if you build it, eventually someone will collect it.

BUILDER:	PN
RELEASED:	CIRCA 1969
OPERATION:	MECHANICAL

VALUES:	
GOOD	**$150**
EXCELLENT	**$350**
MINT WITH ORIGINAL BOX	**$550**

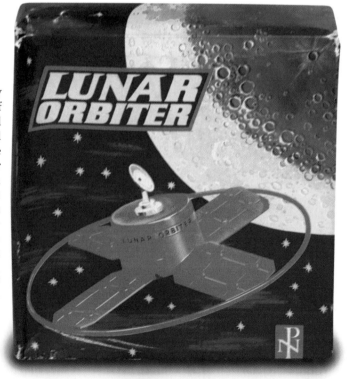

ROSKO-DAIYA
SPACE CONQUEROR
JAPAN • CIRCA 1961

Though we're familiar with their names today, most Japanese toy manufacturers were loath to promote their unAmerican-sounding corporate identities. That's why most toys featured branding like "T-N" (Nomura), "M-T" or "Modern Toys" (Masudaya), and "Y" (Yonezawa). Asahi one-upped their Tokyo competitors by using that all-American icon of toygiving, Santa Claus, in their ATC logotype. And when self-branding wasn't the ticket, most cut deals with importers, many of whom put an American face (and name) on an otherwise Japanese product. Cragstan is the most famous of these, but a close second is Rosko. Known for a handful of space toys as well as items from a host of other toy categories, Rosko "Tested Toys" often followed the lead of the more successful Cragstan. There's no better example than Space Conqueror, a rebranded, identical version of Cragstan Astronaut, by Daiya (1960s). Functionally and visually identical to both the blue Cragstan and standard Daiya-branded version, the Rosko Astronaut comes packed in a box which reuses (in modified form) those two predecessor-products' package art. Due to this identicality, the toy's package brings a far higher value to the toy than a loose example. Plus, all three versions — Cragstan, then Daiya, and finally Rosko — make a tremendous combined display, particularly when original packaging is present. Sometimes toys don't evolve — only their packaging and branding change.

MARKETER:	ROSKO
BUILDER:	DAIYA
RELEASED:	CIRCA 1961
OPERATION:	BATTERY

VALUES:	
GOOD	$1000
EXCELLENT	$2000
MINT WITH ORIGINAL BOX	$4500

ROSKO-NOMURA
ASTRONAUT
JAPAN • CIRCA 1962

Once a toy has run its course in the marketplace, manufacturers are left with tools which, in most cases, are just as serviceable as they ever were — except that they create "tired" toys. But with a few strategic changes here and there, even old toys can become new again. That's the case with the legendary Rosko Astronaut, built by Nomura using the Mechanized Robot (Robby) platform. Legs, feet, chest, and even plastic head dome are all drawn straight from the original stamping and molding tools, with new lithography and interesting actions included to provide differentiation. The result is one of the more desirable toys from the early-1960s period — one so popular that it was an early-1990s subject of reproduction. Of the Rosko originals, two main color variations are known: blue and red, each with distinct lithographed astronaut faces. (Blue Roskos are dark-haired, while red examples tend toward blond.) During operation, the Astronaut walks forward, then stops, raises his arm, and "speaks" silently into his flashing and beeping walkie-talkie. When the communication is complete, the Astronaut again initiates his forward journey. Not inexpensive, Rosko Astronauts are particularly valuable when found in mint condition with original packaging. Note that the reproductions — which are quite faithful to the originals — are marked inside their leg battery compartments with the letters "OTTI."

MARKETER:	ROSKO
BUILDER:	NOMURA
RELEASED:	CIRCA 1962
OPERATION:	BATTERY

VALUES:	
GOOD	$1200
EXCELLENT	$2000
MINT WITH ORIGINAL BOX	$4500

ROSKO-DAIYA — ROSKO-NOMURA

ROSKO-NOMURA — SCHOPPER

ROSKO-NOMURA
MOBILE SPACE TV TANK WITH TRAILER
JAPAN • CIRCA 1962

KALMBACH IMAGES

With television penetration in excess of 50 percent by the early 1960s, it figures toymakers would integrate the newly ubiquitous concept into space toys. "Television spacemen" had been produced since the mid-1950s, but the inclusion of TV cameras was a concept which wouldn't emerge until the early '60s. Rosko Tested Toys marketed their iteration on this theme, called Mobile Space TV Tank with Trailer, around 1962. Built by Nomura, the TV Tank includes an astronaut driver who operates a vintage two-lens camera. During operation, the battery-op rolls along employing mystery action, its tank treads simulating locomotion. As it moves, illuminated space scenes project through the camera's translucent viewscreen. Back on the trailer — which houses two D cells — the stamped-tin antenna dish spins. The all-litho astronaut driver with bubble space helmet is a nice touch. Highly valued in mint-original package condition, even loose examples can be secured at reasonable values. Perfect for television- or tank-themed space toy displays, Rosko-Nomura's Mobile Space TV Tank with Trailer symbolizes the zenith of space toy production.

MARKETER:	ROSKO
BUILDER:	NOMURA
RELEASED:	CIRCA 1962
OPERATION:	BATTERY
VALUES:	
GOOD	$500
EXCELLENT	$1200
MINT WITH ORIGINAL BOX	$2500

SCHOPPER
AROUND THE WORLD
WEST GERMANY • CIRCA 1968

The 1960s were a boom time for tin-litho globe manufacturers. After all, what had formerly been an "educational gift" which bored children out of their skulls, now had an "outer space" feel, thanks to the American and Soviet space programs. Germany's Schopper released Around The World circa 1968. Starting with a globe toy, Schopper designers added a slide-lever mechanical actuator, which causes the globe to spin on its base. The final touch is the addition of three carnival-like spacecraft, grafted onto the globe with enameled-tin "arms." Add miniature space-explorer figures, and it's a mechanical midway ride for the outer space set. As one might expect, this toy was a low-end product from the onset, meaning few were given the respect necessary to survive the intervening years. As a result, Schopper's Around The World is actually a scarce toy today, particularly in mint-original box condition. All values provided necessitate the presence of all three spacecraft and "riders." For a taste of opportunistic globe-toy marketing, it doesn't get any better than Schopper's Around The World.

BUILDER:	SCHOPPER
RELEASED:	CIRCA 1968
OPERATION:	MECHANICAL
VALUES:	
GOOD	$400
EXCELLENT	$800
MINT WITH ORIGINAL BOX	$1600

SY

MECHANICAL WALKING SPACE MAN

JAPAN • CIRCA 1962

BUILDER:	SY
RELEASED:	CIRCA 1962
OPERATION:	WIND-UP

VALUES:	
GOOD	$300
EXCELLENT	$600
MINT WITH ORIGINAL BOX	$1200

Despite the fact that they created a successful line of robot toys, very little is known about Japanese toymaker SY. As some Japanese firms used the "S" prefix on acronymed formal names (e.g., "SH" equals Horikawa), some conjecture that SY might be an alternative brand for Yoshiya, which normally was identified by their "KO" mark. Whatever the heritage, the main tenets of SY include mechanical drivetrains; interesting lithographic design; and a large number of relatively scarce packaging variants across generally identical toys. These features all combine with Mechanical Walking Space Man. A 7½-inch wind-up, the toy boasts swinging claw-hand arms and forward walking motion. Unboxed versions are far more affordable, particularly in lesser conditions. As part of an interesting family of related robotic product, Mechanical Walking Space Man and its variants comprise a challenging group for collectors to identify and own.

ROBERT JOHNSON / COMET TOYS USA IMAGES

SY

MECHANICAL WALKING SPACE MAN

JAPAN • CIRCA 1965

This alternate version of Mechanical Walking Space Man by SY not only exhibits the later-style packaging found during the mid-1960s period, but also the twirling-antenna variation as well.

The toy features the standard swinging claw arms and true walking articulation during action, along with the aforementioned rotating antenna. Note this package is considered somewhat scarce.

Though so little is known about SY, the sheer number of variations on this toy is a well-known fact among seasoned space-toy collectors.

BUILDER:	SY
RELEASED:	CIRCA 1965
OPERATION:	WIND-UP

VALUES:	
GOOD	$600
EXCELLENT	$1200
MINT WITH ORIGINAL BOX	$2100

JAMES D. JULIA AUCTIONS IMAGES

SY
SPARKLING ASTRONAUT
JAPAN • CIRCA 1965

The great SY Mystery continues with Sparkling Astronaut, circa 1965. This basic six-inch paddle-walker features the same kind of drive train and many design elements found on toys manufactured by another enigmatic brand, N (1960s). Could it be that N and SY shared designs, production facilities, even corporate parents? Or, were they simply so enamored of one another's designs that their mutual love fest produced essentially copycat products throughout the 1960s? Or even worse, are these products the bastard stepchildren of companies like Nomura (T-N) or Yoshiya (KO)? Whichever way it falls, one thing is clear: SY made a tremendous amount of variants on this design, including nonsparkling versions and versions with head-mounted twirling antennae. The colorful litho of this toy is marred only by the rendering of the face art; the astronaut's pudgy visage and large, pursed lips don't win many converts. Still, the chest-mounted red gel allows viewing of the prodigious sparkling effect during wind-up operation. In the end, it's obvious that whoever built toys like Sparkling Astronaut didn't care so much about identification as they did profitability. And profit they did — these toys exist in fairly large quantities today, making their acquisition affordable and easy.

BUILDER:	SY
RELEASED:	CIRCA 1965
OPERATION:	WIND-UP
VALUES:	
GOOD	$125
EXCELLENT	$200
MINT WITH ORIGINAL BOX	$450

TPS
FLASH SPACE PATROL
JAPAN • CIRCA 1966

Flash Space Patrol, by TPS, is both mysterious and entrancing. This example dates from the 1966 period, when TPS (Tokyo Plaything Co., Ltd.) marketed it in the United States. The toy's "mystery" surrounds the fact that the eight-inch Flash Space Patrol seems to be from an earlier time. Yet it's quite clear this version was released in the mid-1960s; either TPS had marketed an iteration earlier in its corporate history, or this toy is merely a throwback to a happier, more creative time. Either way, the battery-op is a terrific plaything. Essentially an automated patrol vehicle, it features mystery action, a "whirling rotor blade," "flashing light from eyes," and engine noise. The sweptback styling and angular orientation of the toy's superstructure adds a sense of speed and style not usually found in Japanese space-vehicle design. Best of all, this toy is widely available today. While this isn't beneficial to high valuation, it does make TPS' Flash Space Patrol an affordable example of late-period quality design.

BUILDER:	TPS
RELEASED:	CIRCA 1966
OPERATION:	BATTERY
VALUES:	
GOOD	$100
EXCELLENT	$300
MINT WITH ORIGINAL BOX	$450

BUILDER:	TPS
RELEASED:	CIRCA 1964
OPERATION:	BATTERY
◆	
VALUES:	
GOOD	**$350**
EXCELLENT	**$550**
MINT WITH ORIGINAL BOX	**$850**

TPS
MAGIC COLOR MOON EXPRESS
JAPAN • CIRCA 1964

In the future, when food comes in pill form and everyone drives around in flying cars, Greyhound buses will resemble TPS' Magic Color Moon Express. And why not? This rendition of tomorrow's mass transit merges the style and form factor of a 1930s-era streamlined steam locomotive with the utility of a passenger bus and a touch of Walt Disney-esque monorail styling, for good measure.

Speaking of measure, the battery-operated toy clocks in at a whopping 14½ inches in length. During operation, the toy careens about the floor thanks to mystery action. All the while, its top-mounted cockpit enjoys illumination, as does the whirling rocket toy-sourced plastic tail section. But all the major business gets done up front, where the "magic color" action can be found behind the whirling bulletnose. As the somewhat crude package art depicts, the toy projects a kaleidoscope-like panoply of colors through the translucent-white nosecone during operation, to great effect, no doubt. Easily found, and a little too close to those ultra-common Japanese whistling train toys of the 1960s, Magic Color Moon Express doesn't receive the respect it probably should, resulting in lower-than-expected valuations. Even so, it's a fanciful toy that is one of only a handful of space-related playthings to emerge from Tokyo Playthings Co., Ltd.

UNKNOWN
APOLLO ASTRONAUT
UNITED KINGDOM • CIRCA 1961

Here's a toy that's something of an enigma. While it's not known who built Apollo Astronaut, as it's called, the toy is marked "Made in United Kingdom." The 7½-inch toy itself is one of those painted, jointed-wood "dancing" figures which, when hung by its head hook, can be made to move and "dance" by pulling the string which emerges from the chassis, as it were. It's clearly a space-themed toy by its astronaut-style "headset" ears and silver space suit finish. The crowning touch is the "Apollo" marking (though not a NASA logotype) over the toy's heart region. Yet, all research indicates this toy comes from around 1961; few if any in popular culture knew anything beyond NASA's Mercury and Gemini program names during this period, so it's unclear whether this toy is the beneficiary of a lucky guess, or has been misidentified regarding date of issuance. Whatever, it's a low-value plaything that raises more questions than it answers. As it was originally marketed on a card, the mint-original package reflects this condition.

BUILDER:	UNKNOWN
RELEASED:	CIRCA 1961
OPERATION:	MECHANICAL
◆	
VALUES:	
GOOD	**$65**
EXCELLENT	**$125**
MINT ON ORIGINAL CARD	**$350**

TPS — UNKNOWN

145

UNKNOWN
ROBOT

JAPAN • CIRCA 1969

As plastic began to overtake lithographed tin as the medium of choice, robots began to change in substantial ways. As this four-inch Robot by an unknown Japanese manufacturer demonstrates, everything was suddenly different. In the absence of lithography, details had to come from relief cavities in the tools; flash was dependent on vacu-plated parts; and personality had to come from mold-in-color plastic. But as Robot also illustrates, change isn't such a bad thing when it comes to affordable play value. Wound up and switched on, this toy hops around, while its arms swing to the beat of the unheard robotic music. Believed to have emerged around 1969, Robot comes in plain yellow packaging with neo-realistic illustrated art. In fact, the entire packaging presentation is more like a period Matchbox package than it is a robot's box. And, just maybe, that's exactly how the manufacturer wanted it.

BUILDER:	UNKNOWN
RELEASED:	CIRCA 1969
OPERATION:	WIND-UP
VALUES:	
GOOD	**$100**
EXCELLENT	**$200**
MINT WITH ORIGINAL BOX	**$400**

ROBERT JOHNSON / COMET TOYS USA IMAGES

WACO
NEW SPACE REFUEL STATION

JAPAN • CIRCA 1961

Waco's New Space Refuel Station is a landmark toy for so many reasons. First, it's startlingly prescient in its industrial design, accurately foretelling the design of communications satellites. Next, it boasts terrific operation, with animated figures and glowing illumination. Third, it's believed to be the only space toy by Waco, and one of the few toys even marketed by the obscure Japanese brand. And finally, it's highly scarce. The toy is remarkable in its portending of bounce-paneled orbital objects. Switched on, the toy mystery actions about the floor, then comes to a stop. Suddenly, the toy lifts itself up and begins turning furiously in a circle — like a satellite. Because it's a space station, there are two dockable space vehicles: a delta-winged US fighter, and a bulbous, Russian-style craft. Both can be manually "docked" at any of the four ports by pushing their metal-rod noses into snug-fitting receptacles. Little is known of Waco; the name may be a contraction of a W-initialed Japanese surname. The toy comes in beautifully illustrated packaging which depicts the toy orbiting the rugged lunar surface. Rare and desirable, totally unique, and one of the best.

BUILDER:	WACO
RELEASED:	CIRCA 1961
OPERATION:	BATTERY
VALUES:	
GOOD	**$4000**
EXCELLENT	**$6000**
MINT WITH ORIGINAL BOX	**$8000**

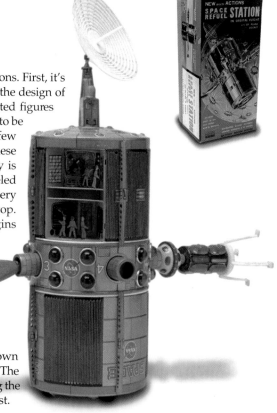

UNKNOWN — WACO

JAMES D. JULIA AUCTIONS IMAGE

YONEZAWA
(CONEHEAD) ROBOT
JAPAN • CIRCA 1962

Popularly known as Conehead, Yonezawa's Robot is the last in that company's four-member product family built around the Robby Robot (1950s) wind-up leg and torso assembly. The line started with 1958's Robby, then progressed to X-27 Robot, the flared-head toy with unruly antennae; was relaunched in 1960 with the release of Roby Robot (1960s); and culminated in 1962 with Conehead. The shared components remain remarkably unchanged: the bulbous, Robby the Robot-style legs and feet; the cylindrical torso with the color-litho gauge chest plate; and the cheap, stamped-and-plated tin "claw hands," which dangle from Robby-style forearms. Where this toy departs from the family with alacrity is in the head region. The giant conical assembly sports comically shaped "eyes," which are actually red gels, behind which sparkling can be seen during mechanical operation. Two rubber "ears" and a rubber head tip project outward, presumably to prevent damage during inevitable tipovers. Original Conehead packaging is extremely difficult to locate, and even more difficult are the package's always-missing cardboard inserts. Some have surmised that Conehead Robot is inspired by a period Japanese television character, but this has not been confirmed. Original Japanese packaging depicted in books by tin-toy godfather Teruhisa Kitahara does depict the toy "launching," *Gigantor/Tetsujin-26* style, into the air while a TV-style boy positioned nearby leaps in approval. Whatever the case, this family of Yonezawa product was developmentally retired after the release of Conehead, their 8½-inch run in the marketplace complete.

BUILDER:	YONEZAWA
RELEASED:	CIRCA 1962
OPERATION:	WIND-UP

VALUES:

GOOD	$1400
EXCELLENT	$2500
MINT WITH ORIGINAL BOX	$4500

YONEZAWA
(DIRECTIONAL) ROBOT
JAPAN • CIRCA 1963

Fame isn't everything. The best-known member of Yonezawa's skirted-robot family is Cragstan's Mr. Robot, the enameled-red, clear-domed brainiac that started it all. Lesser members include Modern Robot, Jupiter Robot, and Talking Robot (1960s). But it's Robot — or Directional Robot, as it's commonly known — who ultimately gets the nod for creative evolution. Directional Robot, it turns out, is the only Yonezawa skirted (no legs, hidden mystery action drivetrain) robot to feature a turning head. That's right: when Directional Robot mystery-actions its way into an impedance, the automaton turns its head and heads out in a newly chosen direction. With its almost clinical color scheme and modernistic, purpose-built face and chest-plate, Directional Robot doesn't have the simplistic charm of Yonezawa's earlier skirted toys, but this single animation feature alone earns Directional its due among today's robot enthusiasts.

BUILDER:	YONEZAWA
RELEASED:	CIRCA 1963
OPERATION:	BATTERY

VALUES:

GOOD	$1000
EXCELLENT	$1800
MINT WITH ORIGINAL BOX	$2800

The toy also features eye and head-signal illumination, and it swings its arms twitchingly during operation. Original packaging is very scarce for this toy, adding a meaningful premium to the value of loose mint examples. For a true head-turning experience, nothing beats Yonezawa's Directional Robot.

YONEZAWA

YONEZAWA

YONEZAWA
(DIRECTIONAL) ROBOT
JAPAN • CIRCA 1964

Yonezawa marketed a second version of Directional Robot around 1964, perhaps a year or so after the first incarnation's release. Essentially identical, including packaging, the toy does feature a small number of superficial changes. In particular, relief-stamped patterns to the left and right of the central lithographed gauge array have been removed, perhaps due to irregularities during the stamping process. Also changed are the tabbed connection points for the mystery-action wheel-drivetrain; on the original, they are located within the central recess of the skirt; on this version, they've been relocated to the two proud (outside) panels of the skirt. It's likely this was the final version of Directional Robot, a toy whose head turns whenever it strikes an object (hence its popular name). Within a few short years, most large-format robots like this (Directional stands 11 inches) would be removed from manufacturers' lines as too costly to produce, relative to marketplace demand and return on investment. It was truly the end of an era.

BUILDER:	YONEZAWA
RELEASED:	CIRCA 1964
OPERATION:	BATTERY

VALUES:
GOOD	**$1000**
EXCELLENT	**$1800**
MINT WITH ORIGINAL BOX	**$2800**

JAMES D. JULIA AUCTIONS IMAGES

YONEZAWA
EIGHTMAN
JAPAN • CIRCA 1966

The end of the classic period in Japanese robot manufacture coincided with the rise in Japanese superhero culture. The progenitors of this trend — *Gigantor/Tetsujin-26*, *Astroboy*, and *Giant Robot* — were all Japanese TV shows which melded the mechanical with the heroic. The resulting concept: a powerful force which battled on behalf of the defenseless. In 1966, Japanese TV debuted its latest from this fold: *Eightman*. Part machine and part man, Eightman was an early Robocop, created by his employers to fight crime on a cyborgian level. Yonezawa's massive 14-inch battery-op captures the look of the character nicely. Animations include forward walking, swinging arms, and an illuminated collar which displays red and green lighting. Original packaging is equally sharp, with an illustration of the *Eightman* character flying across the sky as ICBMs streak through the background. As a toy that was primarily for the domestic market, few examples are seen outside of Japan, except in collections which focus on Japanese superheroes. Rare and highly collectible, Yonezawa's Eightman was a harbinger of the coming change for Japanese toy design and popular culture alike.

BUILDER:	YONEZAWA
RELEASED:	CIRCA 1966
OPERATION:	BATTERY

VALUES:
GOOD	**$6500**
EXCELLENT	**$9500**
MINT WITH ORIGINAL BOX	**$15000**

ROBERT JOHNSON / COMET TOYS USA IMAGES

YONEZAWA
FLYING SAUCER SPACE PATROL
JAPAN • CIRCA 1966

As a bizarre cross between an Everglades swamper airboat and an alien flying saucer, Yonezawa's Flying Saucer Space Patrol is one of the weirder throw-togethers known to space-toy collecting. Made from a basic body stamping shared with another Yonezawa toy, the Mego Mercury X-1 Flying Saucer (1960s), Flying Saucer Space Patrol features standard late-saucer motifs: central domed control area, miniature "astronaut"/alien at the helm; mystery action; flashing lights; "space noise"; and garish lithographic art. But the toy goes one step further, and adds a giant "fan" assembly to the rear of the craft. The effect is nothing short of hilarious; during operation, the toy mystery-actions about the floor as the light-sound show plays and the fan turns. Two versions are known; red fan/yellow enclosure, and yellow fan/red enclosure. Perhaps most notable about Flying Saucer Space Patrol is the shape-of-things-to-come wedge-style package, so created to accommodate the verticality of the fan. Inexpensive and pursued mainly by saucer fans, the toy's valuations represent marketplace scarcity for this late-period product. Yonezawa's Flying Saucer Space Patrol shows what can happen when brain drain finally reaches the development department.

BUILDER:	YONEZAWA
RELEASED:	CIRCA 1966
OPERATION:	BATTERY
VALUES:	
GOOD	$200
EXCELLENT	$300
MINT WITH ORIGINAL BOX	$450

YONEZAWA
MECHANIC ROBOT
JAPAN • CIRCA 1969

One of the very late Yonezawa robots is Mechanic Robot, a battery-operated automaton that combines classic-period elements into a plastic package. By 1969, when this toy is believed to have been first released, Yonezawa was nearing the end of its run as a toymaker. Soaring labor and materials costs were sending most Japanese toy production to Hong Kong and Taiwan, where similar toys could be manufactured for a fraction of the cost required by Tokyo production. It was under these conditions that Mechanic Robot was released, and it shows. Cost reduction is everywhere; what might have been metal only a few years prior is now plastic; play patterns are combined from a disparate variety of formerly successful toys; and packaging reflects the amount of investment Yonezawa put into it (*none*). Still, battery-ops like Mechanic Robot, with its phone-dial play pattern, forward walking motion, and interior lighting through translucent plastic components, would lead the way for those who survived the impending shake-out. The future, as toys like this demonstrate, would be cost-reduced, nonmetallic, and more based on Japanese animation themes than self-designed concepts which had been industry staples for the last 20 years.

BUILDER:	YONEZAWA
RELEASED:	CIRCA 1969
OPERATION:	BATTERY
VALUES:	
GOOD	$150
EXCELLENT	$250
MINT WITH ORIGINAL BOX	$350

YONEZAWA

YONEZAWA

YONEZAWA
MODERN ROBOT
JAPAN • CIRCA 1962

Maybe Cragstan hadn't paid their bill in a timely manner. Perhaps the check was still in the mail. Who knows? What is clear is that Yonezawa wasted little time in marketing their own version of Cragstan Robot, using their own branding and calling it Modern Robot. The toys are essentially identical, with the exception of revised lithography on the chest plate. Even the packaging is identical, with the exception of the toy being called "Modern" instead of "Cragstan." Concurrent reissuing was commonplace during the hey-day of Japanese toy manufacture; some-times distribution partners didn't pay for an exclusive, leaving the door open for a flood of iden-tical toys revised only in brand-ing. Whatever the case, of course, Modern Robot only serves to swell the Mr. Robot-based family (1960s) to larger levels; other mem-bers include the aforemen-tioned Modern Robot (1960s), Talking Robot (1960s), Jupiter Robot, and Directional Robot (1960s). There's a lesson here, no doubt: make sure the distribution agreement includes at least a year of exclu-sivity, or toys like Modern Robot are certain to follow.

BUILDER:	YONEZAWA
RELEASED:	CIRCA 1962
OPERATION:	BATTERY
VALUES:	
GOOD	$1200
EXCELLENT	$1800
MINT WITH ORIGINAL BOX	$2600

ROBERT JOHNSON / COMET TOYS USA IMAGES

YONEZAWA
MR. MERCURY
JAPAN • 1961

The best toy mysteries are the ones that defy conventional wisdom. In the case of Mr. Mercury, it's the three versions and the order in which they were released. Most believe this version (plastic paddle-arms, head-mounted warning light, plastic-relief "Mr. Mercury" chestplate) is the final version. *Wrong.* Research with Japanese toy historians in possession of Yonezawa Mr. Mercury blueprints shows that not only is this Mr. Mercury the first release from 1961, but its design dates to 1957-58. Yonezawa designers wanted to move toward plastic far earlier than most credit them. To Yonezawa, this Mr. Mercury was cutting-edge. Thus, the first run was marketed by Yonezawa and appeared in 1961 (Sears carried it for $5.99). Linemar elected to pick up the second run, but preferred an all-metal arm version, according to these same historians, thus the change to the more traditional arm stamping. The second version, blue with a lithographed chestplate (1960s), was marketed by Linemar in 1962-63, followed by the final gold version (1960s), in 1963-64. Though many will hotly dispute this timeline interpretation, the research is solid and the sources dependable: 13-inch Mr. Mercury debuted with plastic arms, then regressed to tin for its final two itera-tions. Period. (Nothing like a little unequivocation, huh?)

BUILDER:	YONEZAWA
RELEASED:	1961
OPERATION:	BATTERY
VALUES:	
GOOD	$1000
EXCELLENT	$1800
MINT WITH ORIGINAL BOX	$2800

YONEZAWA
NASA ROCKET
JAPAN • CIRCA 1967

The vertical rocketship enjoyed two heydays during the postwar period of tin toy manufacture. The first was during the early-to-late 1950s timeframe, when images from films like *Destination Moon* sent toymakers scurrying to release myriad interpretations on the long, tapered-end rocket standing upright on its stabilizing fins. Later, when reality had caught up with science fiction, the mid- to late-1960s witnessed a second explosion of vertical rocket toys — this time based on the reality of NASA's massive Saturn V rockets, which would ultimately be used to ferry men to the moon. Yonezawa's 16-inch NASA Rocket, from around 1967, is their take on this burgeoning category niche. Like most of its competitors, the toy begins its operational sequence as a wheel-based horizontal toy, rolling around the floor until it reaches the second phase, vertical "liftoff." A camouflaged lifting arm then extends from the toy's chassis, slowly lifting the toy up and back until it rests on its plastic base, at which point a "countdown" commences. Throughout, lights flash in the nose and "cockpit" capsule window. Lithographed in period-standard light-blue for "added realism," Yonezawa's NASA Rocket brings slightly higher-than-normal values, due to its marketplace scarcity. To step back into the majesty of the Saturn V era, look no further than toys like Y's NASA Rocket.

BUILDER:	YONEZAWA
RELEASED:	CIRCA 1967
OPERATION:	BATTERY
VALUES:	
GOOD	**$200**
EXCELLENT	**$300**
MINT WITH ORIGINAL BOX	**$550**

YONEZAWA
ROBY ROBOT
JAPAN • CIRCA 1960

As the third release in Yonezawa's eight-inch wind-up robot/astronaut family, Roby Robot suffers from the same malady as many middle children — lack of attention and differentiation. It's easy to see why, when its peers are considered: the child-astronaut Robby Robot (1950s); flared-head X-27 Robot; and 1962's Conehead Robot each have their own distinctive personality. Roby Robot, with its goofy name and circuit board for a face, just doesn't quite measure up. Of course, collectors see the situation differently; Roby commands solid valuation today, thanks to scarcity and inclusion in that desirable eight-inch Yonezawa family. From the neck down, Roby is like its brothers; sausage-link legs house an eccentric-wheel drive mechanism that allows the toy to waddle forward during operation; sparkling is visible through the red-gel "mouth" region; and the obligatory (and cheap) stamped-claw hands dangle lifelessly from Robby the Robot-inspired stumps. Roby's original package is a dynamite addition to any loose example, with values that reflect its scarcity. Yonezawa would wind this family up, as it were, with Conehead Robot (1960s) in the 1962 timeframe. That more famous sibling only served to further push middle-child Roby into the shadows.

BUILDER:	YONEZAWA
RELEASED:	CIRCA 1960
OPERATION:	WIND-UP
VALUES:	
GOOD	**$1400**
EXCELLENT	**$2500**
MINT WITH ORIGINAL BOX	**$3800**

JAMES D. JULIA AUCTIONS IMAGES

YONEZAWA

YONEZAWA

YONEZAWA
SEA HAWK FUTURE CAR
JAPAN • CIRCA 1964

Future cars have long been staples in the toy industry, beginning with early stylized interpretations in the 1930s and continuing to this very day. But the 1950s and '60s were glory days for this category. It was a time of great forward thinking; Detroit automakers furiously cranked out "futuristic" designs for the auto show circuit; and best of all, future cars didn't

require authenticity. It was during this remarkably accepting time that Yonezawa's Sea Hawk emerged. Styled between the Ichida Ford Gyron of 1960 and the Jetsons' family saucer of 1965, this circa-1964 car speeds along using mystery action to keep it from being held up by impedances. Perhaps the most appealing part of this toy is its package, which depicts an alternative-color version of the Sea Hawk cruising along a futuristic highway, at speed, while the cities of the future whiz past in the background. As a typical hybrid toy, this time merging the vehicle and space-toy categories, Yonezawa's Sea Hawk offers an inexpensive look into the future. Just squint the eyes and see if vehicles like the Triumph TR7, Dodge Charger Daytona, and even Ford Probe don't come to mind.

BUILDER:	YONEZAWA
RELEASED:	CIRCA 1964
OPERATION:	BATTERY
VALUES:	
GOOD	**$200**
EXCELLENT	**$350**
MINT WITH ORIGINAL BOX	**$650**

YONEZAWA
SMOKING SPACEMAN
JAPAN • 1960

Released at the height of the robot craze, 1960, Yonezawa's Smoking Spaceman combines terrific styling with fabulous animation to create one of the all-time favorite Japanese toys. Metal construction gives the 12-inch toy a substantial feel, while expressionless facial styling and blocky design convey the emotionally detached

might of an automaton. But it's smoking that still drives the toy's popularity. During operation, the toy walks, its lights and plastic mohawk dome glowing eerily in the night, while it puffs clean, white smoke from its mouth. The presentation is at once terrifying and hilariously entertaining, probably just the reaction Yonezawa designers were looking for. Two main variations include a Linemar-branded toy and one marketed by its builder, shown here. Sears carried the toy in 1960 for $3.77. Unmarked reproductions exist; be wary. Mint-original package examples fetch strong response from enthusiasts, due primarily to the difficulty today in finding Smoking Spacemen who still smoke, as it were. Reformed or inveterate, Smoking Spaceman is an all-time classic deserving of its accolades.

BUILDER:	YONEZAWA
RELEASED:	1960
OPERATION:	BATTERY
VALUES:	
GOOD	**$1200**
EXCELLENT	**$1800**
MINT WITH ORIGINAL BOX	**$3500**

YONEZAWA
SPACE PATROL
JAPAN • CIRCA 1964

Resplendent in Vietnam-era green, Yonezawa's Space Patrol circa 1964 is wartime toymaking at its finest. During periods of military activity, toys inevitably take on attributes which are identified with the social conflict of the day. In the case of space toys, this means silver-blue lithographic designs gave way to olive drab, as on Space Patrol. It features "non fall action" (mystery action), which lets it travel to a table's edge yet always remain in action, out of danger. For enhanced impact, Yonezawa included a rotating stamped-tin antenna dish and a "disappearing cockpit" feature, which opens and closes during operation. All the while, the toy's insect-like coil-spring antennae flop helplessly. As an inexpensive example of the mid-1960s toy industry, Space Patrol represents an affordale entry-level collectible within reach of most budgets. And that olive-drab green goes with just about any space-themed setting, as well.

BUILDER:	YONEZAWA
RELEASED:	CIRCA 1964
OPERATION:	BATTERY
VALUES:	
GOOD	**$400**
EXCELLENT	**$600**
MINT WITH ORIGINAL BOX	**$1200**

YONEZAWA
THE ROBOT "CAPTAIN"
JAPAN • CIRCA 1968

A late-period toy from a once-great manufacturer, Yonezawa's The Robot "Captain" shows that even a defeated creative genius can still put out good product while in its death throes. That's certainly the case with this 5½-inch automaton, created mainly from plastic with an inexpensive wind-up walking and sparkling mechanism for animated entertainment. The 50/50 mixture of plastic and metal suggests that even in its darkest days, Yonezawa was trying to maintain the perception of quality, even at low price points such as that of Robot "Captain." This down-market plaything features chest-mounted sparkling and scissors-style walking motion, in which legs travel up and over one another, their feet-stabilizers meshing with one another each step of the way. The lithography on the torso is actually quite nice and shows off fine attention to detail — another example of design pride, no matter how cost-reduced the overall plaything. Even the packaging suggests some effort, with a Horikawa-like image of the toy powering along, sparks shooting from its chest. No explanation exists for the toy's name nor its ungainly use of quotation marks. Exceedingly affordable in today's collecting environment, Robot "Captains" can be had in mint-original package condition for terrific values.

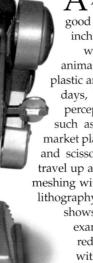

BUILDER:	YONEZAWA
RELEASED:	CIRCA 1968
OPERATION:	WIND-UP
VALUES:	
GOOD	**$85**
EXCELLENT	**$150**
MINT WITH ORIGINAL BOX	**$295**

YONEZAWA

YONEZAWA
X-5 MOON PATROL VEHICLE
JAPAN • CIRCA 1962

KALMBACH IMAGE

Always keep 'em guessing. That's just what Yonezawa's X-5 Moon Patrol Vehicle had going for it upon release around 1962. This tank-based vehicle appears to be benign; it cruises across all sorts of alien landscapes using mystery action while its radar dish and astronaut crow's nest rotate. But what *is* that in the crow's nest? A television camera? Or death ray? Only X-5's adversaries know the real story, and likely most of them aren't talking — or even still around. As a member of Yonezawa's small tank-based space vehicle family of product, the nine-inch X-5 didn't set the world on fire, but it likely torched a few adversaries using its camouflaged "television camera"/death ray. Colorfully lithographed and available in at least two color variations (silver-blue and baby-blue), the Moon Patrol Vehicle is a fine example of early late-period toy design: nice litho, good actions, colorful illumination (particularly in the camera/ray gun), terrific box art, and a minimum of plastic componentry. Though the packaging is quite nice, it doesn't bring the expected premium, perhaps due to a high survival rate. Smile, you're on X-5 TV — if you *dare*.

BUILDER:	YONEZAWA
RELEASED:	CIRCA 1962
OPERATION:	BATTERY

VALUES:
GOOD	$800
EXCELLENT	$1600
MINT WITH ORIGINAL BOX	$2100

YOSHINO
SPACE FRONTIER
JAPAN • CIRCA 1969

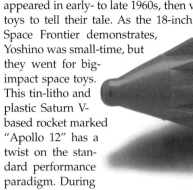

Yoshino, who marketed their toys under the "KY" brand, is yet another enigmatic company on the forgotten landscape of postwar Japanese toy manufacture. They appeared in early- to late 1960s, then vanished, leaving a handful of toys to tell their tale. As the 18-inch Space Frontier demonstrates, Yoshino was small-time, but they went for big-impact space toys. This tin-litho and plastic Saturn V-based rocket marked "Apollo 12" has a twist on the standard performance paradigm. During

BUILDER:	YONEZAWA
RELEASED:	CIRCA 1969
OPERATION:	BATTERY

VALUES:
GOOD	$200
EXCELLENT	$300
MINT WITH ORIGINAL BOX	$550

operation, it mystery-actions its way around the floor, its illuminated translucent nosecone spinning all the while. Then, it suddenly stops, and a small, top-mounted access door opens to reveal an astronaut and his television camera on a folding gantry arm. After capturing needed imagery, the astronaut reenters the vehicle, and it heads out in search of more impedances and adventures. It's likely Space Frontier was one of Yoshino's biggest hits, as this toy exists in fairly large quantities today. As a result, values are in the seriously affordable range, even for mint-original package examples. (The box itself is a good example of late-period, reality-based package design.) Like so many forgotten companies, Yoshino must now rely on its toys to speak for its creative intent, now and into the future.

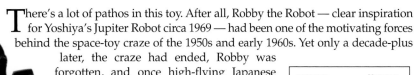

YOSHIYA
JUPITER ROBOT
JAPAN • CIRCA 1969

There's a lot of pathos in this toy. After all, Robby the Robot — clear inspiration for Yoshiya's Jupiter Robot circa 1969 — had been one of the motivating forces behind the space-toy craze of the 1950s and early 1960s. Yet only a decade-plus later, the craze had ended, Robby was forgotten, and once high-flying Japanese toymakers now found themselves crashed on the beach. Which is what makes Jupiter Robot all the more pathetic; made almost entirely from unpainted plastic, the humble little seven-inch wind-up and sparkling walker is barely a shadow of even the low-budget Robby toys from a decade earlier. Perhaps not surprisingly, collectors pursue this rather common toy today, not only as an example of late-period Japanese toy manufacture, but also as a thematic coda for the entire Robby-inspired generation of Japanese toymaking.

BUILDER:	YOSHIYA
RELEASED:	CIRCA 1969
OPERATION:	WIND-UP

VALUES:	
GOOD	$100
EXCELLENT	$150
MINT WITH ORIGINAL BOX	$300

YOSHIYA
KING FLYING SAUCER
JAPAN • CIRCA 1968

When a toy gets named "King" by its builder, it must be good, right? Uh, *right*. Certainly Yoshiya had lofty ambitions for King Flying Saucer, a circa-1968 battery-op. The toy comes in a nicely illustrated package featuring numerous Kings swooping into a desolate lunar landscape. Even the late-period litho design is competent. But overall, the toy weighs in as a lackluster effort, owing to the industrial design — a kind of fattened Frisbee — and goofy actions. During operation, the toy mystery actions about as its top-mounted color gels receive a circular illumina-tion effect. Then, the toy stops and lifts itself slightly, waddling left and right ungraciously. While this dynamic might work for the robots of N (1960s), it's not the most terror-inducing action for a flying saucer. As a late-period toy with decent distribution, King Flying Saucer can be found at very affordable values — which makes that waddle all the more priceless, no doubt.

BUILDER:	YOSHIYA
RELEASED:	CIRCA 1968
OPERATION:	BATTERY

VALUES:	
GOOD	$100
EXCELLENT	$150
MINT WITH ORIGINAL BOX	$300

YOSHIYA

YOSHIYA
SPACE GUN
JAPAN • CIRCA 1964

The "ray gun" as a toy category extends back to the 1930s, when Daisy pioneered the concept with *Buck Rogers*-licensed toy sidearms (PRE-1940s). By the 1950s, however, most inexpensive outer-space weaponry was coming from Japan, and it continued into the 1960s with toys like Space Gun by Yoshiya. A small click-style toy sidearm, Space Gun features nice lithography and interesting, if derivative, industrial design. Most toys like Space Gun were extremely affordable during their initial release periods, and as such, generally were sold to the trade in bulk packs, from which retailers would draw and restock shelves accordingly. Thus, Space Gun's best valuation is simply for "mint" condition, as original packaging (other than master cartons) simply does not exist. Toys like this are prized by toy sidearm collectors, and dedicated ray-gun collectors devote serious study to the variations and iterations of products such as this. For good clicking fun, nothing beats toys like Space Gun by Yoshiya.

BUILDER:	YOSHIYA
RELEASED:	CIRCA 1964
OPERATION:	MECHANICAL

VALUES:	
GOOD	$55
EXCELLENT	$90
MINT	$150

YOSHIYA
SPACE JET RAY GUN
JAPAN • CIRCA 1962

Moving slightly upmarket from Space Gun (1960s) was Space Jet ray gun. Though similar in look, this Yoshiya toy sidearm uses its own stamping tools, as well as the characteristic plastic "emitter" at the barrel's end. Though the toy likely would have benefitted tremendously from illumination or sparkling, it remains a humble click gun. It's believed that Yoshiya used these tools as far back as the late 1950s, but best research places this version in the early 1960s. At 9½ inches in length, Space Jet ray gun can be found with its original packaging, though at a premium, due in large part to its popularity with ray gun and general toy sidearm collectors alike.

BUILDER:	YOSHIYA
RELEASED:	CIRCA 1962
OPERATION:	MECHANICAL

VALUES:	
GOOD	$100
EXCELLENT	$250
MINT WITH ORIGINAL BOX	$550

YOSHIYA

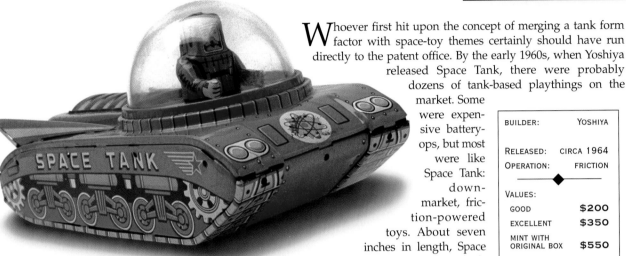

YOSHIYA
SPACE TANK
JAPAN • CIRCA 1964

Whoever first hit upon the concept of merging a tank form factor with space-toy themes certainly should have run directly to the patent office. By the early 1960s, when Yoshiya released Space Tank, there were probably dozens of tank-based playthings on the market. Some were expensive battery-ops, but most were like Space Tank: down-market, friction-powered toys. About seven inches in length, Space Tank rumbles along when pushed, spewing sparks inside a red-plastic gel mounted just astern the control dome. Meanwhile, inside that dome a square-headed astronaut holds on for dear life (or so its grip would suggest). The toy's litho is pure early late-period; primary colors dominate, with neo-realistic lettering and detail. Nicely packaged, Space Tank is one of the more "findable" toys from the early 1960s, with contemporary values which reflect this lack of scarcity.

BUILDER:	YOSHIYA
RELEASED:	CIRCA 1964
OPERATION:	FRICTION

VALUES:	
GOOD	$200
EXCELLENT	$350
MINT WITH ORIGINAL BOX	$550

YOSHIYA
SPACEMAN RAY GUN
JAPAN • CIRCA 1968

Yoshiya marketed a deco variation on the standard 9½-inch Space Jet (1960s) ray gun in the 1968 period, called Spaceman. Altered lithography creates a more fanciful presentation; on the gun's grip is a rocket in mid-liftoff, while the butt of the barrel is home to a spaceman illustration (hence, the gun's name). Light-blue fields provide a background against which Yoshiya designers integrated their spot illustration, while red plastic fills in for the "emitter" portion of the ray gun. Less desirable than the Space Jet piece on which it's based, Spaceman ray gun is a good entry-level toy sidearm.

BUILDER:	YOSHIYA
RELEASED:	CIRCA 1968
OPERATION:	MECHANICAL

VALUES:	
GOOD	$85
EXCELLENT	$125
MINT WITH ORIGINAL BOX	$200

THE 1970S

STAR ROBOT

CIRCA 1978

BY **CDI**

HONG KONG

THE 1970s

In the end, when robots and space toys had finished their marketplace run, there was very little sadness or public display of remorse. Time had moved on; builders and marketers had wrung the life from this once-vibrant category.

Perhaps most important was the change which took place in the consumer's mind. No longer was the concept of an "outer space" toy novel or interesting; in fact, even the American space program would wind down by 1974, the victim of declining popular interest and sagging financial support. Even going to the Moon had become passé.

Rising overhead costs had decimated most of the major names in Japanese toymaking. Many went under, others retooled and became manufacturers of consumer electronics, and a few survived to continue their toymaking ways.

One country's loss is often another's gain, and as Japan's fortunes waned, those in Hong Kong and Taiwan began to rise. Many of the 1970s' more memorable playthings would emerge from these enclaves outside the People's Republic of China. Indeed, throughout the 1970s, it was far more likely to come across a toy marked "Made in Hong Kong" or "Made in Taiwan" than it was "Made in Japan."

And in 1977, with the arrival of George Lucas' groundbreaking *Star Wars*, space toys would once again rise up — but this time, in a completely new and different way. Licensing was the new path toy makers would follow; no more would fanciful, in-house designs be the Next Big Thing. For that, such ideas would have to come from outside. And so it is, to this very day.

AHI
LOST IN SPACE ROBOT
JAPAN • CIRCA 1977

By the 1970s, most people had forgotten about the Irwin Allen classic *Lost In Space* — except for a hardcore cadre of fans who continued to keep the magic alive through fanzines, public shows, and the like. Japanese toybuilder AHI offered something for this group in the 1977 period with the release of the *Lost In Space* Robot. Clocking in at 10 inches in height, the plastic toy spans the distance between the Remco 1968 original and the contemporary, voice chip-equipped models of today. It's unclear whether this AHI is related to the Naito Shoten (1950s) AN/AHI Toys brand, but it is possible there is a descendant role being played here. Valued largely by *LIS* collectors, this toy isn't quite faithful to the television robot's form factor, but it is close enough — and odd enough — to warrant collector attention.

BUILDER:	AHI
RELEASED:	CIRCA 1977
OPERATION:	BATTERY
VALUES:	
GOOD	$450
EXCELLENT	$600
MINT WITH ORIGINAL BOX	$1200

AMICO-HORIKAWA
ROTATE-O-MATIC SUPER ASTRONAUT
JAPAN • CIRCA 1972

One of Horikawa's 1960s innovations was the Rotate-O-Matic feature, phased into the higher price points of their 11-inch Robot/Astronaut product line. Before its advent, Horikawa robots and astronauts walked, stopped in place, and chest-fired cannon at would-be attackers. With the dawning of Rotate-O-Matic, however, attackers located anywhere around such an equipped toy were at their peril; the toy rotates 360 degrees while blasting the chest-fire gun effect. By 1972, this feature certainly added cost in an overly price-conscious market, so Horikawa only used it on their best releases, such as 1972's Rotate-O-Matic Super Astronaut, marketed in conjunction with Amico. It's an interesting toy, as for the most part, Horikawa went its own way when marketing toys. Still, by the lean 1970s timeframe, it was probably just the ticket to help pay the electric bill. And for Horikawa enthusiasts, toys like this Rotate-O-Matic Super Astronaut offer a point of interest and differentiation, all at once.

MARKETER:	AMICO
BUILDER:	HORIKAWA
RELEASED:	CIRCA 1972
OPERATION:	BATTERY
VALUES:	
GOOD	$100
EXCELLENT	$180
MINT WITH ORIGINAL BOX	$250

AMICO-UNKNOWN
ACROBAT ROBOT
JAPAN • CIRCA 1979

Amico was a small-time importer along the lines of Cragstan or Rosko, bringing Japan-built toy product into the United States for wholesale and retail sale. Amico worked with many differing manufacturers, including majors like Masudaya (1960s). But as time passed and the 1970s dragged on, it becomes more difficult for toy historians to accurately determine their manufacturing partners. One key example is Acrobat Robot circa 1979. With key design elements owed to the creations of George Lucas, Acrobat Robot reflects elements of R2D2 and other *Star Wars* droids, particularly from the bowels of the Jawa sandcrawler. Despite its derivative nature, this is a terrific little battery-op. Switched on, the toy performs end-over-end tumbling while its translucent-red "brain" glows approvingly. The vacuum-plated plastic componentry either helps or hurts the toy's nonmetallic nature, depending on one's opinion. A late toy with interesting actions — that's Acrobat Robot, by Amico and an unknown manufacturer.

MARKETER:	AMICO
BUILDER:	UNKNOWN
RELEASED:	CIRCA 1979
OPERATION:	BATTERY

VALUES:	
GOOD	$65
EXCELLENT	$90
MINT WITH ORIGINAL BOX	$160

BEIJING TOY No. 1 FACTORY
SPACE TANK
PEOPLE'S REPUBLIC OF CHINA • CIRCA 1974

Though the worldwide toy industry is now beholden to its Communist manufacturing partners in China, it wasn't always this way. In fact, Chinese toymaking wasn't a known quantity in the 1970s, when toys like Space Tank emerged from the isolation of the PRC. Taiwan and Hong Kong were far better known as toy builders during the 1970s, having captured most Orient toy production from Japan. But state-run firms like the awkwardly named Beijing Toy No. 1 Factory represented the future of Orient toymaking, thanks to plentiful cheap labor and state-subsidized facilities and energy costs. Space Tank is a crude copy of Yoshiya's Space Tank V-2 (1950s). A Robby-like robot grips two tank-tread controllers, while a form of mystery action provides forward motion. It's mainly collected as a visual point of differentiation for the Yoshiya original, but it also portends the future of world toymaking, such as it would become.

BUILDER:	BEIJING TOY
RELEASED:	CIRCA 1974
OPERATION:	BATTERY

VALUES:	
GOOD	$25
EXCELLENT	$50
MINT WITH ORIGINAL BOX	$80

宇宙坦克
SPACE TANK

BEIJING TOY NO. 1 FACTORY
UNIVERSE CAR

PEOPLE'S REPUBLIC OF CHINA • CIRCA 1974

BUILDER:	BEIJING TOY
RELEASED:	CIRCA 1974
OPERATION:	BATTERY
VALUES:	
GOOD	$25
EXCELLENT	$50
MINT WITH ORIGINAL BOX	$80

Though clearly indebted to many Japanese toys of the past, the circa-1974 Universe Car, by Beijing Toy No. 1 Factory, is actually fairly original. The mostly tin-litho toy sports mystery action and flashing lights, and comes packaged in a nicely illustrated box. Various incarnations of this toy exist, having been produced throughout the 1970s, and even early '80s, under a number of names. Indeed, many new enthusiasts focus on the low-end Chinese reproduction

toys as an affordable way to create variation-based collections without seeking the more costly Japanese originals. Whether pursued in its own right, or simply as a counterpoint to the Japanese originals from which it takes its inspiration, toys like Universe Car are indeed a trend for the future of space-toy collecting.

CDI
STAR ROBOT

HONG KONG • CIRCA 1978

The powerful iconography of George Lucas' 1977 *Star Wars* rippled not only throughout the toy industry, but society as a whole. The fact that most people born since 1980 can instantly envision the shape of Darth Vader's helmet drives the point home: Lucas' ability to redefine popular recognition of even minute details is,

BUILDER:	CDI
RELEASED:	CIRCA 1978
OPERATION:	BATTERY
VALUES:	
GOOD	$100
EXCELLENT	$150
MINT WITH ORIGINAL BOX	$250

to this day, nothing short of amazing. The clearest form of this impact is found in knockoff toys, of which CDI's 11-inch Star Robot from around 1978 is a classic. Employing the Horikawa innovation of Rotate-O-Matic chest firing (in itself, yet another example of someone else's creativity), Star Robot walks forward, stops, opens its chest, and "blasts" away with hidden cannon while rotating. And the toy's head

design and overall look are nothing more than a simple steal of Lucas' Stormtroopers from the original *Star Wars* film. CDI was a Hong Kong-based toymaker who thrived during this period, then disappeared in the 1980s. As a knockoff toy, Star Robot by CDI is basic, affordable, and entertaining. But as a symbol for the enduring power of *Star Wars* industrial design, it's priceless.

DUNBEE-COMBEX-MARX
MR. SMASH
UNITED KINGDOM • CIRCA 1975

During the late 1960s, food conglomerates began buying up old-line toy manufacturers to extend their respective profit bases. Nabisco bought Aurora; General Mills bought Kenner, Parker Brothers, and Lionel; and Quaker Oats purchased Louis Marx & Co. Over in the United Kingdom, where Marx maintained a prodigious manufacturing and marketing operation, Quaker sold the rights to the Marx factory and name to rival toymaker, Dunbee-Combex. The newly combined firm, Dunbee-Combex-Marx, soldiered on for less than a decade before an early-1980s dissolution. Prior to this sad ending, however, D-C-M maintained the Marx mantle, licensing the latest and greatest properties from film and television, including *Mr. Smash*, a popular mid-1970s British comedy featuring a bumbling automaton. This all-plastic wind-up is a faithful re-creation of the TV character, shuttling about and moving its arms and head. Note this version lacks its plastic antennae, which are generally missing. Equally important as both a robot collectible and symbol for the demise of Marx, budget-priced Mr. Smash provides a fitting coda to the grand era of Marx tin-toy manufacture.

BUILDER:	D-C-MARX
RELEASED:	CIRCA 1975
OPERATION:	WIND-UP
VALUES:	
GOOD	$100
EXCELLENT	$300
MINT WITH ORIGINAL BOX	$550

EGE
SPACE SHUTTLE COLUMBIA
SPAIN • CIRCA 1979

When the final Apollo mission was completed in 1974, NASA turned its attention to a "reusable" space-flight system: the Space Shuttle. Upon its debut in the 1977 timeframe, numerous toys began to emerge, hoping to capitalize on resurgent interest in the space program. It's doubtful much capitalization took place, but interesting toys from all corners did emerge, including this terrific 14-inch battery-op from Spain. Built by the enigmatic EGE, the Space Shuttle Columbia hails from the 1979 time period and features a slew of nifty actions: mystery action, opening cargo bay, emerging-floating astronaut, flashing lights, and sound. Squat in proportion, the toy's true charm lay in its tin-and-plastic evocation of an earlier era in toymaking. Difficult to find in the U.S., the EGE Space Shuttle Columbia does appear on occasion, and is a moderate-value collectible in today's collecting environment.

BUILDER:	EGE
RELEASED:	CIRCA 1979
OPERATION:	BATTERY
VALUES:	
GOOD	$300
EXCELLENT	$500
MINT WITH ORIGINAL BOX	$1000

DUNBEE-COMBEX-MARX — EGE

HORIKAWA
NEW SPACE EXPLORER
JAPAN • CIRCA 1970

With origins dating back to at least 1966, Horikawa's New Space Explorer is a throwback struggling to survive in a changing world of toymaking. The 11-inch battery-operated "astronaut" sports the backlit "television screen" feature, a space-toy staple since the 1950s. During operation, the toy walks forward, its plastic TV aerial spinning, while the illuminated screen runs Horikawa's tape of space exploration and adventure. The late-style package features typeset lettering and action-lined imagery. An interesting side note to this — and all late Horikawa toys — is how the astronaut faces behind the clear-plastic shields inexplicably evolved into more Bob Newhart-like middle-aged faces. The aging of the marketplace? Probably not — but a good indication of detail-oriented design, even at this late date. Prodigious use of plastic keeps this toy's value low, though earlier examples can bring markedly higher realizations. More than just a thematic bookend to the Horikawa astronaut series, New Space Explorer recalls better days while managing to hang on a little while longer.

BUILDER:	HORIKAWA
RELEASED:	CIRCA 1970
OPERATION:	BATTERY
VALUES:	
GOOD	**$100**
EXCELLENT	**$185**
MINT WITH ORIGINAL BOX	**$350**

HORIKAWA
PISTON ROBOT
JAPAN • CIRCA 1972

As yet another Horikawa survivor into the 1970s, 11-inch Piston Robot still retains much of the same animated action of the original, albeit in mostly plastic form. Like the 1960s original, Piston Robot circa 1972 walks forward, swinging its arms, while a chest-mounted four-banger pumps furiously in rhythm. The head illuminates throughout the action sequence. Not particularly incredible in terms of design or execution, Piston Robot is the kind of toy new enthusiasts start growing collections with; it's affordable, looks good, has entertaining action, and is easy to find packaged. Best of all, despite its relatively low sense of importance on the timeline of Japanese toymaking, it does constitute an entry point through which collectors can begin to learn more about better days.

BUILDER:	HORIKAWA
RELEASED:	CIRCA 1972
OPERATION:	BATTERY
VALUES:	
GOOD	**$100**
EXCELLENT	**$180**
MINT WITH ORIGINAL BOX	**$300**

LOUIS MARX & CO.
ROCK 'EM SOCK 'EM ROBOTS
UNITED STATES • CIRCA 1973

The 1970s were not good to the old Marx empire. Under the ownership of corporate parent Quaker Oats, many of its prized product lines were divested or closed down. Those which remained had to struggle with a life of lifeless reissuing, not to mention truly horrendous packaging. As this 1973-era iteration of Rock 'Em Sock 'Em Robots demonstrates, even the worst packaging is self-redeeming, if only as comic relief. Quaker Oats did manage to affect one change that never had been possible under the old Louis Marx regime: completely standardized packaging across the entire toy line. But at what price?

BUILDER:	MARX
RELEASED:	CIRCA 1973
OPERATION:	MECHANICAL
◆	
VALUES:	
GOOD	$45
EXCELLENT	$100
MINT WITH ORIGINAL BOX	$150

MASUDAYA
BOEING SUPERSONIC JET
JAPAN • CIRCA 1972

It was the ambitious program that guaranteed America would remain at the forefront of aviation technology: the SuperSonic Transport (SST). The future of commercial flight. Tomorrow, today. Science fiction you could take to Cleveland. The only problem was, no one wanted the SST landing at *their* nearby airport — it generated sonic booms each time it broke the sound barrier. Imagine the sound of explosions occuring, oh, say, every six minutes, and you get the idea. Of course, no one was likely more upset than Masudaya, who was readying a nice toy rendition of the new Boeing SST for the child market. (Okay, so *maybe* Boeing was a little more upset than Masudaya.) When the SST program died from lack of government funding and orders, Masudaya was stuck with a white-blue-and-gray elephant. It moved a limited run of preproduction toys through the channel, ending their own SST program. Thus, the Boeing Supersonic Jet of the 1972 time period remains one of the more collectible of all late-period aviation toys, despite its cost-reduced plastic lower fuselage, simple lithography, and basic taxi-and-"takeoff" action sequence. Affordable contemporary sci-fi that is doubly nice when accompanied by its original package — Masudaya's Boeing Supersonic Jet.

BUILDER:	MASUDAYA
RELEASED:	CIRCA 1972
OPERATION:	BATTERY
◆	
VALUES:	
GOOD	$150
EXCELLENT	$350
MINT WITH ORIGINAL BOX	$550

MASUDAYA

MASUDAYA
SPACE SHIP X-5
JAPAN • CIRCA 1978

Long after the space-toy party had ended, Masudaya stayed around, flogging many of the same concepts and animations. Even today, Masudaya still creates toys, primarily for the collector market. As the 1970s wore on, Masudaya designs targeted younger consumers, as Space Ship X-5 demonstrates. The cereal-bowl shape of the saucer is out-kiddied only by the oversized dome and simple lithographic decoration scheme. To be fair, at least the toy still uses tin-litho. Okay, enough fairness: what about that packaging? It's straight from the mini-rainbow-sticker, Mork-and-Mindy era of design tastelessness. Today, late Masudaya toys are a pretty affordable lot — with or without the rainbows.

BUILDER:	MASUDAYA
RELEASED:	CIRCA 1978
OPERATION:	BATTERY
◆	
VALUES:	
GOOD	**$100**
EXCELLENT	**$150**
MINT WITH ORIGINAL BOX	**$250**

MASUDAYA
SPACE SHUTTLE
JAPAN • CIRCA 1978

Just as the Apollo program had provided a spark to the languishing Japanese toy industry of the mid-1960s, so too did the emergence of North American Rockwell's Space Shuttle breathe life into the *Star Wars*-dominated toy industry of the late 1970s. Created by Masudaya, Space Shuttle is a fairly realistic toy, outfitted with "non fall action," "blinking tail lights," and "space sound" — itself something of a conundrum. Packaged using typical 1970s design themes (earth-tone colors, "sci-fi" typography and photograph imagery of the toys), Space Shuttle is actually a nice toy for its time. Best of all, toys like Space Shuttle represent easy point of entry for new space-toy enthusiasts — low price — with the marquee value of the legendary Masudaya name.

BUILDER:	MASUDAYA
RELEASED:	CIRCA 1978
OPERATION:	BATTERY
◆	
VALUES:	
GOOD	**$50**
EXCELLENT	**$75**
MINT WITH ORIGINAL BOX	**$150**

MIKE TOYS
EMPIRE-MONSTER ROBOT
TAIWAN • CIRCA 1978

As yet another *Star Wars* knockoff toy, Empire-Monster Robot is loaded with entertainment value. After all, who would think of ripping off the lovable R2D2 droid character, then add skate-legged walking and satanic horns? In two words: Mike Toys. This unknown Taiwanese company captures what is truly great about knockoffs: to get unlicensed and derivative product through customs inspections, cheesy toymakers usually modify the intellectual property just enough to evade seizure. For Mike Toys, that differentiation came in the form of those head-mounted horns. At 10 inches, the all-plastic toy features standard battery-op walking motion, as well as interior illumination. Plus, its R2D2 dome head opens during one portion of the performance to reveal a lumpy red-plastic head inside. Scary! From today's perspective, it's no wonder the entire walking robot category no longer exists — creatively bankrupt toys like Empire-Monster Robot helped dig the grave.

BUILDER:	MIKE TOYS
RELEASED:	CIRCA 1978
OPERATION:	BATTERY
VALUES:	
GOOD	$80
EXCELLENT	$150
MINT WITH ORIGINAL BOX	$250

MORT TOYS
ROBBIE ROBOT
HONG KONG • CIRCA 1973

Though very much a late-period toy, wind-up Robbie Robot, by the virtually unknown Mort Toys, definitely enjoys thematic connectivity to the toys of a decade earlier — or more. Virtually all plastic, Robbie Robot starts with a legendary name, then adds the standard play pattern of forward walking motion, swinging arms, and "light in eyes," which presumably refers to the sparkling mechanism housed inside the toy. Its blockheaded design, expressionless face, and stiff-legged walk gives the 9½-inch Robbie a classic feel at a time when such toys were definitely the exception to the design rule. Mort Toys, branding for Mort Alexander Ltd., was evidently a U.S.-based import house — something of a latter-day Cragstan, it would appear. Available for some time throughout the 1970s, Robbie Robots are relatively easy to find and make good additions to assemblies of blockheaded wind-up robots, particularly when accompanied by original packaging.

BUILDER:	MORT TOYS
RELEASED:	CIRCA 1973
OPERATION:	WIND-UP
VALUES:	
GOOD	$100
EXCELLENT	$150
MINT WITH ORIGINAL BOX	$250

MIKE TOYS — MORT TOYS

TOMY
VERBOT
JAPAN • CIRCA 1979

The dawn of the microprocessor — thousands of transistors crammed onto a tiny square of silicon — transformed consumer electronics in the 1970s. Digital watches, pocket calculators, mini-sound generators, and even toys benefitted from the new technology. Tomy, a late-period Japanese manufacturer which thrives to this very day, rolled out its version of next-generation robot design in 1979 with the debut of Verbot. A simple robot from an aesthetic point of view, 8½-inch Verbot is a classic battery-op with a twist on an old theme — it responds to voice commands, like Masudaya's Sonicon products did in the early 1960s. Tomy went one step further, however, by integrating a wireless remote control to assist in delivering commands. Verbot's greatest skill is in moving around the floor, but the "you control it" nature of the toy still earns it praise from a select group of robot enthusiasts. Affordable and readily available, Tomy's Verbot stands between the past and tomorrow of robot manufacture.

BUILDER:	TOMY
RELEASED:	CIRCA 1979
OPERATION:	BATTERY
VALUES:	
GOOD	$75
EXCELLENT	$100
MINT WITH ORIGINAL BOX	$200

The programmable robot! Performs 8 functions by remote control. Your VOICE is his command! No. 5401

UNKNOWN
MONSTER ROBOT
HONG KONG • CIRCA 1979

Monster Robot is an unknown Hong Kong manufacturer's take on one of the all-time classic Japanese robot toys: Tulip Robot. And, quite obviously, it's another *Star Wars* ripoff. Switched on, the nine-inch battery op comes to life, walking forward, opening its cranial cavity, and revealing its true, hideous self. The toy is nearly all plastic, and comes packed in a good-quality, late-1970s package. It's highly likely this toy was built using the same tools used to create Empire-Monster Robot by Mike Toys (1970s). In fact, it's possible this toy was created by Mike Toys, but the fact remains that this toy is unmarked. Certainly the tool-swapping, wild-west nature of Hong Kong toymaking could have resulted in some no-name company using the molds for a period. Or, the toy could have emerged as the effort of some post-Mike Toys corporate successor. Whatever the case may be, ripoff toys like Monster Robot certainly helped usher in the end of the robot era.

BUILDER:	UNKNOWN
RELEASED:	CIRCA 1979
OPERATION:	BATTERY
VALUES:	
GOOD	$60
EXCELLENT	$100
MINT WITH ORIGINAL BOX	$200

UNKNOWN
TALKING MAGIC MIKE
HONG KONG • CIRCA 1979

Go looking for Japanese-style robots today, and toys like the 11½-inch Talking Magic Mike are what turn up. All-plastic automata are now the standard form in toy robot design; flashing lights, electronic voices, and limited animation exemplify the contemporary paradigm. But that's okay, for several reasons. First, toys like Talking Magic Mike make the humble robot toy accessible to most budgets, as they sell for very reasonable costs, particularly when new. Second, such toys serve to remind both the public at large and space-toy enthusiasts in particular what an important role robots have played in shaping child play patterns in the latter half of this century. And finally, simple plastic robots keep the spirit of toys like Mr. Mercury, Mechanized Robot, and Smoking Spaceman alive, today and into the future. It's easy to look down on the Talking Magic Mikes of the world; the real challenge lies in seeing the connectivity between what exists today and what history has given us forever.

BUILDER:	UNKNOWN
RELEASED:	CIRCA 1979
OPERATION:	BATTERY
VALUES:	
GOOD	$25
EXCELLENT	$35
MINT WITH ORIGINAL BOX	$75

YONEZAWA
MIGHTY ROBOT CARRING APOLLO (SIC)
JAPAN • CIRCA 1970

One of Yonezawa's final toy products, Mighty Robot Carring Apollo (sic) is a metaphorical whimper from a company that should have exited toymaking with a prodigious bang. This simple wind-up "hopper" — so called because the toy looks as though it's hopping, rather than walking — represents a goofy, squat robot design towing a plastic Apollo rocket to destinations unknown.

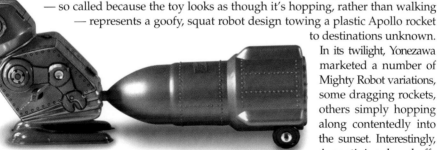

In its twilight, Yonezawa marketed a number of Mighty Robot variations, some dragging rockets, others simply hopping along contentedly into the sunset. Interestingly, Argentinian knockoffs of this toy exist, though no good explanation has yet been provided for why someone would copy such a creatively bankrupt design. Perhaps Yonezawa sold or leased the tooling, or simply outsourced production during its final days as a master toybuilder. Affordable and readily available, Yonezawa's Mighty Robot Carring Apollo is pathos defined for a generation of Japanese toymaking.

BUILDER:	YONEZAWA
RELEASED:	CIRCA 1970
OPERATION:	WIND-UP
VALUES:	
GOOD	$100
EXCELLENT	$150
MINT WITH ORIGINAL BOX	$300

MECHANICAL WIND UP TOY

UNKNOWN — YONEZAWA

GLOSSARY

Alps. Best known by their mountainous logotype, Alps was a top-tier builder of both battery and mechanical toys throughout the postwar period. Alps appears to have abandoned toymaking in the early 1970s during a transition to consumer and industrial electronics, which they continue to manufacture to this day.

Amazing Stories **Magazine.** A pulp-paper publication (1920s-1960s) whose focus was primarily on the fantastic. *Amazing Stories* was one of the first publications to popularize the subject of science fiction and was the platform from which the enormously popular *Buck Rogers in the 25th Century* comic strip was launched.

Amico. A small-time importer who worked with a number of Japanese and Hong Kong-based toymakers. Amico appears to have been most active between the early 1960s and the mid-1970s.

Anker. An East German toymaker who built a wide variety of toys for distribution through the old Soviet bloc. Anker appears to have survived into the 1980s, though its current disposition is unknown.

Apollo. The third main American space program, initiated in 1965 and wrapped in 1974. Highlights of the Apollo program include the tragic launchpad fire of Apollo 1; the historic moon landing of Apollo 11; and the near-fatal catastrophe of Apollo 13.

Asahi. Best known by their Santa Claus logotype, Asahi was a major postwar builder of mechanical and battery-operated toys, with particular emphasis on scale-like models of then-contemporary vehicles. Asahi's disposition remains unclear to this day. Also identified as "ATC" on many toys.

Asakusa. An obscure Tokyo-based toymaker who released a very limited selection of products in the late-1950s timeframe. Its current disposition is unknown, but is presumed to have ceased operations in the early 1960s, as no later-period toys marketed under their brand are known. Asakusa is a manufacturing district on the outskirts of Tokyo, presumably the original location of the company.

ATC. See **Asahi**

automaton. Robot or mechanical being.

Bandai. A powerhouse of Japanese toymaking, Bandai ("B") thrives to this day as Japan's largest and most successful toymaker, best known for its line of *Mighty Morphin Power Rangers* action figures and accessories. During the postwar period, Bandai specialized in vehicle toys, dominating that segment for more than twenty years.

battery box. A location for installing a toy's batteries. Also generally used as a "remote control" or control box.

battery-operated. As it suggests, this term is applied to toys which require batteries to operate. During the postwar period, D cells were the dominant form of battery power, though C cells (with their slightly lower electrical potential) held sway initially and in some lower-cost toys. Batteries supply direct current to miniature motors housed within battery-operated toys — motors which, under power, connect to intricate and often complex gearboxes and transmissions to create toy animations.

Birth of a Nation. The landmark feature film of 1915, by D. W. Griffith, which established the form and style used to create long-form cinematic films. Criticized today for its period, negative depictions of blacks, *Birth of a Nation* remains highly regarded by cinematic historians for its impact on successor filmmakers and films.

Buck Rogers. A spinoff from *Amazing Stories* Magazine, *Buck Rogers in the 25th Century* was the first and most successful of early science-fiction properties. Along with copilot Wilma Deering, Buck battled evil. Much of Buck's appeal was derived from the fact that he was a 20th-century man who, Rip Van Winkle-like, had been preserved for nearly 500 years before being revived to enjoy adventure and intrigue in the distant future. The original *Buck Rogers* comic strip ran from the late 1920s through the 1960s, and was revived as a television program in the late 1970s, as well.

bump and go. Mystery action.

capsule. An orbital or reentry vehicle.

Captain Video. An early sci-fi television series which ran from 1949-1955 on the failed DuMont network. Captain Video and his youthful sidekick, The Video Ranger, are best remembered for their ability to defeat daily adversaries using their intellect rather than ray guns.

circa. Around or about; used in this volume to help denote the approximate time of a toy's release.

clockwork. See **wind-up**

Command Module. The orbital portion of Apollo moonshot-era missions which stayed above the lunar surface during astronaut landings. The nosecone section of the Command Module doubled as the reentry vehicle, also known as the "space capsule."

Cragstan. A New York-based toy marketing and distribution firm which specialized in the importation of mechanical and battery-operated toys from postwar Japan. Cragstan was likely the creation of toy-industry veterans; the name "Cragstan" is believed to be a homolgation of two principals' names. Cragstan appears to have operated from the late 1950s through the late 1960s.

Cubism. A school of design which emerged from early twentieth-century France. Cubism reduces natural forms to their geometrical foundations. Many robots and space toys employ variations on the Cubist school of design.

Daisy. Formerly based in Plymouth, Michigan (just outside Detroit), Daisy Manufacturing Co. still exists as a toymaker, now based in Rogers, Arkansas. Best known for their 1950s-era line of "Red Ryder" B-B guns, Daisy continues to market a full line of toy sidearms.

Daiya. An important toymaker from Tokyo, active throughout the postwar period. Daiya appears to have been most active from the late 1950s through the early 1970s, after which it disappears from view. Daiya's current disposition is unknown, but it is presumed to have succumbed to marketplace pressures of the early '70s period.

Destination Moon. The epic 1950 film produced by George Pal which presented the subject matter of space travel in a serious fashion, setting the stage for later depictions of sci-fi topics in equally mature lights.

Dux. A West German toymaker best known for its metal construction sets similar to Erector and Meccano products.

E.T. An obscure Japanese corporate entity believed to have been either a distributor of nonbranded toys or an industry trade group similar to the Toy Manufacturers of America. Its tiny, enigmatic "E.T." logotype can be found on literally thousands of Japanese toys and packages, but little more is known beyond this small scrap of information.

easel-back. A wire-based form of support used to keep Linemar robots in an upright orientation during walking. The term comes from the fact that the wireform resembles an easel's support legs.

East/Eastern Germany. The former Soviet-controlled section of Germany, seized after the fall of the Nazi regime in 1945. With the fall of the Berlin Wall in 1990, the eastern and western portions of Germany were reunited, bringing to a close the divided nature of the German state.

eccentric-wheel. This is a form of locomotion used on many "walking" toys which do not have separate legs or actual leg-based articulation. Instead of moving legs, toy designers integrated two wheels which are offset on their axes. During operation (generally mechanical wind-up), these "eccentric" wheels spin slowly, with their apexes offset 180 degrees, causing the toy to wobble forward slightly, creating the impression of "walking." An alternate version of eccentric-wheel locomotion is eccentric-pin walking, which uses the same wheel concept, but employs pins to actually contact the walking surface instead of wheels.

Eightman. A 1960s-era Japanese television program about a *Robocop*-like cyborg character. Immortalized by Yonezawa ("Y") in toy form.

excellent condition. A grading condition applied to toys that are free from scratches and scuffs; such toys show no real evidence of wear, and appear to have been hardly played with.

Flash Gordon. The "second" big name in early science fiction, Flash Gordon was a swashbuckling hero who battled the evil Ming the Merciless in the outer space of the future. *Flash* was created in response to the success of *Buck Rogers* by the Hearst Corporation for distribution in its newspaper syndicate. The original *Flash Gordon* comic strip appears to have run from the mid-1930s through the 1960s, and was the subject of a 1980 feature film of the same name.

flying saucer. A space vehicle, presumably piloted by extraterrestrial life form(s), shaped like a plate (or "saucer") and employing an unknown, highly advanced method of propulsion.

Forbidden Planet. The 1956 Metro-Goldwyn-Mayer (MGM) sci-fi classic starring Leslie Nielsen, Walter Pidgeon, Anne Francis, and Robby the Robot. This film and its automaton star were a catalyst for the 1950s sci-fi toy craze.

friction. This method of conveyance is generally found on vehicle toys. Friction motors employ flywheel-equipped mechanisms which rely on the "revving" of a child — for example, the repeated pushing of friction wheelsets across the floor to generate progressively more inertial power. As the name suggests, friction assemblies use the presence of friction between the drive mechanism components to sustain the short period of operation.

Gama. A toymaker based in West Germany, known for a variety of metal playthings.

Gang of Five. A group of "skirted" robots built by Masudaya during the 1950s, '60s, and possibly as late as the '70s. They include Giant Sonic (Train) Robot, Target Robot, Non-Stop (Lavender) Robot, Radicon Robot, and Machine Man. Exceedingly valuable and incredibly rare toys from a revered Japanese toybuilder.

Gemini. The second main American space program which laid the groundwork for the moonshots of the Apollo programs. Unlike the "get a man into space" missions of the Mercury launches, Gemini space flights gathered necessary data to help NASA engineers create the vehicles which would sustain a successful flight to the Moon — and back.

Gigantor. Tetsujin-26, a large mechanical being who fights on behalf of its human operators, good or bad. Derived from a Japanese 1960s-era television program which was called *Gigantor* in the United States.

good condition. A grading condition applied to toys that show evidence of having been played with; small, minor scuffs and marks are present, but the toy is generally well cared for.

Haji. A small Tokyo-based toymaker which focused on the vehicle-toy category but dabbled in other styles as well.

Horikawa. One of the most successful of all postwar Japanese toymakers, yet also one of the least respected. Horikawa ("SH") specialized in robot/astronaut battery-operated toys with great marketplace success, surviving to this day as a specialty niche builder of vintage-style playthings for the collector market.

hot stamping. A decoration process used in manufacturing where a heated plate is pressed onto plastic, transferring colored tape in the shape of the plate's art design.

Ichiko. A small Japanese toymaker known mainly for vehicle toys. Their current disposition is unknown, but they are presumed to have stopped toy production in the early 1970s.

Ideal. Ideal Toy Company was a New Jersey-based toymaker during the postwar period, known for a wide variety of products in many differing categories. Ideal later merged with Sawyer's ViewMaster, and was ultimately taken over by Tyco, which itself was consumed by Mattel in recent years. The Ideal brand is no longer used.

illumination. Tiny light bulbs displaying light during battery-powered operation.

Kitahara, Teruhisa. A legendary and influential toy historian whose groundbreaking work in Japanese tin toy manufacturing laid the foundation for successive research. Without Kitahara's work, enthusiasts of vintage Japanese toys would be much poorer, unquestionably.

Ley, Willy. An influential futurist and scientist whose depictions of space vehicles helped inspire both toys and actual NASA designs.

Linemar. The import subsidiary of Louis Marx & Co. Marx was an early adopter of overseas manufacturing and distribution relationships, and established Linemar to facilitate the importation of mechanical and battery-operated toys from Japan. Though notable here for its robot and space-toy offerings, Linemar's primary focus was on character and licensed toys. Linemar appears to have been in business from the late 1950s through about 1968, when Marx ostensibly disbanded the organization and assumed corporate responsibility for subsequent imported products.

lithography. The process used to print a design on a flat surface. "Tin" lithography involves sending large sheets of steel or tin through massive printing presses, which apply one, two, or four colors in rapid succession. The flat sheets are then sent through stamping machines which die-cut the toy components. The final step before assembly involves forming the flat sheets to their final shape, using hardened-steel forming tools and compression stamping machines. Also known as "tin-litho."

lunar module. The Apollo-era space vehicle that performed the actual landing on the Moon's surface. The module also included a return vehicle for repatriating the astronauts with the orbiting Command Module. Also called the "lunar lander."

M-T. See **Masudaya**

Marusan. A small Japanese toymaker whose products featured accurate design and colorful lithography. Best known by their circular "SAN" logotype. Marusan's current disposition is unknown, but it is presumed to have gone under in the 1960s.

Marx. A giant in American toymaking, Louis Marx & Co.'s corporate history spans the late 1920s through the early 1980s. Best known for tin toys, playsets, and licensed product, Marx was ultimately purchased by Quaker Oats, then later dissolved at auction in the '80s. A successor company, which owns many Marx plastic tools and its marks and name, exists today.

Masudaya. The venerable Japanese toybuilder whose corporate history dates back hundreds of years (according to their website). Masudaya was a leading builder of mechanical and battery-operated toys in the postwar period, and unlike most of its contemporaries, managed to survive to this day. Masudaya normally identified their toys using the "M-T" or "Modern Toys" logotype.

Masuo. A small Japanese toy builder best known for its mechanical and friction toys marked with the firm's "SM" or "MS" (depending on one's interpretation) logotype.

Mattel. An American toybuilder whose roots extend back to the early 1950s in Hawthorne, California. Best known for its Barbie and Hot Wheels lines, Mattel is the largest toymaker in the world, and is based in El Segundo, California.

mechanical. This method of actuation relies on physical input by the child — for example, the pulling of a trigger or the revving of an inertial motor. Mechanical toys were the norm from the late post-Industrial Revolution period through the late postwar period, though by that late date, they had fallen to occupy the lower echelons of price points and desirability.

Mercury. The first of the American space programs. Mercury astronauts include Alan Shepard, first American in space, and John Glenn, first American to successfully orbit the earth.

Metropolis. A silent classic from 1926 by German filmmaker Fritz Lang which helped cement popular fascination with science-fiction subject matter, particularly in filmed format. Though rather melodramatic by contemporary standards, *Metropolis* is best remembered for its stunning visual effects and dark, brooding, and dismal depictions of future life.

Milton Bradley. An iconic American toy brand, now part of Hasbro. MB dates to the late 19th century, when it was founded by its namesake in Beverly, Massachusetts. Best known for its huge historic line of board games which span all genres of toy subject matter.

mint-original box condition. A grading condition applied to toys that are absolutely pristine and have never been played with; such toys are considered factory-new and are accompanied by all their original packaging, inserts, and instructional sheets.

Modern Toys. See **Masudaya**

mystery action. A method of conveyance for battery-operated toys in which the plaything automatically alters its course whenever an impedance is struck. Mystery action (also known as "non-fall action" or "bump and go") employs a small one-axle wheelset mounted on a 360-degree spindle, all of which is driven by a gear assembly connected to a battery-powered can motor. Whenever an object or table edge is encountered, the wheelset immediately turns and reverses drive-wheel direction, causing the toy to head in an alternative direction.

N. An obscure Japanese toymaker who may be known as Noguchi, or may be a subbrand of Nomura (T-N). Best known for its diminutive paddle-walking wind-up robots and astronauts.

Naito Shoten. An enigmatic Japanese toy builder whose name was determined by legendary toy historian Teruhisa Kitahara. Naito Shoten toys are generally marketed under the brands "AN" or "AHI." It is believed that Naito Shoten worked closely with Nomura.

NASA. National Aeronautics and Space Administration, formed in 1959 when it transformed from the National Advisory Committee on Aeronautics. NASA oversaw (and continues to oversee) all major American space programs, including Apollo, Space Shuttle, and outer-world exploration efforts.

Nomura. One of the biggest and most prolific of all postwar Japanese toymakers. Also known by their mark "T-N." Nomura is believed to have built toys from the late 1940s through the 1970s, though its current disposition is unknown. It is believed Nomura transformed itself into a manufacturer of other subject matter.

non-fall action. See **mystery action**

Occupied Japan. The term applied to products which emerged from Japan between 1946 and 1952, the period in which United States military forces occupied and controlled the country as a result of Imperial Japan's defeat in World War II. In 1952, with the ratification of the new democratic constitution, control of Japan was relinquished by the U.S. military to the Japanese people. Product released after 1952 are marked "Made in Japan."

Ohta. Best known by their "K" logotype, Ohta was a small, short-lived Tokyo toymaker who created a small collection of playthings under their own brand, mainly during the late 1950s and early 1960s. Ohta's current disposition is unknown, but it is presumed to have failed during the 1960s shakeout of the Japanese toy industry.

Pyro. A small, New Jersey-based injection-molded plastic toy manufacturer who competed with Louis Marx & Co. in the bottom-feeding plastic figure segment. Pyro is best remembered today for its military flatcar loads on 1960s-era Lionel trains. The company ceased operations in the 1970s; its tools are still in production at a variety of firms.

Remco. A once-major American brand during the postwar period. Remco specialized in cheap, yet flashy, plastic toys. The brand survives to this day as a division of Azrak-Hamway International.

remote control. A corded control box which allows the child to actuate and control a battery-operated toy's features.

Robby the Robot. The automaton character from the Metro-Goldwyn-Mayer 1956 classic, *Forbidden Planet*. Robby the Robot inspired a generation of space-toy design, and remains to this day the most recognizable icon for both automaton and toy robot design.

robot. A mechanical being; an automaton.

rocket. A man-made space vehicle, usually cylindrical in nature, which, when filled with gases and ignited, provides propulsion, facilitating the manned exploration of the heavens.

Rosko. An American toy importer, similar to Cragstan, which specialized in the importation of Japanese mechanical and battery-operated toys. Rosko appears to have been most active from the late 1950s through the late 1960s, when it disappeared from view. Best known for their child-faced "Rosko Tested Toys" logotype.

Sanyo. A little-known Japanese toymaker who thrived during the 1950s and seemingly vanished thereafter. Primarily a builder of penny toys and other cheap playthings, Sanyo diversified into slightly upmarket playthings during the '50s. Their current disposition is unknown, but they are presumed to have gone under by the 1960s.

Showa. A small-time subcontractor who worked with a variety of builders, most notably Nomura (T-N). Showa's mark can be found on many different toys and packages.

skirted. A style of robot design which does not include separate legs. Instead, the toy's lower region employs a tapered rectangular design, which allows toy designers to integrate lower-cost means of locomotion instead of more complex, separate-legged walking assemblies.

smoking. A feature used on many battery-operated toys in which a small smoke generator puffs clean, white smoke during operation. Smoking toys are often dependent upon no-longer-available smoke pellets or fluids, though some "smoking" toys are believed to actually use powder to simulate the look of billowing smoke.

SNK. Also believed to be known as "Sankei." A small-time Japanese toybuilder, SNK is best known for its Zoomer-like robots. Little is known of SNK, and its disposition remains unclear.

Sonsco. This firm is believed to have been a small-time distributor, akin to the more famous Cragstan or Rosko. They appear to have been in business for roughly ten years, spanning the late 1950s through the late '60s.

space noise. Mechanical thumping or clicking.

Space Patrol. A completely overused term which is ostensibly derived from the *Space Patrol* television series which ran from 1950-1955, and featured the Commander Buzz Corry character. The "Space Patrol" term was appropriated by Japanese toymakers and used to describe virtually any kind of sci-fi-themed plaything, from the early 1950s through the late 1960s.

Space Shuttle. The American post-Apollo space vehicle used to ferry astronauts and equipment to and from space in a reusable format.

sparkling. Flint-produced spark effect. This pre-battery form of "illumination" was popular with many manufacturers, including Marx. Sparkling toys were almost invariably mechanical wind-ups. During operation, part of the toy's drive mechanism would supply power to a stone which rubs against a flint, producing the spark (or "sparkling") effect. By the late postwar period, sparkling toys had been relegated to the lower echelons of toydom.

Sputnik. The first man-made satellite successfully launched into Earth orbit, on October 4, 1957, by the Union of Soviet Socialist Republics (USSR). The first Sputnik satellite sustained a 98-minute orbit. Sputnik II, launched in November 1957, contained a heroic Soviet dog, named Laika, who survived until the satellite's air supply gave out prior to a fiery re-entry. Sputnik's successful launch is the seminal event which initiated the modern space race, culminating with Apollo 11's July 1969 manned landing on the Moon.

Star Wars. The massively influential 1977 film by George Lucas which reintroduced vintage serial-like adventure storylines against a sci-fi backdrop. *Star Wars* also heralded the modern phenomenon of licensed-toy focus, which has dominated the American toy industry ever since the film's release.

SY. A little-known brand believed to be related to either N or Yoshiya ("KO"), remembered today for its walking spacemen wind-ups.

T-N. See **Nomura**

Tetsujin-26. See *Gigantor*

The Day the Earth Stood Still. A 1952 opus directed by Robert Wise and starring Michael Rennie and Patricia Neal, wherein alien visitor Klaatu lands on the Mall in Washington, DC, to warn Earth's inhabitants about the dangers of nuclear weapons. A serious, mature approach to science fiction that helped legitimize this formerly child-oriented genre with a widespread audience.

tin litho. See **lithography**

Tom Corbett Space Cadet. This television show (1950-1955) followed the adventures of a futuristic youth attending a space academy set in the year 2350. Thanks to a successful licensing program, *Tom Corbett Space Cadet* remains one of the best-known early-period TV shows about sci-fi.

Tootsietoy. A brand of the Dowst Manufacturing Company of Chicago, Illinois. Tootsietoy helped establish the "pocket money" toy segment during the 1930s with its affordable line of die-cast vehicle and aircraft toys. With the arrival of Matchbox vehicle toys in the early 1950s, Tootsietoy moved downmarket and dominated the bottom levels of die-cast for many years. Tootsietoy remains one of the few independent major toymakers.

TPS. Tokyo Playthings Ltd., best known by their "three fingers" logotype and initials. A third-tier manufacturer, TPS was most active in the late 1950s and early '60s, focusing mainly on younger-child market segments and colorful lithography.

Trip to the Moon, A. A silent film by Georges Mélies, from 1902. This three-reel film depicted a group of upper-crust citizens who embark on a journey to the lunar surface, where they encounter a race of "moon people" and engage in a series of adventures before returning to Earth. Regarded as the seminal depiction of science fiction, particularly in cinema.

von Braun, Werner. The rocket scientist who helped create Nazi Germany's infamous V-2 rockets which pummelled Britain during World War II, and after the war, headed up the United States' rocketry program.

Waco. Another enigmatic Tokyo-based toymaker whose products represent the only information known about them. Waco released only a handful of toys during a short run that spanned the decade transition from the 1950s to the '60s.

West/Western Germany. The former western portion of Germany which was occupied by American and British forces after the surrender of the Nazi regime in 1945. Many toys can be found marked "Western Zone," "American Zone," or "British Zone," as well. With the 1990 fall of the Berlin Wall and the reunification of Germany's eastern and western territories, the "west" term ceased to be applied.

wind-up. A form of actuation used in toymaking which requires the child to wind an internal mechanism to provide power to the toy. Generally speaking, wind-ups rely on clockwork mechanisms, which are nothing more than assemblies of gears powered by the inertial potential of keywound steel coils. Also known as "clockwork."

Wyandotte. A pressed-steel toy manufacturer from Wyandotte, Michigan. This company dates back to the 1920s, and appears to have survived until the late 1960s.

Yonezawa. One of the biggest and certainly the most creative of all postwar Japanese toymakers. Yonezawa ("Y" or "Yone") was a prodigious toymaker indeed, responsible for literally thousands of different battery-operated and mechanical toys in all categories from the early 1950s through the early 1970s. Its current disposition is unclear, but Yonezawa is believed to have transformed itself into a builder of industrial electronics, though this is unconfirmed.

Yoshiya. A major Japanese toymaker from the postwar period. Yoshiya (known by their mark "KO") specialized in mostly mechanical or wind-up toys featuring fanciful designs, but also is known for its extensive line of Robby the Robot knockoff toys. Tokyo-based Yoshiya appears to have been in business from the early 1950s through the early 1970s; its current disposition is unknown.

INDEX

183

In the desert that is vintage-toy reference,

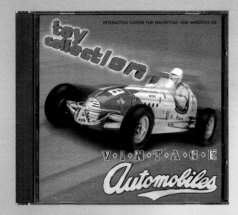

TOY COLLECTION — VINTAGE AUTOMOBILES
interactive CD-ROM
for Windows 95/98/NT, iMac, PowerMac

TOY COLLECTION ART CELS
Nomura Moon Space Ship
museum-quality art

TOY COLLECTION — ROBOTS & SPACE TOYS
interactive CD-ROM
for Windows 95/98/NT, iMac, PowerMac

trust the Eagle.
Nobody does it better.

AMERICAN EAGLE
entertainment
INCORPORATED

WWW.AMERI-EAGLE.COM

PMB 866
1223 WILSHIRE BOULEVARD
SANTA MONICA, CA 90403